Vasantha sam

May ... be
with you and your family
Sri Ram
Sujitha Reddy

MILK, HONEY AND GRAPES

MILK, HONEY AND GRAPES

SIMPLE HINDUISM CONCEPTS FOR EVERYONE

KIRAN MEHTA

SHARDA BOOKS

MILK, HONEY AND GRAPES

Simple Hinduism Concepts for Everyone

Printed, Published, and Distributed by:

SHARDA BOOKS

ISBN-13: 978-1438209159

We would love to know about your reading experience and get your comments and suggestions: milkhoneyandgrapes@gmail.com

Available on Amazon.com

Price: $ 15

Printed in the U.S.A.

Materialism matters in the world but

Spirituality is the essence of human Life.

Elevate yourself.

CONTENTS

Simple Hinduism Concepts for Everyone

SCRIPTURES

MISCELLANEOUS

FOREWORD

Hinduism

Hinduism is the third largest of the world's religions today, with only Christianity and Islam followed by more people. It extends to about one-sixth of the world's population or over a billion people, not just in India but also now in all the main countries of the world. Most notably, Hinduism is the largest of the non-Biblical traditions, and the largest of the older native and pagan traditions that once dominated the world and still exist in many forms and in many countries. Hinduism is larger than its offshoot of Buddhism, which is also still widely practiced throughout the world today.

It is also the oldest of the world's major religions with its origins over five thousand years ago looking back into prehistory itself. Hinduism formulates itself as *Sanatana Dharma*, a universal and eternal tradition of truth, not limited to any particular book, teacher or institution, but having a great variety of teachings relative to the changing needs of time, person, and culture. Yet there is much that is modern and futuristic in Hinduism as well.

Hinduism has a pluralistic view of the spiritual life, accepting one truth underlying all existence, but also recognizing a diversity of paths and approaches in order to reach it. This "Hindu spiritual pluralism" fits in well with modern civilization and its cultural, social, and political pluralism that is necessary for any global peace and harmony among the many countries, ethnicities, languages and cultures of the world. This broad Hindu view of truth aids in the development of tolerance and mutual respect for all people, not only for those of different religious backgrounds but also including those who may not follow any particular religion at all.

Hinduism, however, does not simplistically equate all the religions of the world as being the same. It recognizes that there are notable and important differences between religious teachings and doctrines, and various formulations of Divinity or spiritual reality, and of the ultimate goal of human life. Hinduism can accept theism as one path among these, but can also accept polytheism, monism, pantheism, or even atheism as having a role in the human spiritual experience. Hinduism resembles the vast banyan tree with many leaves, branches, and its roots both in the air and in the ground. It accepts the abundance of nature and does not try to make reality conform to the limitations of the human mind and its need to promote conformity.

Perhaps because of this very abundance, Hinduism remains probably the hardest to understand and the least appreciated of the world's great religions today. Hinduism is often looked upon relative to what we could call "old missionary and colonial stereotypes." These include looking at Hinduism according to charges of idolatry, superstition, caste, oppression of women, worship of cows, poverty, and lack of education.

Today Hindus have spread globally and have revived their position in India since it was freed from foreign rule. Hindu immigrants in the western world have higher levels of income and education than the average person, including the USA and UK, showing anti-Hindu stereotypes to be misleading and wrong. There are beautiful Hindu temples in many cities of North America and UK, along with thriving Hindu communities that are tolerant, law-abiding, affluent, and intelligent, including a high percentage of such professionals as doctors, engineers, software technicians, and those working in the media.

Hindu based teachings of *Yoga*, meditation, mantra, and Ayurvedic healing have spread globally over the last century and brought many benefits and insights to numerous people. Millions worldwide follow or study the teachings of India born Hindu teachers. Such Hindu teachers, following a universal view, may not overtly promote conversion to Hinduism, but they are sharing teachings from the Hindu and greater *Yoga* tradition that are relevant to everyone. Many people in the world also hold to the concepts of *Karma* and rebirth that dominate Hindu thought. Hindu based concepts of non-violent resistance by Mahatma Gandhi have gained a large global acceptance.

This new resurgence of Hinduism worldwide means that we need new studies of Hinduism that show Hinduism as it is today, as well as its long and rich history, and its spiritual and cultural abundance over time and space. Perhaps the main difficulty in approaching Hinduism is that it does not fall into western stereotypes as to what a religion is supposed to be. It does not follow a pattern of one book, one main teacher, one prophet or savior, one God, salvation by belief, or the need to convert the world that dominate in Biblical traditions that have ruled the western world for many centuries. Hinduism is not based upon any exclusive belief but on an inclusive approach to the whole of life.

Yet Hinduism is not the only religion to fall outside of western religious stereotypes. Along with Hinduism can be placed Buddhism, Taoism, Shinto, and related traditions of Asia. All native and pagan traditions fall in this category as well, including the pre-Christian traditions of Europe like the Greek, Roman and Celtic, extending to current native traditions in Africa, America and the Pacific. Such traditions are still practiced by large groups all over the world.

This means that we must look at Hinduism in a new light, with both a new cultural sensitivity and a deeper spiritual insight. Fortunately there are many western educated Hindus, including a younger generation, who can be better placed to articulate its traditions.

The current book *Simple Hinduism Concepts for Everyone* is a good example of that new blossoming of the Hindu mind on the global stage, and how Hindus are defending, expressing, and sharing their great teachings in a wider context. The book covers Hinduism as *Sanatana Dharma* in both a comprehensive and broad manner that counters current distortions and presents a clear picture of this vast tradition and its many facets.

The book explains the main deities and practices of Hinduism extending from Veda to Tantra, including their philosophical and psychological depth in various *Yoga* teachings. It shows that Hindu deities are formations of a higher universal consciousness, part of a great spiritual science, and not simply folk images as they are often portrayed to be. Unveiling the great treasures of Hindu literature like the Ramayana and Mahabharata, the book shows the importance of the main Hindu scriptures or source teachings and their deeper Vedantic philosophy.

The author, Kiran Mehta, has composed an excellent guidebook to Hindu thought and practice that is relevant for anyone interested in higher spiritual knowledge and Self-realization. It should be carefully studied and contemplated by all those who want a better understanding of this great tradition and its relevance for the whole of life.

Dr. David Frawley (Vamadeva Shastri)
Director, American Institute of Vedic Studies
www.vedanet.com

PREFACE

The Purpose of this Book

I am extremely happy that a decade old desire, years of research, and earnest attempt at an appropriate narration has come to fruition with this book. It is my humble effort to present various beliefs of Hinduism accentuating its most popular deities of worship and accepted concepts of God. It also describes the ancient practice of Tantra covering subjects like the ubiquitous power of Mantras, psychic centers in our body called Chakras, and the mother power of *Kuṇḍalinī*. It is the result of my serious and sincere work, an endeavor aimed to achieve four-fold objective while catering to the spiritual appetite of the readers.

Primarily, it is to explain the three major concepts of God by introducing and acquainting them with its many divine portraits. These sacred deities carry an underlying essence, each personifying a subtle principle that sustains such view and vision ultimately converging on the same Ultimate Truth called *Brahman*. The emphasis throughout is to provide an insight and understanding into the specific aspects of *Brahman* that assume these deity forms and faces. I have tried to cover this unique and outstanding feature of the religion in a palatable language for pedestrian appeal. These traditional beliefs are also highlighted with the basic laws of cosmology that give metaphysical insights into their spiritual relevance. Specifically, it addresses those stumped minds who wonder about the endless index of deities populating this great tradition.

These concepts have given rise to the three most common theistic orders of Vaishṇavism, Shaivism, and Shaktism that regard Lord Vishṇu, Lord Shiva, and Devī or Divine Mother respectively as the Ultimate Reality. The second aim of the book is to show that these diverse strands of the religion though appear to be quite different, essentially evolve from, revolve around, and uphold the same fundamental principle that underlies all physical phenomena. They all accept that there is only one God, *Brahman* who appears as the casual sound Aum. It then spontaneously and transcendentally polarizes into the eternal throb of pulsation called *Nāda Brahman* which is the source of all material manifestation. They only differ in stressing different aspects of this universal vibratory field which they recognize and worship preferentially with utmost faith.

The third aim of the book is to show the way in which this subtle sound, *Nāda Brahman* effects the entire creation. This living cosmic intelligence consists of two interdependent opposites, the passive self-illuminating Consciousness, *Bindu* from which arises the ever active energy of its Being which propagates as the subtle sound waves, *Nāda*. These waves are cyclical in nature as, though moving away from the source, they eventually return to it. This primary principle of bipolar Reality gives rise to all the polarities of nature as they institute countless interpenetrating energy cycles like sunrise and sunset, expansion and contraction, spring and autumn, crests and troughs. They are also the source of innumerable shades of dualities like pleasure and pain, birth and death, white and black, gain and loss of which the entire creation is essentially made of.

These waves inherently carry two quite inseparable characteristics, the energy of propagation which carries the latent trait of a form. At every stage of creation that follows, the object they create is known by the sound of its underlying energy which is heard as, and deemed to be its name. Thus, they simultaneously give rise to the mental and physical planes. As these *Nāda* waves spread, they differentiate into the prime root powers of gross sounds, each a deity called mother, *Mātrika* as they carry the innate potential to create specific physical forms. Sanskṛit alphabets articulate these sounds and therefore, Sanskṛit is called the language of creation. These divine sounds variously combine giving rise to the sacred sound-codes of creation. Many of these were revealed to the ancient sages in their deep state of meditation who compiled them as the Vedas, the Holy Scriptures.

These sounds further combine and recombine by three modes well recognized as *Sattva*, *Rajas*, and *Tamas* to grow into various step-down categories of mental and material principles called *Tattvas*. These subtle and gross elements are various building blocks of the universe each of which is duly explained in the chapter on *Kuṇḍalinī*. The chapter goes on to describe how the spirit descends into matter through the divine play of their organized integration. It is a quantum process which ultimately projects each life in a physical form having appropriate mind and body. How discreet parts of subjective Consciousness, *Atman* are obscured by various limiting principles to make individual souls is dealt with in the chapter on Shiva and Mahesh. They manifest as an entity duly embodied through these *Tattvas* to enjoy life and have various experiences.

Hinduism is based on *Vedānta* philosophy which is well intertwined with the esoteric tradition of Tantra. The chapter of Tantra introduces its unique approach which sets it apart from the ways of all religions in pursuit of spirituality. By harnessing the power of ubiquitous energy around us, within us, it directs everyone to the path of Self-discovery. Many secret initiations, abuse and misuse of the occult powers acquired by its practitioners, and such projections as its invariable association with sexuality though, has tainted its image. But if studied and understood in proper context, it offers deep insight into the operation of our subtle system, its regulation through the psycho-energy centers called Chakras, and their creation through the power of *Mātrika* sounds.

It is the deity power of *Mātrika* energies which first establishes various Chakras that develop our subtle system prior to their creation of our physical self during gestation. *Prāṇa* of each breath animates Chakras that regulate all aspects of our life as they constantly externalize awareness through these sound energies. Their vibrations are the source of thoughts and mental powers that give us ideas and raise desires upon which we plan and act. Their presence and mode of operation is common to all humans. The fourth aim of the book is to show that this knowledge and understanding offers true insight into all aspects of our being. It has universal application and therefore, transcends the boundaries of all religions.

It is interesting to know that the grace of each deity power explicated earlier is encapsulated in its mantra. Mantras are also made of *Mātrika* sounds that come together in specific set of a formula which constitutes its unique deity power. They are the phrases of spiritual wisdom that embed within the energy of their conscious effect. Mantra chanting creates vibrations that effectively resonate with Chakras to influence, stimulate, and empower our inner self. Their impact is direct and natural due to the interaction of the same *Mātrika* energies that easily correspond. It attunes our mind to the cosmic mind, protects us from negativity, and influences our thought and perception such that we follow the rightful way of life. The knowledge of this esoteric subject is inspiring and equally useful to everyone irrespective of their religious affiliation. It expands the vision of all seekers leading them to the foremost frontiers of spiritual wisdom.

I have enjoyed developing conceptual framework of the book by giving this presentation a very concise form and a contemporary perspective. The content is based on the compilation from various selected sources like authoritative religious literature, personal spiritual experiences, and teachings of the great spiritual masters, true beacons of the mankind from time immemorial. Just as milk, honey, and grapes are the simple foods consumed by everyone, and are easy to assimilate, this short introduction is intended to serve as a simple to understand source for all. It offers an excellent view of the multidimensional makeup, immense depth, resolute nature, and sophisticated approach of the wide spiritual stream that is Hinduism. I hope it clears doubts about its polymorphism, generates genuine interest in this 'beyond our daily world' subject, and duly motivates the readers to seek more details about this most intricate science of the soul by pursuing the path of spirituality, in the chosen way.

Kiran Mehta
Atlanta

INTRODUCTION

HISTORICAL OVERVIEW

An All-comprehensive Religion

As the world's oldest living religious tradition, Hinduism is most enduring. It is the third largest in terms of the number of followers pursued by an extensive range of racial groups, social classes, and regional communities. Reflecting its great age extending over several thousand years, it is incredibly vast, deeply variegated, and quite vexing at times. And yet, it is extremely vibrant, naturally versatile, and truly viable all the time. So elusive is this cumulative ancient and esoteric religious tradition that no single succinct and satisfactory definition can be given. It is impossible even for a Hindu to practice all of Hinduism. A rich, varied, and fluid theological system, it is without rigid boundary between the philosophical fruits of its large loom. Also, it invariably carries the kind that suits, stimulates, and satisfies the spiritual appetite of a seeker.

In an absence of a single source of founding principles, appearing at a particular time, it has not evolved as an organized or unified belief system. The vast breadth of its mighty course powers through a confluence of countless practices streaming in from the centers of several schools of philosophies. They run together within the liberal confines of Vedic principles to create an intricate flow gushing towards the same goal. Adding designer doctrines trending with the occasion of an era, it has constantly expanded its philosophical wardrobe. Also, it sports a huge collection of dramatic masks like images and icons, sects and cults, deities and symbols. Thus, it is quite intriguing yet interesting, often contradictory yet captivating. It easily confirms to have an archaic yet amazingly alive, colorful chameleon character that defies the power of imagination.

However, potpourri of such attires enlivening its appearance conceals great depths of character. Local literature, sectarian beliefs, native deities, and regional disparities are veils of diverse surface expression. Under it runs a common thread of immutable principles, a cohesive force strong enough to connect, hold, and unify them together. For instance, there is strong belief in reincarnation and transmigration of the soul. Absolute conviction in destiny, *Prārabdha* based on the law of cause and effect, *Karma* guides everyone to live by following their duty, *Dharma*. Also, everyone has a chosen deity, *Ishta-Devtā* as the face of God to worship. Time honored and tested, it is a proven way of life. It provides the followers a myriad of methods and means like ceremonies and celebrations, dedication and devotion, rites and rituals, *Yoga* and meditation. There is an incomparable wealth of philosophical literature to gain metaphysical insight and spiritual illumination. It helps everyone to find the rightful way of life, harmonize their lives, and experience inner peace and happiness while guiding them to achieve the ultimate goal of human life: Self-Realization.

Vedic Age (3000+ BC)

Its core philosophy, heard in the voice of self-existent Absolute, *Brahman* is known as *Śruti*, what was directly revealed to ancient sages enfolded in enlightenment. The ingenious mix of these vibrations was conceived as the breath of *Brahman* who achieved immanence as the phenomenal body of cosmos through these subtle sound energies. Epitome of sacred knowledge, it was well remembered as *Smṛti*. Narrated by word of mouth, it was duly preserved with profound integrity over several millennia through generations. Much later, with the beginning of literary tradition in 2nd-1st millennium BC, it was first written down by sage Vyāsa. This collection is the holiest spiritual texts known as the Vedas. It has a sense of intimate communion between the nature and those Self-Realized sages. This spiritual treasury consists of mantras and hymns that invoke and adore various elemental powers of life with awe. Eventually they came to be resolved in the form of cosmic entities and deities.

Each of these natural forces was visualized with a name and form. As none of them had supremacy, each was elevated, in turn, to the highest rank at the time of its worship and eulogized. A few of them are Indra, Agni, Varuṇa, Soma, Sūrya, Mitra, Rūdra, and Vāyu. They were duly recognized as various aspects of the transcendental Supreme. However, in the contemporary deity group of worship, none of them has a role, though some are recognized differently. Sacrifice was central to ceremonial and propitiatory rites conducted under the auspicious of the Vedas to gain spiritual and worldly powers. The number three appears to be sacred as ***Ṛgveda***, the premier and foremost of the four Vedas has a reference to thirty three such deities. Grouped under three leading categories, their leaders presumably rose as the presently predominant Trimurti Concept of God. Of all the mantras of the Vedas, Gāyatrī mantra is considered to be the essence as it encapsulates the entire knowledge of the Vedas.

The purpose and goal of the Vedas were described in abstract philosophical texts at the end of each Veda known as Upaniṣad. There is a transition from hymnology and liturgy of the Vedas that adore and worship nature to the metaphysics of thought, reason, and reflection on the Supreme in Upaniṣads. They essentially teach pantheism submitting subtle theories of evolution and existence based on the principle of natural law and universal order called *Ṛta.* An independently operating authority, its reign is infallibly effective. It equally embraces the physical as well as the spiritual realms directing all worldly things and events. *Ṛta* is a kernel with two cotyledons, the major doctrines of *Karma* and *Dharma*. *Dharma* is a relative term with a wide meaning, quite different from the word religion that it is generally believed to stand for. Applied to special circumstances surrounding everyone, it carries different meanings that govern the specific responsibilities and action, *Karma* of an individual. Under its broad canopy, it covers all aspects of privileges, duties, and obligation at every stage of human life. It touches such timeless truths as service and sacrifice, moral values and ethics, natural law and justice, duty and righteousness. These guiding principles called Perennial Philosophy, ***Sanātana Dharma*** directed everyday matters of life. They are relevant to everyone, at all times, even today.

The seeds of *Sanātana Dharma* were sawn in prehistoric period. Though the germs of this uncompromising way of life got rooted, sprouted, and developed during the Vedic age, it did not explicitly express the limited idea of a religion. Nourished and nurtured by people over centuries, they grew in stages over ages weathering vagaries of time and various storms of human discord and degeneration. As the saplings grew taller and became stronger, the ensuing classical age afforded them an unbelievably robust impetus. They were transplanted with the grafting of newer theologies, doctrines, and disciplines. Such hybridization created novel reconfigurations significantly transforming its body and character. As it renewed, revived, and reinvented itself, it acquired newer appellation of a religion. Branching in all directions, it spread out like a vine to have morphologically heterogeneous and incomprehensibly entangled body known today as Hinduism. It is a name of broad description which is more of a linguistic convenience that carries geographic connotation.

The early view of divine conceived during the Vedic period eventually led to Brāhmanism (800 to 500 BC). It gave rise to professional class of priests. They led people by creating social identity based on caste system. A well stratified system of social relations, it divided people into four main categories based on their profession and lineage. They were Brahmans, the priests; Kshatriyas, the warriors; Vaishyas, the merchants; and Kshudras, the serving class. Relevant to that time, it was quite effective laying foundation of hierarchy and order. But this layered social structure slowly degenerated giving way to contemporary sensibilities, though it is quite significant even today. While conducting fire ceremonies, priests performed rites and rituals offering oblations and sacrifices to appease and propitiate deities. It became widely prevalent, essential, and deeply ingrained doctrine central to the worship of divine.

Classical Age (200 BC – 1100 AD).

The Vedic era of intuition gave way to the era of reasoning and critical inquiry, suspicion and skepticism. People raised questions about excesses of ruthless immolation of animals, occurring in large numbers during sacrificial practices. With a new found awareness, they wanted answers to questions like who am I, what is the purpose of my life, why people experience so much pain and suffering, how did God create the world. Answer to such philosophical questions was not directly offered by the Vedas or available Upaniṣads. Hence, many sages like Yajnavalkya responded to such queries by expanding the existing line of Upaniṣads. Out of many that were composed, 108 are available today of which 12 are considered to be the major. Laws of Manu, *Manusmṛti* compiled around this time lists ten points of duty, among other laws. It is considered to be the most authoritative and sacred text after the Vedas.

Several other orthodox schools of philosophies also variously shaped up with such a shift in the psyche of people. Of these, succinct comments of the six classical schools called ***Darśana***, each suitable to specific grade of mind are well recognized. They all accept the Vedas to be authoritative. They are the *Nyāya* by sage Gautama, the *Vaiśeshika* by sage Kanāda, the *Sānkhya* by sage Kapila, the *Yoga* by sage Patanjali, the *Mīmānsā* by sage Jaimini, and the *Vedānta* by sage Bādarāyaṇa. Converging on specific metaphysical speculation and addressing it in its own unique way, each had hugely profound and lasting implications. Despite postulating graded standards, points, and opinions, they all highlight equally valid views, each being complementary in nature. Vedic culture was an all-tolerant, all-compliant, and all-absorbing ideology having universal receptivity. Therefore, accretion of such ideas and appropriation of these doctrines worked their way through to widespread acceptance. As these six 'limbs' anchored to the Vedas were fully incorporated and duly integrated, it assumed the form of a perfect religious body having an abundantly mature character. By getting multi-dimensional perspectives on divinity, it gradually thrived and prospered as an all-comprehensive breath of a religion, Hinduism.

Nyāya investigates by reasoning and analysis whereas *Sānkhya* employs the method of enumeration and synthesis. *Sānkhya* also preaches dualism and propagates the philosophy of the union of two principles, spirit and matter which is very well received. It had a tremendous influence on Tantra. *Vaiśeshika* supplements analytical tools of *Nyāya* while dealing with the elements of earth, fire, water, air, ether, soul, mind, space, and time that make the universe. *Yoga* may be regarded as a branch of *Sānkhya* that teaches means by which human soul can unite with the Supreme. *Yoga* practices popular in the west are mostly limited to the physical fitness exercises specifically known as *Hatha Yoga*. *Mīmānsā* offers inquiry and interpretation of the art of Vedic rituals, considered to be the stepping stones to spirituality. ***Vedānta*** enunciates, explains, and elaborates upon the philosophy of non-dualism of the Upaniṣads. It is considered to be the crown jewel of all doctrines, philosophical foundation of Hinduism, universal in its application. It believes that the whole universe is a form of one eternal Essence. Brahma Sūtras are the principal texts of *Vedānta.*

Besides these classical philosophical texts, distinct genre narrations called **Purāṇas** were authored over a period of several centuries. They consist of the ancient, historical, and mythological stories, tales, and legends. Having an authoritative background, each enlarged to be an encyclopedia by accretion of content edited over time. It was written for the grasp of unlettered, those who could not study the Vedas, and find the knowledge of *Darśana* too abstract. All Purāṇas contain essence of the Vedas and stress the importance of preserving genealogy of gods, great sages, and glorious kings. To generate pedestrian appeal, interesting narratives with the stories of various deities focused on their life, love, play, and divine powers that routed demonic rulers were written. They were interspersed with allegories to illustrate the reign of cosmic order while elucidating eternal principles of religion. With their assimilation in social and cultural situations, it kindled interest, flared up imagination, and led people to spirituality through devotion well serving their purpose.

The strength of this stream developed a new tradition of folk religion running parallel to the elite and orthodox philosophical systems pursued by the learned. The line of their demarcation is quite indistinct which constantly changes all the time. Narratives of mythological lore created popular ideas associated with images in the minds of average people. It blurred many subtle concepts like that between Lord Shiva and Lord Mahesh as both came to be known as the same deity. This literature is dominated by deities other than those of Vedic era, though they are also populated with reduced rank. Eighteen of the Purāṇas, often grouped in three divisions are considered major. The Bhāgavat Purāṇa giving details about the life of Lord Kṛṣṇa is the most accepted, read, and celebrated whereas the Mārkaṇḍeya Purāṇa is one of the oldest and the least partial.

Āgamas are yet another class of scripture that presents the teachings of the Vedas in its own ways. They are the operative manuals having directions and specifications for temple construction. They show the ways to install and consecrate deities, the method of their worship, the associated rites and rituals, and the philosophy behind it. Each of the three major theistic systems, Vaishṇavism, Shaivism, and Shaktism has its own *Āgama.*

Buddhism and Jainism

Two other doctrines thrived and grew as an off-shoot of Hinduism due to their non-orthodox character. In fact, each was a rebellion against the dominance of Brāhmanism and caste system. One of them is well recognized as Buddhism named after its founder Gautama Buddha, the enlightened one. Though having striking parallels with Hinduism, Buddhism rejected the authority of the Vedas not approving the sacrificial ceremonies. It is a system of duty, morality, and benevolence without having any deity or prayer and therefore, a unique religion without any theology. It lays great emphasis on the teachings of Buddha, path of *Dharma*, and the community called *Sangha*. These three jewels of spirituality stress self-inquiry in order to attain *Nirvāna*. Having great influence on Hinduism, Lord Gautama was recognized as an incarnation of Lord Vishṇu, one of the deities of Trinity Concept. Most of its precepts were also assimilated to mark a period of renaissance. It saw decline of the Vedic cult, dwindling of sacrificial practices, and transformation of ritualistic tradition into devotional system. However, later, after the revival of Brāhmanism, Buddhism perished by the thirteenth century in the land where it took birth. It was mainly due to overemphasis on monastic life and absence of deity of worship.

Like Buddhism, the other system that sought a separate identity came to be known as Jainism. It claims to be eternal though it is largely believed to be contemporary to Buddhism. Based on the teachings of 24 liberated souls called *Tirthankars*, it believes in non-violence, truth, non-stealing, celibacy, and non-materialism. It also does not have any concept of God while deeply embedding the elements of deep compassion and fasting. It advocates renunciation of the world and regards knowledge to be relative in the complex scheme of nature. Their scriptures elaborate various methods of meditation for liberation from the *Karmic* bondage. Later, the youngest religion, Sikhism was established in the fifteenth century by Guru Nanak Dev, first in a lineage of ten spiritual leaders. Its coherent corpus was later compiled as the holy text, Guru Granth Sahib. It attaches great importance to truthful living for Self-realization.

The gradual transition of ritualistic system to devotional stream concurrently transformed the nature of Vedic deities. It is widely believed that Agni took the form of Lord Brahmā whose role was expanded as the creator. Lord Vishṇu, mentioned as a God of grace in *Ṛgveda* superseded Sūrya as the prominent pervader and preserver. Rūdra, depicted as ruthless destroyer represented rule of nature upon man. He got elevated by acquiring the lofty position of Lord Mahesh, the transformer. These deities form the most accepted concept of Trimurti today. Each of them personifies a specific mode of action called Guṇa the three strands of which combine in various ways to weave all types of creation. Each deity also has a spouse who duly represents their active energy. Over time, Lord Brahmā got sidelined whereas Vaishṇavism and Shaivism grew to be the two most predominant theistic systems of the modern time.

In the 7th-8th century AD, the philosopher Ādi Śankarācārya played a major role in the revival of Brāhmanism. He advocated the Vedic theory of non-dualism, *Advaita* where all beings are believed to be one with God. He has authored vast number of treaties and his commentaries on Vedic philosophy are held in the highest esteem. He also established four monasteries, *mathas* to spread this philosophy. By this time, the ancient practice of Tantrism also found its roots eventually coming to the fore by the medieval period. Though closely intertwined with Hinduism, it is a unique system open to everyone as it accepts all worldly ways of life. It harnesses ubiquitous energies in order to purify the subtle system that catalyzes spiritual elevation and also gives paranormal powers. Its most profound contribution is *Kuṇḍalinī* Yoga; to raise the energy lying dormant at the base of spine for the ultimate spiritual experience. However, it is commonly viewed as magical and mystical due to various secret practices and the occult powers acquired by its practitioner, often used for questionable purposes. It has several schools and is widely practiced even in Buddhism.

Shaktism developed over the past couple of millennia to be one of the major sects today along with Vaishṇavism and Shaivism. This ancient doctrine stayed dormant during the Vedic Age but resurfaced and brilliantly expanded during the period of renaissance. It propitiates Devī as Divine Mother, the female God-head as Ultimate Reality who is visualized and worshiped in her countless forms. Embodiment of primal energy, she is the dynamic aspect of *Brahman*, the efficient and material cause of all creation. As this doctrine is an exponent of the predominance, power, and play of energy, it is intimately associated with Tantrism. Shaktism is also well interconnected with Shaivism as her spouse, Lord Shiva personifies static aspect of *Brahman*.

Contemporary Hinduism

Hinduism constantly battles deterioration caused by ignorance, lower human nature, and misinterpretation. Spiritual leaders, at times, interpret scriptures and profess truths tainted and tilted to their advantage. The tools offered to a common man for his grasp of spirituality often leads to superstitious beliefs, idolatry, and false notions of the divine. Vested interests of people who use religion as a means of living do not hesitate to exploit the misplaced faith and innocence of these people. Casteism, child marriage, female feticide, and life of seclusion for widows were some evil and obsolete practices. Various social reformers and spiritual leaders of modern India condemned them to rejuvenate, reinvigorate, and revive it with their broad vision and insight.

The strength of Hinduism lies in variety of ways of salvation it offers and its deep roots in *Sanātana Dharma*, faith illuminated way of life. It has countless paths, doctrines, philosophies, and traditions. With an unbelievable continuity of mindscape, they all are duly recognized as well-knit network of different cognitive systems of the religion. Religious precepts, social standards, moral values, and cultural expressions are finely knit together as science and art of living within the psyche of people. It has survived through descent and lineage, power of kinship and community spirit creating a unique outlook of life. In an ever shifting paradigm of social and cultural norms, it is, therefore, truly commendable that the traditional beliefs and practices of Hinduism hold sway over all aspects of life even today. Home shrines are common symbols of unshakable faith. Daily worship, temple visits, and faith based activities are few of the steps guiding the path of people. It bears testimony to its influence and centrality in their life. Contemporary Hinduism is a confirmation that truths of the past not only prevail but are also relevant to the present.

The modern Hinduism slowly and steadily but surely continues to evolve on the principles of heredity and adaptation. Adaptation is the natural law to survive and succeed, to ascertain ways to cope with the present realities. In fact, the entire history of Hinduism reflects this trait through which it has survived to this age. The guiding principles of life, *Dharma* are constantly redefined to find new meanings with the ever demanding dimensions of life in the modern era of civilization. Hinduism has truly become a universal religion with migration of people and establishment of Hindu communities all over the world. As an old Hindu doctrine says, the whole world is but one family, *Vasudhaiva Kutumbakaṃ*. How true it literally has come to be in the present age of shrinking boundaries, narrowing distances, and rapid globalization.

With enhanced interaction of diverse ethnic groups and cultures, ever increasing number of people get a glimpse of Hinduism. For these curious viewers in the gallery, its vast arena may variously appear to be strange, mysterious, fascinating, or simply awesome. It may be equally challenging for them to appreciate the fine way in which mantra chanting, meditation practices, and meticulous methods of deity worship harness the universal cosmic energies. Such routines exhilarate and empower, illuminate and elevate having material as well as spiritual benefits. Yet, to all rational minds, it may defy logic and hence, lack conviction. But riding the subtle influences of these esoteric practices is a part of the experiences of an out of the world journey of spirituality. It is only made possible by determination, dedication, and devotion of a nescient mind.

AUM

Sonic Absolute, Nāda-Brahman

Aum is an extremely sacred syllable in Hinduism. It represents a soundless sound that casually exists in the void of space eternally encapsulating vibratory nature of the entire universe. An unmanifest, *Nirguṇa* aspect of *Brahman*, it is a seed sound which, upon spontaneous polarization pulsates as its manifesting, *Saguṇa* aspect called *Nāda Brahman*. This subtle sound is a self-emanating impulse, the creative potential of the Absolute that ultimately gives rise to all physical creation. The living intelligence of this universal substratum has no beginning and no end. It embraces everything that exists in the phenomenal world, from the grossest to the finest. Therefore, it is the holiest invocation invariably intoned by everyone in mantras and prayers during religious ceremonies, rites, and rituals.

Entire creation is the ultimate phenomena initiated by *Nāda Brahman*. It is the source of subtle sound waves, *Nāda* that spread around to create the vibratory field, *Spanda*. *Nāda* waves gradually differentiate into the key cosmic sounds endowed with the prime power to create specific physical forms. They further combine into typical derivative sounds that create various building blocks of the universe. Many of these were revealed to ancient sages who compiled them as the Vedas, Holy Scriptures. It constitutes the divine knowledge that upholds this manifold universe. As Aum is the source of these sounds, its incantation is universally held as holy and supreme. It connects the body, mind, and spirit and therefore, an integral part of all *Yoga* and meditation practices. Often written as OM, it has a unique symbol having a significant meaning. All Hindu temples and places of worship customarily carry this symbol.

All living beings carry vibratory energy humming around them that produces a droning sound. Normally sound is produced when an object strikes another. However, the natural vibrations of this eternal sound are unstruck, *Anāhata*. Devī *Kuṇḍalinī*, the divine energy is the source of this indistinct murmuring sound. She lies dormant at the base of spine in the subtle body, which interpenetrates the physical body of every human being. Though it is not audible to us, sages clearly perceive this vibratory Reality during their transcendental state of meditation. The whole universe resonates in harmony as its pulsating energy connects all life forms. It is the imperishable throb of primordial sound Aum which is also well known as *akśara*.

Praṇava mantra

When we pronounce Aum, the audible sound so produced most closely resembles this unstruck sound of the life force of the universe. Its vibrations pervade all our subtle energy channels transmitting an enormous amount of spiritual energy. While meditating, as we chant Aum and align our inner self with their evolutionary energy, it catalyzes our spiritual elevation. Being in correspondence with the eternal energy flow of cosmos, they harmonize our energies with nature to have a healing and soothing effect. Since the vibratory field of *Aumkāra* is the source of primordial energy, *Prāṇa* which sustains the breath of life, Aum is also called *Praṇava* mantra. Its sounding is the field of living cosmic intelligence, eternal aspect of God, source of our self.

The sacred sound Aum is mentioned in all the major Upaniṣads, concluding part of the Vedas. *Māṇḍūkya* Upaniṣad is entirely dedicated to this syllable as it interprets and offers an in depth insight into its sacred meaning. It describes Aum as an imperishable, eternal, and universal sound that transcends the past, the present, and the future divisions of time. It further states that it is not merely a sound but the entire cosmos, sonic body of the Absolute. All creation visible to us, perceived by our senses, and comprehended by our mind is the ever pulsating field of Aum. This subtle substratum continuously resounds, resonates, and reverberates supporting all existence. No matter what changes take place in the external shapes and forms, animate or inanimate, this creative and life sustaining force of universe always remains the same.

The monosyllabic Aum has three phonemes 'A', 'U', and 'M'. They bear the same harmony of correspondence that prevails between the gross, the subtle, and the casual planes underlying all forms of existence. Their vibrations travel through all major psycho-energy centers, Chakras strung along the spine in our subtle body. The least differentiated sound 'A' originates in the first Chakra, *Mulādhāra*. It is near the base of the spine from which the vibrations initiate in the throat region. With the sound 'U' moving to the middle of the mouth, these vibrations gradually move up to *Anāhata* Chakra near the heart. As they further move forward to create sound 'M' with lips gently closed in the front, they reach the last Chakra, *Sahasrāra* in the crown of brain. It is then followed by a silence which underscores the three aspects of our existence signified by these phonemes that ultimately unite with the Absolute. With the articulation of Aum, all Chakras of our subtle body resonate and all areas of our vocal chords vibrate, in succession. It encompasses all such sounds that can possibly be produced within our mouth. Therefore, Aum is the source of all alphabets, words, and spoken languages forming the basis of all types of communication. It is extremely important to know, especially to understand the effect of mantra chanting that Aum is the progenitor of all other sounds.

In any language, the use of specific sound combinations creates an accepted medium of communication for the people. The idea conveyed and information provided, as understood by the listener invokes an appropriate response. Similarly, a mantra combines specific sounds of Sanskṛit alphabets in such way as accepted by the related deity for communication. Dedicated chanting of mantra effectively addresses the deity, invokes its grace, and releases its auspicious energy as a response. In other words, mantra is the sound body of divine cosmic energy represented by a deity. As Aum is the progenitor of all sounds, including Sanskṛit alphabets, all mantras originate from Aum. Chanting Aum invokes energies of the whole universe, our entire subtle system, and the grace of all deities collectively constituting the Absolute. Therefore, Aum is considered to be the mother of all mantras. Recitation of Aum at the beginning of any mantra imparts potency to it, brings it to life, and makes it truly effective.

Three states of existence

The three letters 'A', 'U', and 'M' carry more than one symbolic meaning with them. In one interpretation, 'A' expands further into *Ṛgveda*, signifies devotion, and is associated with the cosmic plane of the earth, *Bhūh*. 'U' differentiates into *Yajurveda*, symbolizes action, and represents the cosmic plane of the sky, *Bhūvah*. 'M' develops into *Sāmaveda*, represents knowledge, and the cosmic plane of the heaven, *Sūvaha*. Also, they signify the three states of our existence - waking, dreaming, and deep sleep one of which prevails at any given time. Each state is identified by specific level of activity of the mind and consciousness.

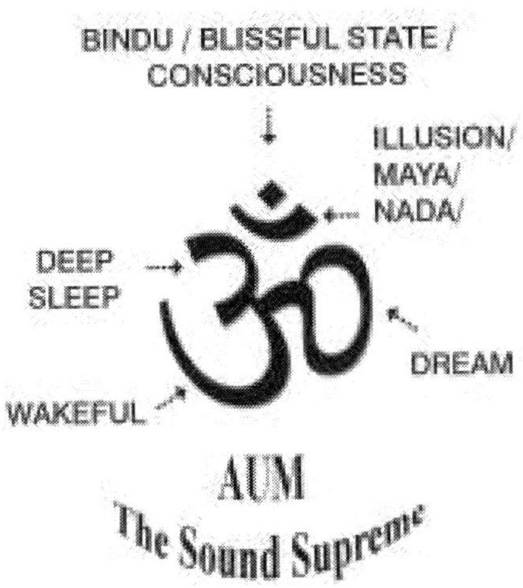

Our body is considered *Tripura* as our consciousness operates in one of these three states and also experiences through the corresponding body or city (*pura*) – gross body while waking, subtle body while dreaming, and casual body while in deep sleep. They represent the three integrated states of our manifestation.

Our soul, as *Ātman* or *Sanctus Spiritus* is a part of the Absolute, *Brahman* personified by the portrait of Lord Shiva. He is, therefore, worshipped as the ruler of the three cities, *Tripurari*. To have finite experiences, Lord Shiva manifests as embodied souls through his formative energy, Shakti. Therefore, Shakti is also known as *Tripureshi* and *Tripurasundari*.

The silence that follows after pronouncing Aum is the fourth unheard sound. It represents the gradual melting into the source of our being, the most blissful state that unifies these three conditions. Achieving this state is the aim of all spiritual practices like *Yoga* and meditation that allow us to raise our awareness beyond the limits of mind and body. Human life is a boon and a blessing as, of all the living species, only humans can achieve this ultimate goal of life.

The iconography of Aum is a graphic representation of this meaning. The large lower curve symbolizes the predominant **waking state (*vaishvanara*)**. It also symbolizes the physical body we acquire upon birth for worldly experiences. This state is prevalent during the daytime in which our mind as well as consciousness is fully active directed to the external world. Within the limitations of time and space, we work, enjoy, and suffer through the gross body as shown by ‘A’ of Aum. Our consciousness dominates and controls as it uses the mind as a tool fully exploiting its potential. According to its level of awareness, it enjoys the world having appropriate experiences. Throughout the life, it evaluates various options at each moment, makes a considered choice, and then decides the course of action. Thereby it characterizes our *Karma*.

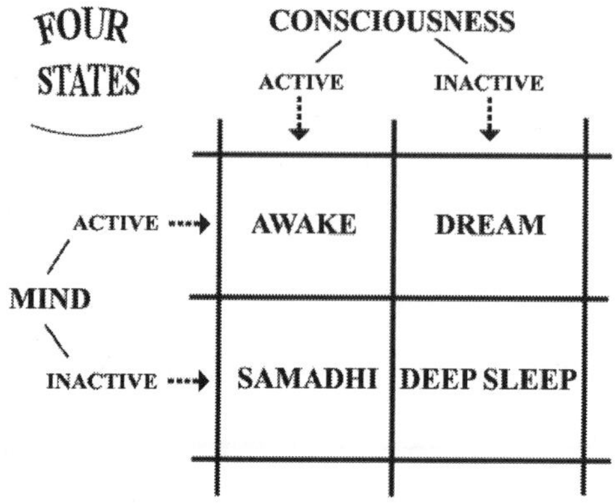

The upper curve shows the deep sleep, **unconscious state (*prajna*)**. In this state the desires are dormant as mind as well as the consciousness is absolutely inactive. It also symbolizes the time of death when our soul ultimately merges with the divine. It is the state of absolute silence represented by ‘M’ of Aum. Only the deepest aspect of subconscious mind prevails as we dwell in the casual body. Casual body is the repository of past *Karma* which carries all impressions in its latent form. We do not think or do, remember or know anything in this most peaceful and restful experience. Deep sleep is the pristine state of total harmony with the divine where there is no distinction between the subject and the object, the observer and the observed. Basking in this most blissful period unbound by the time, space, or causation our soul quietly recharges, renews, and revitalizes itself. Though apparently nothing happens during the period of deep sleep, it is considered to be the domain of supreme knowledge.

However, while sleeping, when the mind awakes and becomes active whereas the consciousness is still inactive and dormant, we are thrown into **dream state** (***taijasa***). It also corresponds to the intermediate state of the soul after the death and the time before it reincarnates. Here the senses are inactive as well. The sound 'U' of Aum and the curve in between, on the other side in the symbol represents this dreaming state. Without the guiding field and force of the consciousness, mind is free to move around. It wanders into different worlds where the subject and the object, though separate, coalesce together in absence of the boundaries of time and space. Latent impressions, infatuations, and imaginations of the inner world lead us to indulge in strange visions. We enjoy, experience, and suffer through the subtle body only to realize that it was a dream, a different level of reality, when we wake up.

We often experience a brief transition period of consciousness known as *Unmani* during the change between the waking and the dreaming states. A similar transition of consciousness between the dreaming and the deep sleep states is known as *Aladani* which, though, is never experienced.

Cosmic Consciousness

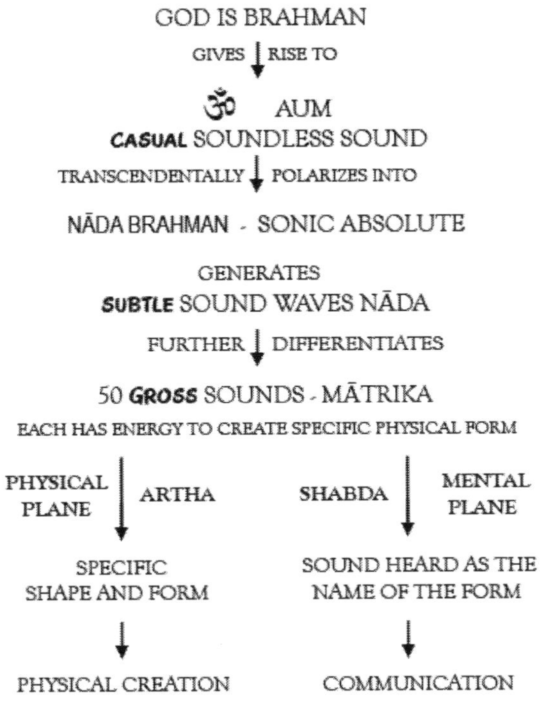

The dot at the top, *Bindu* represents the fourth state of **Samadhi (*Turiya*)**. It is the most blissful state of total peace, quiet, and purity symbolized by the silence that follows after uttering the sound Aum. As the sound gradually fades away and becomes inaudible, so do the countless thoughts of mind and endless experiences of existence which finally leads to a state of perfect trance. It is the most conducive state where, in an absence of interruptions and interferences of the mind, consciousness finally succeeds in transcending the limitations imposed by the body to realize the Truth. Permeating all the three states experienced through the gross, the subtle, and the casual bodies, it expands to infinity melting and merging the individual soul, *Ātman* with the dot, *Paramātma*.

Nāda waves that create the subtle substratum of *Spanda* inherently carry the divine desire, intent, and ability to create. Spreading around, they develop embryo of the universe, *Hiranyagarbha* containing all latent names and forms. Within the dual characteristic of these waves, energy of propagation which sustains their shape lie the secret of their creative potential. Its energy is the source and cause of ***Shabda***, expression of an idea and a name on one side whereas the shape it creates and the object it denotes is ***Artha*** on the other. It is the core principle underlying all physical phenomena where all physical forms are sustained by their underlying energy. These two connected characteristics are the cause that simultaneously develops the physical and mental planes each of which represent the same thing, but in their own particular way. As *Nāda* waves differentiate and combine, they develop typical sonic units having ability to create various building blocks of the universe called *Tattva*. They are the basis of all creation, source of all names and forms in the entire manifestation.

The semi-circle in the iconography represents the emanation of *Nāda* waves from *Bindu*. It also stands for the veil of illusion, *Māyā* that separates and prevents us from reaching the dot. Ever active mind and the senses, always focused outwards and entangled in the web of the world is the biggest hindrance in reaching the source. Meditation practices calm the vibratory field of mind and redirect it inward. But only a blessed few succeed in their spiritual practices to establish such control as to withdraw them from the outer world. By moving towards the inner higher self, we 'awake' from the wakeful state and reach the origin. As consciousness expands, it enables us to see the futility of physical phenomenon and transitory nature of worldly experiences. In the most elevated state of *Samadhi*, we get the realization of the Ultimate Truth.

Vibrations of the endless stream of desires, past memories, thoughts of all kinds, feeling of anger and irritation cause restless and turbulent mind. Recitation of Aum creates such vibrations that abate them making us calm, quiet, and relaxed. Chanting of Aum, as we contemplate on *Brahman* or Consciousness is conducive to Self-knowledge. It illuminates the higher mind, elevates the spiritual state, and establishes us in that realm. Aum also indicates many other triads like the three modes of nature; the mode of ignorance, *Tamas;* the mode of passion, *Rajas;* and the mode of goodness; *Sattva*. Also, it represents three levels of existence; in the heaven, on the earth, and in the netherworld. In yet another meaning, 'A' represents creation, 'U' represents preservation, and 'M' represents dissolution signifying the three aspects of the Trinity concept of God. Lord Gaṇesha is considered '*Aumkāra Swarūpa*' as he personifies Aum. Aum is also a part of the most sacred, widely recognized, and commonly chanted mantra '*Aum Mani Padme Hum*' in Buddhism.

IMAGE and DEITY WORSHIP

Personal God with Aspects

Monism is the basis of Hinduism. There is only one God without the second; *Ekam eva advitīyam*. It is well recognized as *Brahman*, Cosmic Consciousness without having a name or form. The cause of all causes, what we see, including ourselves are its various transitory effects. Its will configures various life forms through its energy by attuning five archetypal elements, *Panchamahābhuta* that creates living landscape of all the plants and animals. Through immutable laws of nature, it also governs different sentient levels that operate in harmony to ensure orderly function of the entire creation. Besides the physical plane of our existence, there are also other supersensible and higher mystical realities. These other worlds simultaneously exist and operate at frequencies beyond ordinary understanding, common knowledge, and daily experience. It is the force of nature that cannot be comprehended in its totality by human mind, an excellent tool but for use limited to the material plane in which we live.

The experience based human view-point is partial and flawed due to the finite intelligence and limited perception. Being restricted by the limitations of the senses conditioned with personal traits, *Saṃskāra*, even the entire resume of collective human experiences remains imperfect. Supreme Self has inconceivable potencies so vast in their implications and complexities that it is beyond the conceptual knowledge of the mind based on data of the senses. *Brahman* has infinite faculties of ever-evolving creative intelligence. Also, it unfolds in unpredictable ways in such dimensions that cannot be anticipated or foreseen, visualized or understood. It is the eternal, all-pervading, all-encompassing Reality, cause of all transitory physical phenomena.

Dilemma and the solution

For a common man, it is difficult to appreciate this abstract principle of God and the philosophy that *Brahman* is the core of everything. The three main theistic orders of Hinduism refer to it, in general, by names like *Pārā* Shiva, *Pārā* Shakti, and *Mahā* Vishṇu without having any attributes (***Nirguṇa)***. But to worship an invisible Self is a daunting task, like searching in the dark. In absence of any perception of his presence, it is not motivating or involving, assuring or satisfying. People need a personal God with a form that can be seen and relate with so that their minds can hold on to his divine presence. Ancient seers, highly evolved saints, and Self-Realized sages resolved this issue.

They had performed severe austerities, *tapas* to establish complete self-control over the mind and body. By successfully harmonizing their energies with the nature, they were able to conquer it. Realizing the innermost essence of Transpersonal Self, they were blessed with micro-clairvoyant vision. During their profound meditative state, various celestial beings of higher plane appeared as identifiable personalities, each an aspect that manifest at specific frequencies in subtle realms of existence. Within their inner space, *Cidākāśa* they could see them, hear their subtle sounds, relate with them, and communicate with them. These sounds of direct revelation, *Śruti* were compiled as the Vedas, the basis of Hinduism. This state of being is well illustrated by Arjuna when he saw Lord Kṛṣṇa in his universal form after acquiring the divine vision. Though quite difficult to achieve in this age and time, this state of awareness is available to everyone. It is reached by living the life of purity, following the path of *Dharma*, and undertaking the spiritual practices like worship and devotion, *Yoga* and meditation. Śrī Rāmakṛṣṇa Paramahaṃsa and Śrī Raman Maharishi are the most recent examples who achieved this ultimate state of Self Realization.

Knowing that God of limitless potencies cannot be shaped, those seers presented his various anthropomorphic forms as deities based on their secret sacred vision. They were introduced for an effective outer worship to create a spiritual sense of inner discipline for initiates. Each form is a differentiated view of the divine having some specific attributes (***Saguṇa***), the basis of that image. The sages had also Realized their underlying energy encapsulated in the vibrations of various mantra sounds. The secrets of binding these energies were then embedded in specific rites and rituals constituting unique methods of liturgy. Finally, the deity images were consecrated using these methods to invoke the divine and impart potency to them. These great masters of the past, supreme scientists of the soul and spirituality perfected this whole system. Enthused to be able to share their vision and so inspired by the saints and sages, people recognized these embodied deities and carried out their worship.

Consecration of Images

Āgama is the specific class of scripture that deals with the exact details of temple construction and consecration of deity images. Priests carry out ***'Prāṇa Pratishthā'*** ceremony whereby 'life' is installed in the statues of deities in Sanctum Sanctorum in a temple. An elaborate process, it involves several rites and rituals including Homa, the sacred fire ceremony. Stepwise, it gathers and channels the specific energy from the subtlest cosmic level to the grossest physical level of the image. After invocation of the deity, as the ceremony proceeds, the potency of vibratory field created by mantra chanting is raised by the Homa fire which energizes water filled in ***Kalasa***, special pots arranged nearby. They act as receptors that absorb this energy to hold, carry, and transfer. They are covered with turmeric paste and have a coconut placed over the mouth surrounded by mango leaves along the rim. Finally, the energized water is poured over the statue to sanctify and bring it to 'life'.

Once consecrated, the image so energized carries the same potency and power of the deity it represents in a vibrant state. The embodied deity becomes a source of direction and inspiration for devotees as it reinforces their faith and re-energizes their lives. Therefore, it has become an integral part of all types of ceremonial worship, a feature that is unique to Hinduism. As devotees reverently stand before a now visible God, they really feel his divine presence due to the surrounding air, aura, and energy. To see, have *Darśana* and be seen by the gazing deity is an all-powerful, touching, elevating, and blissful experience. It effectively attends to the spiritual aspirations of devotees who heartily carry out his worship and emerge blessed, fulfilled, and empowered.

Polymorphic System

Obviously different deities are intelligible forms representing various aspects of the Truth. It makes a polymorphic, not polytheistic system where part of the same Truth is represented in their sacred physical forms. Different aspects of life are governed by different cosmic forces, each visualized in the form of deity thus creating multitude of images. At times, they have multiple arms symbolizing their extraordinary powers. Even if an image is not consecrated, it is worthy of worship as all forms are valid manifestation of the Reality. To get initiated into spirituality, worship of a deity having attributes of the divine is the first stepping stone. This simple method is the core practice and an integral part of all devotional paths. It helps to initiate a sense of commune, develop a flow of energy that cultivates a bond, and establish a personal relationship with God. Of all the different paths like the path of action, *Karma*, the path of knowledge, *Jnāna* etc., the path of devotion, ***Bhakti*** is considered to be the easiest, the best, and the most appropriate path for the current Dark Age.

In devotional service, the worshiped deity image is bathed, dressed, fed, and prayed with deep faith and feeling. All these actions are directed by heartfelt love, affection, and reverence to connect with and unify with it. A person with the logic of a rational mind fails miserably either to appreciate or benefit from underlying subtle influences. A matter of feeling and perception, it is a directive of the heart and the intuitive mind. Devotion means unflinching dedication and total surrender, absolute love and complete faith. Mind and the senses are the biggest obstacles in the path of spiritual advancement. When the mind becomes quiescent then only we make progress in spirituality.

Ishta-Devtā

Worshiping the deity of choice, *Ishta-Devtā* is yet another facet of the religion. We have a plethora of choices when it comes to buying cloth that basically covers our body or choosing our foods that basically nourishes it. We select the best we can to suit the time and occasion, a sign of our advanced taste, culture, and sophistication. Likewise Hinduism, highly evolved and sophisticated system that it is, offers plenty of choices of deity and methods of worship. Diversity of deities and paths accommodate different psyches of devotees, provide a selection, and an alternative to accomplish the same goal. A person chooses the one he is exposed to, comfortable with, and appeals to his spiritual appetite consistent with his level of consciousness.

Deity worship has a dual purpose; success in the material world and progress in the spiritual path. Regular worship transforms, centers, and aligns perception to the higher inner self, raises awareness, and brings about spiritual elevation. Divine grace can also change the surrounding circumstances in the objective world to create situation that gives material wealth, grants success, and fulfills desires. Achieving one is not necessarily at the exclusion of the other. There is no disparity between worldly involvement and spiritual evolvement. Therefore, it is possible to achieve simultaneous growth.

Each deity is an aspect of the Absolute having a name, associated energy, legend, significance, and symbol. Therefore, at any time, an appropriate deity is worshiped to seek its blessings for fulfillment of a specific desire or a particular purpose. Students pray *Mahāsaraswati* Devī, Goddess of inspiration and knowledge to seek her grace for success in their studies. Wrestlers and fighters need strength and courage and therefore, they pray Lord Hanuman. For wealth and prosperity, Lord Gaṇesha and *Mahālakshmī* Devī are the deities of choice. Naturally, they are the most favorite deities of all.

The major deities of worship are Lord Vishṇu, Lord Shiva, and Devī. Their worshipers are known as Vaishṇava, Shaivait, and Shakta respectively. Lord Vishṇu is worshiped in his various forms and incarnations, Lord Shiva in the shape of small pillar called Linga, and Devī or Divine Mother in innumerable forms; some benign and gentle, others quite dynamic and ferocious. However, they all recognize, revere, and invariably worship Lord Gaṇesha first before they begin their worship of the deity of choice.

CONCEPTS OF GOD

CONCEPTS OF GOD

IMPERSONAL GOD – COSMIC CONSCIOUSNESS
is recognized as
Brahman

As an abstract principle, God is known as *Brahman*, the Absolute. Omnipresent, omnipotent, and omniscient, it is all pervading Reality.

ॐ

PERSONAL GOD – WITHOUT ATTRIBUTES
is recognized as
Pārā Brahman which is unmanifest.

Personal God without having any attributes, ***Nirguṇa*** is variously recognized as *Pārā* Shiva, *Pārā* Shakti, and *Mahā* Vishṇu by three main theistic orders; Shaivait, Shakta, and Vaishṇava respectively.

ॐ

PERSONAL GOD – WITH ATTRIBUTES
Is recognized as
Nāda (sound) ***Brahman*** which is manifest.

Personal God with attributes, ***Saguṇa*** is the spiritual essence worshiped in the form of a deity. There are three major concepts of God, each having one or more deities. Many deities are common between these concepts.

PERSONAL GOD

Saguṇa Brahman

God with attributes

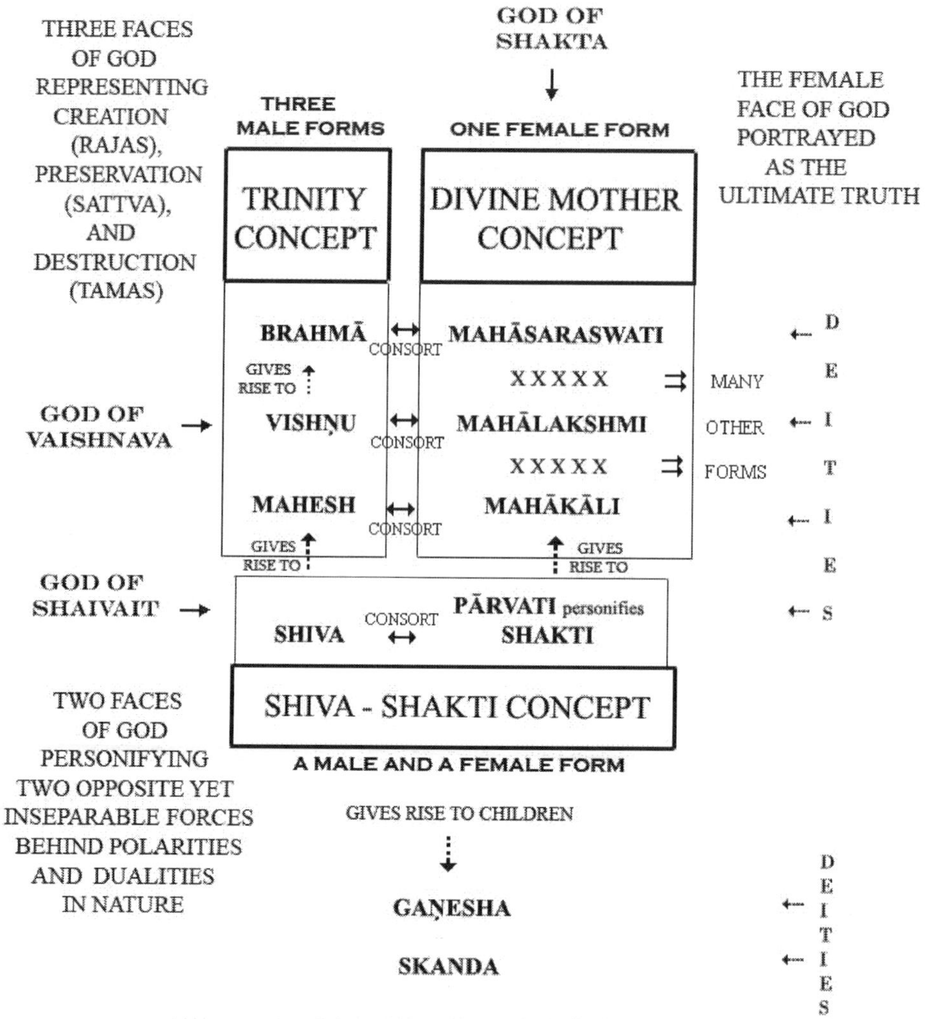

THREE MAIN CONCEPTS WITH DEITIES

1. TRINITY CONCEPT

Three Male Forms

Trinity concept refers to three aspects of God, each concerned with the cosmic function of creation, preservation, and dissolution.

---

1. **Lord Brahmā** – He portrays creative energy of the cosmic mind – Represents *Rajas* Guṇa. He emerges from Lord Vishṇu at the beginning and dissolves back in him at the end of each cycle of creation. Generally not worshiped. *Mahāsaraswati* Devī is his consort.

---

2. **Lord Vishṇu** – Ether of Consciousness that fills the space as the subtlest element ether – Represents *Sattva* Guṇa. He facilitates and supports creation, maintains its continuity, and transcends dissolution. Supreme and eternal. Most worshiped deity. *Mahālakshmī* Devī is his consort. Worshipers are called Vaishṇava. His two most worshiped incarnations -

   - **Lord Rāma** – The seventh incarnation – An ideal man who followed the path of righteousness throughout his life and set an example for everyone to follow.

   - **Lord Kṛṣṇa** – The eighth incarnation – A reservoir of pleasure, he fascinated the world by his favorite past-times, *Leela*. He was a statesman who killed evil forces and restored *Dharma*.

---

3. **Lord Mahesh (Shiva)** – As Time Consciousness, he is the elusive flow of time that measures movement and modification – Represents *Tamas* Guṇa. He rules the matter and incessantly carries out its transformation which renews and purifies whatever exists. Transcends dissolution. Supreme and eternal. Most worshiped deity. *Mahākāli* Devī is his consort. Worshipers are called Shaivaits. His most worshiped incarnation -

   - **Lord Hanuman** – Incarnation as Monkey - He set an example of strength, knowledge, humility, and devotion by serving Lord Rāma.

TRINITY CONCEPT

Brahmā, Vishṇu, and Mahesh (Shiva)

Gurur Brahmā, Gurur Vishṇu, Guru Devo Maheshvaraḥ
Guru Sākshāt Parabrahma, Tasmai Śrī Guruve Namaḥ.

Guru is Lord Brahmā, Lord Vishṇu, and Lord Mahesh.
I bow to the attributeless Brahman who is Guru.

Each faith and religion has achieved its own vision of God by portraying the Ultimate Truth in a form consistent with their specific beliefs. Since the Vedic period around 3000+ BC, Hinduism has viewed God as the Supreme Reality called *Brahman*, One without the second. The whole universe is its ever evolving expression in which, having a growing desire to have multiple experiences, it envisages the world and creates the names and forms of various entities. The Trinity concept, one of the three most accepted concepts of God visualizes it to have three anthropomorphic forms that operate this phenomenal world. They are well recognized as Lord Brahmā, Lord Vishṇu, and Lord Mahesh (Shiva) who incessantly carry out the three complementary cosmic functions of creation, preservation, and dissolution respectively. Expressions of these deities represent the universal and eternal nexus of three functional modes of the Absolute through which it finites and creates life of ever changing forms. They operate in tandem to project the powerful play of this entire physical phenomenon.

Lord Brahmā, the creative aspect of *Brahman* is a portrait of passion, the energy of action called *Rajas* Guṇa. Being the driving force of the universe, he represents creative intelligence of the cosmic mind who rules the unified field of all productive powers and potencies. He is the seed that not only sprouts new beginnings but also sustains their growth until they fully exploit their promise and potential. He appears as the subtle sound vibrations, *Nāda* in the universal substratum of ether; an undeveloped, sentient, and super-conscious ground state of Lord Vishṇu. Lord Vishṇu symbolizes the principle of purity, *Sattva* Guṇa that sustains all manifestation originating from it. An ocean well exemplifies him from which, time and again, waves of creation arise only to eventually recede in it. All creative forces of Lord Brahmā, *Nāda Brahman* arise and operate within the realm of his domain giving rise to the lives and forms he envisions. Lord Mahesh governs the eternal power of transformation measured through the function of time. A quiet and patient operator, he acts on the forms Lord Brahmā creates constantly changing the material nature of the physical world. An embodiment of the mode of darkness, *Tamas* Guṇa, he constantly creates grosser physical limits that finally contain the ever active creative forces of Lord Brahmā. As all evolutionary forces materialize, they progressively reach the peak of their potential, stabilize and sustain the forms they create for a while, and then gradually subside. Thus, Lord Mahesh invariably brings them back to the source over a period of time eventually completing each cycle in creation. These are the three most recognized deities denoting the power of evolution, existence, and elimination. Although they appear to be acting independently, they are well interconnected and fully integrated greatly influencing each other.

There exists an intrinsic relation between the nature of matter and the energy it carries. All visible forms are sustained by the invisible power of underlying energy. Energy not only creates a variety of material names and forms but also empowers the life of all entities. Accordingly, each of these sacred male deity forms has an equally eminent consort who signifies the associated subtle energy essential to accomplish their divine cosmic roles. They are very well recognized as *Mahāsaraswati* Devī, *Mahālakshmī* Devī, and *Mahākāli* Devī respectively. As an active force, these Goddesses prompt and provoke, cajole and compel them to act. They execute their wish, duly assisting them in pursuing their defined cosmic roles. Hence, each Goddess equally shares the veneration and worship offered to them. Together, they represent the most recognized and revered group of deities within the galaxy of Gods and Goddesses of Hindu pantheon.

Lord Vishṇu

All pervading esoteric element ether occupies the entire space. It is an eternally manifesting aspect of Ether of Consciousness represented by the picturesque portrait of Lord Vishṇu. An unintelligible, unconceivable, and unfathomable element, it does not have a beginning or an end. It is the purest and subtlest of all elements, an ultrasonic core that exists beyond the limitations of space and time. As it resonates with the emptiness of the unitive field of cosmos, it pervades everything, including our entire body. Therefore, the mode of purity, *Sattva* Guṇa is the domain of Lord Vishṇu who is well recognized as all-pervading Reality. Manifestation of the entire universe takes place by countless complex combination of various elements. All other elements gradually evolve from the potency of ether occupying space, which also holds and carries them. Therefore, Lord Vishṇu is widely worshiped as the source and origin of the whole physical creation that he also gracefully supports.

Light is the finest vibrational energy which travels through ether within the endless expanse of space. It is an electromagnetic disturbance of ether which also gives rise to vibrant and vividly colorful spectrum by splitting into rays of different wavelengths. Thus, it not only imparts visibility by illuminating the objects in its path but beautifies them as well. The stream of its photons carries bundles of energy that produces a veritable field essential to perpetuate life. Bright and benevolent ***Mahālakshmī*** **Devī** represents this light energy. As she propagates in ether and is invariably associated with it, she is the consort of Lord Vishṇu. In iconography, she can be seen by his side or near his feet. Hence, Lord Vishṇu is also regarded to be the master of space and lord of the light.

Upon birth, our soul acquires the physical form of a body embedded in space. It is made of elements evolved from the subtlest substrate, ether. It is due to the vision, command, direction, and grace of Lord Vishṇu that it comes into being. He carefully considers, as he assesses the casual realm of inner causes before visualizing discrete forms of manifestation as their effects. As he identifies those whose time is ripe, he issues directive for their development. For the purpose, he willfully allows the creative potency of Lord Brahmā to arise who has the cosmic compulsion of creation and carries the power of its appropriate and efficient execution. All functions in creation proceed within the realm of Lord Vishṇu's domain, with his guidance and blessings. During gestation, the potency of his distinct etheric template provides the blueprint, the basis upon which Lord Brahmā begins to create with his passionate moves and delivers. He actively incorporates various evolute elements through the subtle channels, *Nādis* to create our gross body which he also constantly energizes throughout the life. Thus, Lord Vishṇu is the discerning authority and divine source, the director with vision who facilitates the formation of all individual lives.

Conscientiously ensuring our existence by constant presence and support, he also quietly watches our life with deep interest. From microscopic organelles to visible organs, he permeates the entire space of our being to connect and unify the whole system. His etheric energy is the medium through which the primal energy, *Prāṇa* that we breathe in sustains all vital functions. *Prāṇa* is the breath of Lord Brahmā, vibratory field of *Nāda Brahman*. It energizes body and raises endless thoughts and desires in our mind that embeds within the energy of our conscious action. Influence of the ethereal energy of Lord Vishṇu purifies our thoughts and illuminates our mind raising the state of awareness. It affects the way we think and act directing us to follow the right path. He holds the ultrasonic core of body, the fire of life, constantly balancing the dual aspects of our life energy; the manifesting power, *Bhukti* and the releasing force, *Mukti*. By pervading the inner space of our heart, he sustains the effulgence of life. He personifies the ground state of unitary energy field descending from the depth of cosmos. Our life force is duly anchored and well attuned to its high vibrational matrix.

Mahālakshmī Devī illuminates the space of our self that he pervades. She also colors various aspects of our life by showering us with different types of wealth like food, fame, fortune, health, children, and money. Complementing Lord Vishṇu's effort, she provides for the basic needs, bestows variety of resources necessary to preserve life, and even leads us to prosperity. Her grace though, varies with time. It reflects Lord Vishṇu's decree and directive based on evaluation of the individual state of subtle realms; purity of the present and past thoughts and deeds. Sharing his essence, she executes her royal authority with compassion to make life possible, worthwhile, and meaningful.

Mahālakshmī Devī and Lord Vishṇu are intimately associated as luminiferous ether. While supporting our existence on the material plane and guiding our awareness, they not only fulfill our basic needs but way surpass them allowing us to live in comfort, engage in diverse activities, and enjoy our life. Naturally, they carry out the cosmic function of preservation. The followers of Lord Vishṇu or any of his other incarnations, in general, are called **Vaishṇavas.** They consider him to be the Supreme, follow the way of life he advocates by engaging in such activities as to create *Karma* consistent with their duty, *Dharma*, most exclusively pursue the path of devotion, and worship his image.

Lord Brahmā

Assuming the role of creative aspect of *Brahman*, Lord Brahmā emerges as the first offspring in all pervading ether. In iconography, he is seen having four heads and long beard, seated in the pericarp of a lotus which arises from the navel of Lord Vishṇu. It graphically illustrates that Lord of creation evolves from, and has a direct relation with Lord of preservation. Lord Vishṇu represents the unmanifest original state of neutral plane in which Lord Brahmā appears as an impulse. Then, duly inspired by Lord Vishṇu, enjoying his continuous support, and under his full guidance he begins to move and create with passion.

Lord Brahmā represents *Rajas* Guṇa, the ever expanding breath of energy and action. It unfolds spontaneously and expands universally as the subtle sound waves, *Nāda* having an intent, ability, and intensity of creation. They generate vibrations, *Spanda* knitting the subtle substratum of the universe. It is the polarized inner-outer movement of *Brahman*, a blissful throb of *Nāda Brahman* having potential to create various dualities of nature with distinctions of subject and object, observer and observed. It is also the source of *Prāṇa*, life force of the universe that not only sustains our life but allows us to indulge in the wide spectrum of its colorful experiences. As these waves spread around in all directions, their active front reaches various limiting points, each giving rise to a particular building block of the universe called *Tattva*. The creation of these mental and material principles follows through an orderly process of their integration. They confine the differentiated and diversified awareness, duly spread in time and space into variety of life forms having mind and matter.

All creation essentially involves simultaneous manifestation of the physical and mental planes as *Nāda* inherently carries the latent trait of a form sustained by its energy. Lord Brahmā creates through these wave forms, the source of all material shapes, cause of all physical creation. The energy of their propagation is portrayed as ***Mahāsaraswati*** Devī, an extremely intelligent consort of Lord Brahmā. She composes comprehensive sound-codes as the seeds of creation, the basis upon which he acts and creates. Many of the codes were revealed to us which are compiled as the Vedas, Holy Scripture. Inherently carrying the sacred knowledge of secular creation, she very well knows the forms he creates through underlying energy, heard as its sound, which becomes its natural name. Thus she rules the mental plane, her grace allowing us to recognize the objects of the physical plane. It also raises thoughts, forms ideas in our mind, and generates endless index of desires. Our awareness is constantly drawn outwards by them to seek, identify, and build the kind of world they choose within the limits of our existence.

The most powerful aspect of Lord Brahmā is our sexual desire through which he perpetuates human existence. It is an extremely potent force through which our DNA extends life and continues to live by transferring information to the progeny. Two different sources of the combining genes, each time, afford him an opportunity to remodel the new creation. The most natural phenomenon, it happens in various modes in all the plants and animals species. Our other desires lead us to personalize our lifestyle by building the world of our choice. They provide the spark that kindles fire enthusing, educating, and empowering us to design the fabric of our life. It is the force that directs us to act, earn, and accomplish or relax, entertain, and enjoy as we indulge in research and recreation, farming and finance, medicine and music. It is his power of passion operating through us which motivates us to produce *Karma* as the cause of all material fruits of the world that we aspire to reap and enjoy. Through our active engagement in the chosen field of profession, he sustains the network that supports the structure of society. His grace also inspires us to design and develop various articles and objects having tremendous impact on our lives.

The vibratory, dynamic, and cyclical nature of subtle *Nāda* waves is inherited, without exception, by everything that they eventually create. *Spanda* further evolves into countless self-organizing subtle systems of nature that operate at various sentient levels to sustain this entire physical phenomenon. The whole universe is an ultimate projection of innumerable interwoven polar systems. Various kinds of energy, always in a state of flux, constantly flow through it. The complex synergy of their interaction imparts definite attributes to shape the structure, define the dimensions, and create the manifold universe. It is a cycle of creation that lasts a specific time period of cosmic dimension. At its inevitable end, it is entirely annihilated and a period of lull prevails. Then, once again, formation of another universe begins starting the next cycle.

Thus passion of Lord Brahmā creates our physical self and empowers our life duly held by Lord Vishṇu. As he constantly energizes it through *Prāṇa* of our breath, breathing is established as the basic Life Principle. He skillfully rides and develops its course by the stream of passion and pleasures, motives and actions, deeds and desires as we constantly strive to survive, earn, achieve, and enjoy. *Mahāsaraswati* Devī is the source of higher, spiritual as well as lower, worldly knowledge which shapes the nature of desires. She is also the source from which the alphabet sounds of all languages evolve upon further differentiation, the basis of all forms of communication. It allows us to learn, know the world, and interact with others. Thus she affords endless inspiration, unmatched assistance, and full time support to Lord Brahmā in his cosmic role.

Lord Mahesh (Shiva)

The Time Consciousness is another eternal aspect of God symbolized by Lord Mahesh, often known by his higher form, Lord Shiva, the primary deity of Shiva-Shakti concept (Page 38). It is a difficult deity to understand whose consort is commonly visualized as ***Mahākāli* Devī,** an embodiment of the power of time. The energy of her gentle and auspicious form, *Bhadrakāli* creates perpetual flow of time known as *Kāla*. Together, this divine couple gives rise to the streaming state of Consciousness having unique dimension of directedness. Also, it neither has a beginning nor an end quite like the esoteric element ether. In essence, it measures continuous change of material nature which gives rise to the order of succession. Though unidirectional, each moment of its endless flow carries the benevolent as well as malevolent power of transformation.

A profoundly mysterious force of progression, what involves passage of time is truly unknown. It measures movement and change as it alters things and makes them appear and disappear. By presenting series of successive changes of the outer material world to the receptive faculty of our mind, it powers the current of our life experiences. Each streaming moment of its enigmatic flow duly balances various aspects of our life between the past and the future. It simultaneously tracks creation as well as dissolution of what was created earlier. Its auspicious aspect marks new beginning, brings happiness, gives birth, grows and nurtures whereas the inauspicious aspect ultimately brings death at a future point denoting a period of determined life for the soul. It is a journey meant for every 'being' to elevate and 'become' as this elusive current also streams down the path of liberation. The entanglement of *Karma* in pursuit of successful life is the cause that keeps us entrapped in the cycle of birth and death. Lord Mahesh provides every soul an incredible period of lifelong opportunity to exercise the power of volition and resolve past *Karma* in order to evolve and eventually liberate.

Lord Mahesh personifies the quiet rule of nature upon man. As director behind the curtains, he endlessly, often ruthlessly carries out changes transforming our life. His power demonstrates both, a positive and auspicious aspect as well as a negative, wild, anxious, and unpredictable side of life. Hence, our future has the potential to bring peace, progress, and prosperity as well as pain, problems, and paucity. Normally the streaming current of the couple is benign, a regenerative force that steadily and relentlessly transforms the material nature. However, given to quick temper, they easily acquire a fearful stance in rage. At times, Lord Mahesh assumes the terrible form of dark and dreadful Rūdra causing indiscriminate death and destruction. The portrait of *Mahākāli* Devī graphically illustrates her formidable power that destroys everything.

All causes and their effects arise at an appropriate point in time, reach its prime while existing for a period, and eventually decay with its flow. Occurrence of an event, fulfillment of a desire, or consequence of an action – they all are at the mercy of time as divine grace and merit are insolubly linked with time. It is the overriding factor that governs success or failure of all our endeavors and enterprises regardless of our energy, efforts, and efficiency. Time on our side finally translates into success; time on the other side explicitly entails failure.

Flow of time is absolutely uncontrollable, unstoppable, and unpredictable in terms of its future unfoldment. Each arriving moment has inherent potential to change the state of our existence. An unseen, ever-active, and never-failing catalyst of an ongoing phenomenon, it causes changes in our body, things in our surroundings, and the entire manifestation. Defining a state of transition, it constantly and continuously modifies whatever exists at any given moment. While carrying out the cosmic function of material transformation, it also affects dissolution of life. It brings back everybody to ground zero making way for new creation. Naturally, Lord Mahesh is associated with the material nature, *Tamas* Guṇa, mode of darkness. The votaries of Lord Mahesh are called **Shaivaits** who consider him to be the Supreme. Generally, they pursue the path of *Yoga* and meditation that he teaches through scriptures like Shiva Sūtras.

Space, Time, and Causation

Space is the domain of Lord Vishṇu and time is the power of Lord Mahesh. These are the two essential coordinates that order things and events, the basic organizing principles upon which anything and everything is built in the universe by Lord Brahmā. All causes of creation and their effects, inherent to all matter and form constituting the outer phenomenal world occur within these two dimensions. Life and matter assumes three dimensional shapes and exists in space as time provides the fourth temporal dimension. With its process of recurrence as it ticks by, time also acquires a meaning of duration that constantly displays all the material changes under the influence of other causes. Our material experiences are mental impressions of such diligent changes, limited by space in extension and time in intention. In the world art theatre, space partners with time to construct an incredible invisible platform. It stages a very exciting and stunningly spectacular show that Lord Brahmā creates in which all variety of life forms constantly appear and exist, live and enjoy, interact and perform.

The subtle influence of the streaming flow of time occurs at a steady pace on all the objects in this theatre. However, this rate surprisingly varies with location as time exhibits a flexible dimension in different realms of existence. For instance, duration of a year on Saturn equals 30 years of Earth which is quite different. Therefore, various time units like hours and years measure different periods on earth and other higher planes. It is believed that our year equals a day in the realm of the departed souls. In general, we need to know that the time lapses at a different pace in different realms of manifestation.

Our soul remains confined within an ultrasonic container, the subtle core which permeates our physical body and holds it as we live in a place at a time. During lifetime, we cannot change it though the body itself constantly changes all the time. We freely move about in space to visit and revisit different places but we cannot do so going back and forth in time. Thus we experience time and space quite differently. However, as it is possible to be at one place at a time, our consciousness often experiences constrains of spatial dimensions. Also, all our activities and sensory experiences are limited to the place of being, our life being absolutely impacted by the place of living.

Life is a long journey of moment-to-moment experiences. Though transition of moments is steady, uniform, and constant, each arriving moment is veiled in secrecy over its power to bring pleasure or pain. Not knowing what the future has in store for us, each moment is a challenge of existence that opens the doors to the unknown. Accustomed to such uncertainty, we witness the arrival of each second that crystallizes future possibilities into the present actualities. And with these realities quickly turning into the past memories, that moment is gone forever making each life experience unique to the moment.

Temporal passage has no spatial counterpart. In fact, the influence of these two metaphysical elements, static space and dynamic time is quite contradictory to each other. Space is a non-discrete continuum that intervenes as well as interpenetrates all discrete things while holding them in their relative positions. Time measures movement and modification as all sensible matter undergoes change and transforms. But even after such variation in condition, they stand apart in their specific place. As space preserves their location, it creates the notion of spatial dimension, distance, and direction. Obviously these two complementary mediums are very different and yet, quite a few characteristics are shared by them. Both are intangible, entirely relative, uniform, and continuous in nature. Space can potentially be divided by specific location and dimensions whereas time by the past, present, and future. We distinguish space as here and there, near and far; time as now and then, before and after. Though complete nonentities, they are absolutely necessary for the manifestation of all causes and their effects which enable our existence and all life experiences.

Our existence, arranged and supported at a place by Lord Vishṇu, at a time ruled by Lord Mahesh is broadly determined by destiny, *Prārabdha*. We arduously chiseled it out to its current shape by enactment of *Karma* directed by passion, ruled by Lord Brahmā. He not only creates our life based on the resume of past *Karma* but also ensures our continued participation in the future by his power of passion presently operating through us. It is his driving force which, guided by our ego motivates us to act and achieve, have pleasure and power, and find ways to indulge and gratify. After death, we inevitably reincarnate by the cause of accumulated *Karma* that determines the destiny of yet another life. Time renews the location and boundary of its body, sustained by Lord Vishṇu as we continue such enactment. Thus all our worldly passion and consequent acts of *Karma* keep us entrapped in perpetual life-cycles. Each life though, is a blessed opportunity in which Lord Mahesh teaches us spiritual lessons through critical life experiences at various times. Lord Vishṇu also guides our ego and directs our passion to enact *Karma* consistent with our duty, *Dharma*. They constantly help us to get a release from such endless wandering fueled by our worldly passion, material attachments, and unending desires created by Lord Brahmā.

Temporal and spatial dimensions are the determinative forces that 'hold and contain' our existence as to live outside either of them is equally impossible. Our presence or absence though, has no effect on either of them. Also, they have different dimensions in different planes of existence; experiences of dream state cannot compare with those of our wakeful state. All our actions based on the purity of our inner intentions and consistent with our destiny, *Prārabdha* bear fruits of success, fulfill our desires, and bring happiness. It is, however, subject to timely execution at the place of our being. The way we use our time at any place determines our placement in the future. Failing to reach a place may be a missed opportunity, or a blessing in disguise, which time only can tell. Being at the right place, at the right time, translates into success. Synergistic effect of these two important, infinite, and interconnected forces, motion in space and motion of time enables all varieties of life experiences. Invisible and invincible in nature, they operate ceaselessly, perform seamlessly, and influence us continuously without our being aware of them most of the time.

Lord Brahmā, Lord Vishṇu, and Lord Mahesh (Shiva)

The creative aspect of Lord Brahmā is not limited to our physical creation; to incorporate elements, encase our soul in the physical body, and bring us to this world. His influence equally extends to the subtle mind, ground of passion, and the force that creates the field of our life by defining its dimensions. Our breath, attuned to the life sustaining breath of Brahmā is the source of impulse and energy that constantly translates into the sound of thought and articulate speech. The knowledge it carries determine the nature of desires upon which we plan and act. Emanating from the source of our life force, Lord Vishṇu and coloring our awareness, they direct us to the outer objective world propelling the energy of action. This outward act is the essence of our existence, the basis upon which we embrace the wave of life. *Mahāsaraswati* Devī assists us in developing literary and communication skills in order to acquire worldly knowledge necessary to surf this wave, survive in this world, and satisfy all our desires.

Desires build the world. It is the fire that motivates people and keeps them going. It functions at various levels with an aim to achieve different goals. Most commonly, it operates in such modes where survival, pleasure, and power are the dominating objectives. Lord Brahmā sustains our conscious efforts as we commit to career, meet obligations, and reach our goals. This passion for worldly achievements and self-gratification directs us to produce *Karma* that not only supports our existence but adds excitement to it. The fruits of all our deeds, however, depend on the chronicle of *Karma* which shows whether the worldly goals were pursued by rightful acts of life. Its evaluation lies in the hands of Lord Vishṇu and *Mahālakshmī* Devī who govern the subtle realms and reward us accordingly. In an absence of their grace, all our endeavors and enterprises are misdirected efforts that ultimately hit a wall. Their blessings direct our passion to the path of our destiny fulfilling the aim of our life. Therefore, worship of Lord Brahmā is not considered beneficial. It is primarily limited to Lord Vishṇu and Lord Mahesh. However, *Mahāsaraswati* Devī is commonly worshiped as she grants worldly as well as spiritual knowledge.

Lord Vishṇu and Lord Mahesh apparently operate quite differently but as two aspects of *Brahman*, they are intertwined as space-time continuum. One exists within and is relative to the other. The transformative power of Lord Mahesh carries a regenerating side which naturally involves the creative aspect of Lord Brahmā. Hence, Lord Brahmā and Lord Mahesh coalesce. Also, as Lord Brahmā has his origin in Lord Vishṇu, they are not separate from each other. Thus, these three aspects of the Absolute are well interconnected and wholly interchangeable. They are so identified as to understand the constant play of three strands of *Brahman* ruling the whole manifestation. Lord Brahmā creates names and forms, life and matter having three dimensional shapes in space essentially in the fourth dimension of time. It is their concerted effort and cumulative influence which governs the entire physical phenomenon.

Passion of Lord Brahmā sprouts new beginnings whereas fierceness of Rūdra burns whatever exists to ashes. These extremes mark an era of evolution and existence, well sustained by Lord Vishṇu. His ethereal energy is the conduit by which casual realms step-down, pass through the subtle realms, and assume physical forms catalyzed by the creative energy of Lord Brahmā. Ether is the unifying force that connects, as it embraces the life energy of all beings. As all waves arise in ocean and belong to it, all individual life energies are part of him, attuned to him. Lord Vishṇu believes in existence, guides our passion, and cheers our action celebrating the power of life. He lets our awareness flow outward to matters of the world, expects our rightful participation in its affairs, and ultimately rewards us with the fruits we deserve. Having a positive attitude of world affirmation, he administers daily affairs with absolute authority, deep interest, and direct involvement. He also upholds the cosmic order and rhythm of righteousness by overtly establishing the code of conduct in society. He always portrays a positive, benign, and considerate character.

Conversely, Lord Mahesh is oblivious to mundane matters as he continuously carries out the process of generation and regeneration. Being carefree in nature, he exhibits an attitude of indifference whether it is new creation or its ominous dissolution. It may be due to his awareness of temporality of the material world, passing nature of its thrills, and inadequacy of existence. He is wise and knows the futility of physical phenomena. Therefore, he even accepts inaction, ineptness, and ignorance of his devotees. He advocates meditation which directs awareness inward and away from the world helping us to elevate the spirit and get a release from the worldly attachments and bondages. His power of time makes us realize the hopeless nature of worldly life as we learn through life changing situations, events, and circumstances. By living in isolation, he expresses his detachment from such impermanent, and therefore, illusory existence. Master of the world show and well involved in all its affairs, Lord Vishṇu is more personal, humane, and sympathetic to human needs and wants. Mindful that it is just a show and absolutely uninvolved in any matters of the world, Lord Mahesh is quite impersonal, stern, uncompromising, and lofty.

Their anthropomorphic forms, as worshiped in temples are a study in contrast. Lord Vishṇu portrays an opulent and lavish, majestic form of a king who lives in a palace, watches over all manifestation, and governs worldly matters. He even incarnates to restore the world order and balance of righteousness. He motivates people to do *Karma* by following their duty, *Dharma* without surrendering to any concern about the outcome of their action. He wears silk, pearls, and jewelry and is offered fragrance of perfumes, sandalwood paste, and sweets. Lord Mahesh represents renunciation and absolute freedom from worldliness. An embodiment of contemplation, he is an ascetic living on snowcapped mountain always staying away from affairs of the world. His eternal, boundless, and unchanging nature is represented by a simple pillar called Linga. He covers his body with ashes of crematory and becomes happy with austere offering of flowers, Bilva (*Aegle marmelos*) leaves, and bathing with water and raw milk.

Lord Vishṇu is worshiped on full moon days with faith, trust, and love for all worldly achievements, health, wealth, and success. Lord Mahesh is approached with awe, respect, and gratitude on new moon days to realize the transitory nature of our experiences. He imparts superior knowledge leading to eternal bliss, peace, and Self-Realization. Obviously, Lord Vishṇu is the deity of choice for most people. Lord Mahesh is the ideal for saints, sages, and spiritual seekers of Truth. Worship of Lord Vishṇu fulfills our worldly desires as it brings joy, happiness, fame, and prosperity. On the other hand, grace of Lord Mahesh enables us to conquer unending desires. He teaches compassion to share the pain and suffering of others and, in doing so, not to aspire for an award or recognition. Lord Vishṇu advocates action and applauds achievements. Lord Mahesh does not care for material wealth and worldly success and hence he is indifferent to gain and glory. Overseeing world affairs, Lord Vishṇu qualifies and accepts only those devout souls who follow the path of purity and righteousness he advocates. Being kind, merciful, and impersonal, Lord Mahesh is devoid of any type of discrimination. He blesses everyone who worships him with reverence and faith, spiritually elevated or ignorant, without such prerequisites.

Vaishṇavism and Shaivism are two of the three main theistic orders today, the third being Shaktism which considers Divine Mother, *Jagadamba* to be the Supreme. Vaishṇavas worship Lord Vishṇu by calling him **Hari** with utmost devotion and love. They mark their forehead with two vertical lines between eyebrows that join below in curve. Shaivaits have absolute faith in the power of **Hara,** Lord Mahesh (Shiva). As they follow his teachings, they deeply meditate upon the inner self marking their forehead with horizontal lines above the eyebrows. Often time these followers clash over the ideology of their supremacy. This battle between the horizontal and vertical lines is a contentious issue that has been raging on forever. It has not been resolved to date.

The fact is that life preserving power of persistence, Lord Vishṇu who holds matter and life transforming power of conversion, Lord Mahesh who renews it operate and influence us quite differently. Coequal and coexistent they are interdependent and closely interwoven. Governing the spatial and temporal dimensions, they complement each other while always working in coordination as one works upon the other. As we exist in their unified domain and dimension, they allow us to indulge in the chosen way of life. They also teach us spiritual lessons based on our *Karma* through typical life experiences at various points of time. Though independent, as space-time continuum they embody the same spiritual essence and therefore, quite inseparable.

When so recognized, they are called **Hari-Hara** and worshiped together. They put us at places, at times, to experience life events according to our destiny, *Prārabdha.* It operates in cycles of favorable and unfavorable, expansion and contraction, ups and downs. Operating according to the metaphysical laws of nature, it makes us struggle for existence with all the trials and tribulations tied with the tide of time. Often times it tosses and tests us in the space of this mundane world. Charting of this course through *Karma,* using the power of picking is an evolutionary process for the soul. Everyone seeks their blessings to make the right choices of thought and action while exercising free will to lead a successful, prosperous, and spiritually uplifting life.

Nugget of Wisdom

Each life is manifestation of soul molded by unique set of circumstances and therefore, to judge anyone based on the finite knowledge acquired through our set of circumstances is wrong.

2. SHIVA - SHAKTI CONCEPT

A male and a female form

Shiva-Shakti concept refers to two opposing yet complementary, distinct yet inseparable forces of nature always united as one.

---

1. **Lord Shiva** (Male) – Timeless Spirit and Consciousness – The source of the physical phenomena. Immutable infinite intelligence that exists beyond time, space, and causation. Transcendent as well as immanent. He personifies the self-illuminating awareness. Most worshiped deity.

2. **Shakti** (Female) – Primal Energy – As the efficient and material cause of all manifestation, she represents energy and matter. She constantly moves, transforms, and evolves in various ways giving rise to all names and forms - animate and inanimate. Most worshiped deity.

- **Lord Gaṇesha** – The force of Gravity and inertia. – A son of Lord Shiva and Shakti. He removes obstacles, grants wisdom, and bestows prosperity. Most worshiped deity.

- **Lord Kārtikeya** – The force of Electromagnetism – A son of Lord Shiva and Shakti. God of warfare and higher knowledge. Also known as Murugan, Subramanya, and Skanda.

SHIVA-SHAKTI CONCEPT

Two Diverging Yet Inseparable Forces

Shiva-Shaktyātmakaṃ vishvaṃ.

Lord Shiva and Shakti are the innermost essence of the universe.

Shiva-Shakti is a very profound concept visualizing Lord Shiva and Shakti as the two deities expressing dual aspects of *Brahman*. They are the faces of two functional forms assumed by the Absolute that not only initiates the process of creation but also sustains what it creates. This primordial couple portrays two opposing forces that create polarity, which also establishes the duality of nature. They are unique in the fact that despite having a diverging stance, one exalts and glorifies the other. Though acquiring two separate identities, they are always united being mutually interdependent, coexistent, and therefore, quite inseparable. Lord Shiva is the stationary male form who portrays the unchanging aspect of boundless spirit. Centripetal in nature, it is an ascending and liberating force. The exciting female face of Shakti represents the ever active descending energy. As a centrifugal current, she is the power of manifestation.

It is quite similar to the Chinese philosophy of yin and yang, unity of the opposites. The whole universe with cascading array of multiplicities arises out of the contrasting, complementing, and combining energies of this divine couple. They carry intuitive insight, common purpose, and well defined roles in the evolutionary process of this ever changing creation. Therefore, though opposite in character, they always operate as a couple creating harmonious pulsation, *Spanda*, in rhythm, to the beat of time. A timeless throb, it knits the subtle substratum of the universe, the source of all physical phenomena. By getting immanently intermingled in diverse degrees and variety of ways, they appear in variety of forms and exist in everything, from grossest to the finest, in the phenomenal world they create. All animate and inanimate objects, visible symbols of their eternal love and togetherness, owe their presence to them. Shakti as in-breath and Lord Shiva as out-breath, together as respiration are the universal force that constantly animates our life.

Shakti personifies energy and Lord Shiva holds this energy. Just as fire and its burning power or water and its ability to wet go together, one has no existence without the other. They dwell in each other united like the two sides of a coin. This relationship is an apt metaphor commonly used in society to describe the capacity, position, and extent of power, Shakti held by a person, embodiment of Lord Shiva. They are quite like the two primary digits, 0 and 1 of the binary system. These digits create the engaging experience of the entire digital world through their innumerable innovative combinations. Source of new formats and improved content, they constantly enhance its experience by overwriting and obliterating the old overtime. Likewise, the whole universe is an ultimate projection of countless energy plays of Shakti. She creates new configurations eternally reveling in her ever changing relations with Lord Shiva. They are also like the two poles of a powerful magnet; Lord Shiva is the static pole whereas Shakti is the dynamic one from which energy constantly flows.

SHIVA-SHAKTI AS OUR SOURCE

Their perpetual play is the true source of our being, the determinant code of all our characteristics. It is well exemplified by the mysterious power of DNA; the double-helix form of two complementing strands tightly winding around each other that run in opposite directions. Each anti-parallel polymer may be visualized as Lord Shiva embracing Shakti which often multiplies, modifies many a times, merges in meticulous ways, and even mysteriously mutates. The divine play of their endless love making encodes variety of information as genome, gene by gene which creates, holds, and transmits unique codes of life. By appropriately adjusting the length of ladder and altering its configuration, they ingeniously embed specific genotypes within their structure. Thereby, they give rise to countless variety of classical blue-prints that ultimately create the living landscape of all the plant and animal species.

To humans, they impart the most advanced state of life that enables us to have its ultimate experience. Characteristically they stay united together in all varieties of differentiated cells in our body. However, with the specific intent to create, they separate in the germ cells only to come together, as planned, when sperm fertilizes the ovum. It is a moment of real excitement for them at the yet another success to assume a new form. Such an ecstatic reunion activates Shakti to actualize the so reconfigured intelligence into its new being by developing, dividing, and differentiating cells. With an urge to manifest and bring this endeavor to fruition, she gradually polarizes the head-tail axis while incorporating various elements to create the physical body ultimately giving rise to the phenotype of humans. There is an endless graded variety of plants and animals species that inhabit the incredible world art gallery. They are live exhibits and fool-proof evidence of an incomprehensible evolutionary power of the same genetic source. It is an ever improving, exceptionally innovative, and extremely intriguing work of just one eternal source, Shiva-Shakti.

In an unmanifest integrated state, they exist together as one Ultimate Reality, *Brahman*. Due to sectarian distinctions, Shaivaits, worshipers and believers of Lord Shiva recognize this Supreme Being as *Pārā* Shiva whereas in the eyes of Shaktas, the followers and devotees of Shakti, it is *Pārā* Shakti, also recognized as Divine Mother. In this unitary state of ecstasy, they exist together as an abstract principle of God enjoying endless bliss and peace. However, it develops a rising desire (*Icchā* or will) to have multitude of experiences, in various ways, by having different names and forms. Consequently, it spontaneously makes an appearance as the casual sound Aum. This sound-less sound is their first expression ever, in a latent state that carries the divine desire to create.

Visualize the unmanifest *Brahman* void of content to be zero. Though Zero has no value, it has an infinite potential to create world-full of numbers that fall beyond the comprehension of mind. For a number to appear, zero polarizes into two equal and opposite numbers such that when brought together, they recombine to disappear in the neutral origin. For example, +5 comes out with a -5 so that together they remain the balanced whole. Thus, countless such numbers, including fractions having opposite polarities can be populated which always add up to zero. Similarly *Brahman* polarizes into two equal and opposite forces in order to create. Originating from the casual sound Aum, this law of opposite carries an endless potential to expand, evolve, and exhibit the extravaganza of gigantic universe. These two divine forces are the positive and passive Lord Shiva balanced by the negative and active Shakti.

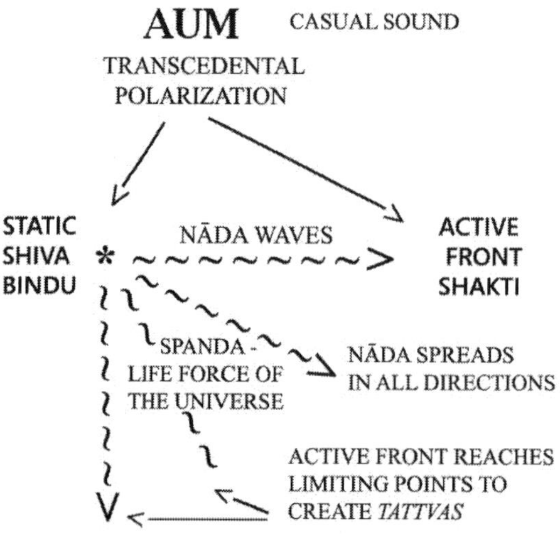

CONSCIOUSNESS EXPRESSES AS MATTER THROUGH NĀDA AND EXPERIENCES IT THROUGH SPANDA

AUM TO SHIVA-SHAKTI

The primal sound Aum spontaneously and transcendentally polarizes into the functional creative ideation of *Nāda Brahman*. It is the process of bursting, *Sphoṭa* in which Lord Shiva is separated and localized as center, ***Bindu*** from which emanates his creative potential as subtle sound waves, ***Nāda***. The active front of *Nāda* is Shakti which moves away and spreads in all directions. Lord Shiva emerges as Self-illuminating light of Consciousness who begins to see himself and experience through the ever growing sonic field of his own Being. From the point of potentialised universe, *Bindu* begins the act of its expression and expansion as *Nāda* gradually actualizes it to its full potential and magnitude. The dot at the top in the symbol of Aum represents *Bindu* and the semi-circle represents the active front of *Nāda* waves, Shakti. *Bindu* is an anchor that preserves the location. *Nāda* waves propagate in all directions to create vibratory field of energy, a throb of pulsation called *Spanda* which is visualized as the dance of Lord Shiva and Shakti. This is the dynamic, subtle, recurrent, and creative state of *Brahman* which is actively involved in every level of existence and its experience.

Nāda waves spread out with cycles of evolution opposed by involution as Shakti, the active front of *Nāda* that moves away from Lord Shiva always returns to him over time. Excited to hold each other and tirelessly performing together on the cosmic floor, they enjoy the routine of each ecstatic move in moment. These vibrations establish their eternal transitory state in creation. As Shakti moves forward, she constantly forms, and transforms, outer gross matter. It is her ever changing expression of accomplishment, in action, each connected with the inner subtle realm in which Lord Shiva dwells. It gives rise to the constantly evolving spectacle of material world in all its motion and shapes consisting mind and matter. Thus, Self eternally acts through the intelligence of its seed sound, *Nāda* having tendency to create various fruits of matter, which it tastes through the mind of *Spanda.* In doing so, it oscillates between the poles of manifest and unmanifest, duality and unity, matter and spirit riding the vibratory energy of *Spanda*. As this divine couple tirelessly performs, their dynamic engagement creates a subtle substratum of living cosmic intelligence. It is an endless source of primal energy, *Prāṇa,* which is present everywhere.

Lord Shiva is the self-illuminating spirit who establishes a base and secures the ground. He holds, inspires, and supports Shakti, the active front of *Nāda* in charge of creation. Knowing their shared desire (***Icchā*** or will), she explores means (***Jnāna*** or knowledge), and acts in ways (***Kriyā*** or action) to ultimately make it a physical reality. As *Nāda* spread around, Shakti exercises her creative ability to identify unique limiting points that makes *Tattvas*. These are the different principles of mind and matter in which she veils Lord Shiva to create various names and forms. Discreet parts of Lord Shiva, the cause of life appears as effect of entities embodied in these *Tattvas*. They experience life sustained by the universal power of her energy, *Prāṇa*. Thus, Shakti is the efficient as well as material cause of creation. She is the one who creates and she is the objects of creation. *Spanda* is the pulse of Consciousness that carries out the process of **observation** for embodied Lord Shiva, the **observer** who enjoys and experiences the finite objective world, the **observed** so created.

Lord Shiva is the spirit, an unchanging Reality that remains the same forever. Shakti is time dependent, ever changing physical phenomenon, powered and projected as world of distinctions. Lord Shiva is the power to persist whereas Shakti is the power to change. Her act establishes various stress points in the static and boundless background of Lord Shiva, like stars in the sky giving rise to the material world. Lord Shiva is the transcending force who enjoys the eternal power and enduring play of ever active Shakti. For her, there is no rest or permanence as she constantly moves and continuously creates in self-repeating cycles. Lord Shiva represents guiding principles, the divine 'will' of the cosmic mind that aims at an appropriate target it sets. Shakti is the divine 'power' who is always aware of the established objective. She finds appropriate ways while exploring available means through which to execute and achieves the goal. The word 'willpower' embeds this dual principle commonly used to describe strong determination of a person in relentless pursuit of his set objective.

Lord Shiva and Shakti establish the primary principle of bipolar Reality, source of other thirty four ontological categories of existence called *Tattvas*. These are the various building blocks of the universe that appear in a cascading fashion, in a descending order to effect the entire creation. It is a quantum process carried out by Shakti which begins with her finitising Lord Shiva into discreet parts, each called *Atman*. Her power of *Maya* then obscures them through various limiting principles to make a soul. (Page 90) At the time of its manifestation, her creative aspect, *Prakṛti* duly veils it in the confines of physical body consisting mind and matter and projects it as an appropriate entity. (Page 144)

THE WORLD OF DUALITIES

Shakti fully exploits her unique finitising power and variously obscures Lord Shiva through her ever changing modes. In inconceivable ways and innovative combinations, she designs countless forms to sport the entire creation. For the purpose, upon spontaneous polarization, as she begins to move away from him, they apparently diverge and depart breaking away from each other. Therefore, they are distinguished as distinct forces well recognized, accepted, and worshiped as two deities. However, these two expressions of God that appear as primordial couple for the purpose of creation effectively compromise their unitary state of primal Being having eternal bliss, peace, and ecstasy.

Such polarization of *Brahman* is absolutely necessary as it gives rise to the dynamic play of countless dualities of which the entire creation is essentially made of. It steadily evolves and occurs through the power of this divine couple personifying the fundamental principle of dichotomy, *Dvaita*. From the static

I'ness, *Ahaṃ* of Lord Shiva emerges the active other, *Idaṃ* of Shakti, everything else in this phenomenal world. Her moving away is the repulsive power which is duly balanced by the attractive power as, constantly attracted to Lord Shiva, she eventually returns to him. It establishes regular patterns of movement in nature creating a realm of life and matter scattered all around, dispersed far and wide. The whole world of conditioned reality, without exception is filled with various shades of dualities like mountains and valleys, crests and troughs, days and nights. The entire manifestation is an explicit expression of endless varieties of interpenetrating energy cycles giving rise to creation and destruction, sunrise and sunset, summer and winter, inhalation and exhalation.

All dualities consist of countless opposites which are all relative in nature. They allow us various comparisons to have different life experiences based on the perception of change. We routinely compare mine and yours, present and previous, one and another to picture, perceive, and participate in the current state of realities. Such dualities are necessary as it is only after passing through the night that we begin to appreciate, value, and enjoy the day. It also gives rise to action as one indulges in various interactions with the other like give and take, send and receive involving exchange of money and matter. As we know, it always takes two to Tango. Between the two extremes of black and white, we experience innumerable shades of gray created by the kaleidoscopic range of situations in our life. Experience of dualities, therefore, is an integral part of life.

Principle of duality even extends to individual character as everyone inherently carries the positives like love, compassion, charity, and benevolence as well as the negatives like hate, greed, lust, and anger. A higher as well as lower self exists within each of us who surfaces at times, and often surprises, to confirm such opposing forces within. The dual power of mind to like, *Rāga* and dislike, *Dveśa* constantly plays out our thought, speech, and action which decides the state of our everyday situations. The positive of pleasure, happiness, and joy inevitably, equally, and simultaneously exist with the negative of misery, pain, and grief in the world. Appearance of Shiva-Shakti establishes the polarity principle of interdependent opposites. The entire universe they project, evenly and quite consistently displays both, the positive as well as the negative.

Being a part of the world, we constantly face the dominating influences, and often distressing experiences of such dualities. To immunize ourselves against unwanted, undesirable, and unfavorable experiences of life, we need to achieve a higher state of equanimity. It is acquired through the practice of meditation. As we concentrate on the 'Third Eye', the center of clairvoyance between the eyebrows in the forehead, it bridges the transient dualistic world with the enduring non-dualistic *Brahman*. As we gradually rise above our current realm of relativity in time to the state of spontaneity and unity with the divine, it helps us to transcend all disturbing dualities. Happily surfing the fluctuating currents and tides of time, we successfully cross the ocean of life.

Divine Consciousness of Lord Shiva called '*cit*' is always associated with, as it pervades all matter created by Shakti called '*sat*' in the entire universe. Therefore, Shakti is often called *Cidrūpinī*, the formative energy of consciousness. We are a part of this object-subject and action-awareness play of '*sat-cit*', universal principle of polarity. It defines the vibratory nature of all polar systems which is the casual matrix and common substratum of all manifestation. Lord Shiva is the light of Consciousness, ***prakāsha*** and Shakti is the creative awareness of its own Being, ***vimarsha***. Just as an object in a dark night becomes visible only when the light illuminates it, the objective world is recognized and made visible by the power of subjective consciousness.

SHIVA-SHAKTI, THE AXIS OF OUR BEING

Lord Shiva rules the subtle center of consciousness, *Sahasrāra* Chakra lying above the crown of brain of every individual. As he exists in timeless, dimensionless state, this subtlest center is attuned with the depth of Cosmic Consciousness. *Ātman*, a part of this Consciousness identifies itself as separate entity due to individual ego. As it gets shrouded with more such impurities, *Malas*, it assumes the state of an individual soul. Thus, part of Lord Shiva, limited as a soul takes birth to indulge in the experience of life as an appropriate entity. Shakti, the active energy of consciousness helps it to self-actualize into a being. As primordial energy, *Prāṇa*, she initiates the process of its manifestation. It begins with the development of subtle mental faculty in accordance with the destined life experience, *Prārabdha.*

Then, Shakti successively creates various seats of matter, subtle psycho-energy centers called Chakras that develop and later associate with the central cerebral-spinal system. It is affected by selectively distributing the energy of her root sounds among them, in progressively increasing order of density, in attunement with spirit. These primeval sounds are the mother powers known as *Mātṛkā* that arise from differentiation of *Nāda,* each carrying powers to create a specific physical form. Infused with these energies and based on the intelligence they carry, each Chakra proceeds to incorporate various subtle elements called *Tanmatras* that develop the subtle system. Finally, as the last step, the gross evolute elements are incorporated by them to make our physical self. The residual power of Shakti then grounds it on the material plane and holds it for lifetime by innately lying dormant as *Kuṇḍalinī* at the base of spine. She is located in the lowest subtle center called *Mulādhāra* Chakra, the terminal point of her evolution which rules the gross matter.

Part of the self-repeating evolutionary cycles of existence, life is a blessed opportunity, a pilgrimage for the spiritual growth of our soul. It exists between two dimensions; the transcendental plane above ruled by Lord Shiva and the earthly realm below ruled by Shakti. Though poles apart, they constitute the two functional extremities of the Supreme Reality who creates our body and holds our being between them. Between their two diverging vortices manifests the active and life sustaining axis of our existence, the cerebro-spinal column that holds our body and powers all aspects of our life. The wheels of thoughts and action, cause and effect, events and experiences revolve around it moving life forward with time. Between them, these opposite poles also hold and support other pulsating fields. They prevail at progressively subtler and higher levels of consciousness as we move up from the center of matter. These realms simultaneously exist and operate as patterns of energy currents flowing from various other Chakras located between the two. However, they are beyond our sensory experience as our awareness is confined to the earthly level of existence. It is brought down and attached to the material world by the power of *Kuṇḍalinī.*

Spanda is the divine dance of Shiva-Shakti, the subtle rhythm of movement and pulsation in nature. It is this unitive field of living consciousness which not only creates our life but also sustains it through the breath. Breathing is the basic Life Principle through which Shiva-Shakti animates our life. Shakti as inhalation and Lord Shiva as exhalation are well attuned to this inexhaustible energy source. Each breath of our life witnessing soul draws *Prāṇa* into the two major subtle energy channels called Ida and Pingala, each connected to a nostril. It sustains the circuit of energy between the two subtle centers, that of spirit, above and the matter, below flowing through these channels. The downward current of passionate Shakti flows through Ida in equilibrium with the upward current of dispassionate Lord Shiva which flows through Pingala. It powers all our mental, emotional, and spiritual realms. It also generates spark in the heart which creates rhythmic movements like systolic (Shakti) and diastolic (Lord Shiva) heart action. The pulse and pressure it produces provides the blood flow in the body which sustains all biological and physical functions. Rhythm of such pulsating fields enables various functions of all our physical systems.

Consciousness and subjective ideas of Lord Shiva are energized, enabled, and expressed through the passion of mind and matter created by Shakti whose action brings them to their fruition. Their harmonious synergy sustains all aspects and activities of our life. As the divine couple choreographs the enigmatic play of our life between their undulating cycles of vibrations, they constantly strive to unite and be complete, *Pūrṇa* to attain their original unitary state of eternal bliss and peace. Such desire, therefore, also manifests in our thoughts and actions as we always seek the same in our life. Unfortunately, we do not seek it within but in the outer phenomenal world, in the wrong things and places, often using improper means that, if at all, gives us just its passing experience. Therefore, our search for happiness continues throughout the life.

The subtle psycho-energy center, *Anāhata* Chakra is located in the middle, near the heart. Divine center of equilibrium between the spiritual center of Lord Shiva above and the gross center of Shakti below, it is the still point where they find a perfect balance. A seat of Consciousness, the heart of everyone, therefore, eternally radiates their endless love and bliss, '*ānanda'*. It is this force emanating from pure hearts which sustains all humanity and makes us whole that we want to experience and actually seek. But our externalized awareness is generally directed downward to the lower levels of self and survival. It seeks power and pleasure of the world through sense gratification and material achievements guided by individual ego. When it is directed inward and upward, it rises to the level of this heart center. As and when it reaches out from here and touches the hearts of others, we enter the realm of such blissful experience.

SHIVA-SHAKTI IN NATURE

Two luminaries in the sky, sun and moon are the most convincing proxy to the eternal play and powerful presence of Shiva-Shakti in the world. They visibly demonstrate their undeniable influence on all existence on earth. Ever brilliant sun always remains the same quite like the timeless Consciousness of Lord Shiva. It is a radiant representation of our unchanging, bright, and sparkling spirit. Alternating appearances of full moon and new moon, with waning and waxing phases mimic the ever-changing manifestation of Shakti which also occurs in similar cycles. And just as brightness of moon is the reflection of sunlight, all creation mirrors the Consciousness of Lord Shiva. Interestingly, various phases of the moon represent our mind and its moods as well that constantly oscillate between the extreme feelings like agony and ecstasy. Also moonlight depends upon the extent of reflection which varies with the phase of moon. Likewise, our thoughts, speech, and action indicate the reasoning, emotions, and awareness of our mind that reflects the state of our inner self to the outer world.

All existence on earth thrives due to the appropriate warmth generated by the combined influence of sun and moon which sustains the fire of life. Whereas they represent Lord Shiva and Shakti respectively, the earth truly represents the physical body of our being. The radiating energy of sun represents our casual self-illuminating **spirit** which is a part of the eternal Lord Shiva. The subtle and ever active **mind** which always keeps on changing like the phase of moon characterize the manifesting or withdrawing energy of Shakti. It is through the mind that our embodied consciousness experiences life, knows the world it lives in, and duly presents our self to the others. An integrated play of their energies makes our existence on earth possible as they not only create and sustain our gross **body** but also govern all aspects of our inner self. They power the circuit of energy that sustains our being, energize the subtle wheels of life, and translate the inner traits of our soul into variety of human experiences.

Shakti is worshiped on full moon nights that dispense delightful luminosity showering like the grace of a kind mother. Her tender love creates, holds, and nurtures all creation. On the contrary, the transcending spirit of Lord Shiva is worshiped on new moon nights. It symbolizes the quiescent mind and absence

Ascending Energy of Shiva

Descending Energy of Shakti

of action necessary to get a glimpse of his eternal light. Fire is an igneous element that rises like a pillar whereas mountains have the shape of a triangle, their apex pointing up. They represent the ascending energy of Lord Shiva flowing towards the depth of Cosmic Consciousness. Streams and rivers flow down the valleys that have the shapes of inverted triangles between two mountains. They duly represent the power of creation which is the descending energy of Shakti, flow of nectar. The endless expanse of sky devoid of dimensions is the unbound Consciousness of Lord Shiva. The grossest form of matter, the solids and place of all existence, the earth symbolize the power of Shakti. In languages, consonants are Lord Shiva whereas vowels are Shakti.

THE WORLD ART GALLERY

Consciousness of Lord Shiva pervades everything and everybody in this entire creation. However, as an embodiment of each individual soul, his trickled down consciousness holds the limited powers of Shakti in different capacities having unique combination of mind and matter. Each soul, attracted to existence, takes birth in order to explore, enjoy, and experience life. Each life also provides it an opportunity to advance by learning spiritual lessons, elevate, and eventually liberate. The souls that evolve and mature over several lifetimes ultimately qualify for a release from this cycle of reincarnation. Human life is a boon and a blessing which is meant to achieve this goal. Those that still have unfulfilled desires and attachments, continue to indulge and gratify.

Lord Shiva is the source of 'I' in all individuals for whom everyone else is 'the other' and distinctly separate. Due to the veil of such ignorance caused by the power of delusion, an aspect of Shakti, everyone acts with 'ego' and 'identity' while interacting with each other. They look after the limited 'self-interest' in dealing with the rest of the world. But when they follow the path of spirituality, they start to expand their awareness. Over time, they realize the limits of individual self and futility of self-centered activities. As their awareness expands, their interest begins to grow encompassing not only the society and the nation but the whole of humanity. In the huge world art gallery, different people are like live exhibits of beautiful paintings. Though made on different pieces of the same canvas, Consciousness of Lord Shiva, each has a unique color combination, appeal, size, theme, appearance, and value. The canvas provides basis and the background that holds these paintings but does not impart any differentiating character. All souls are a part of the same Consciousness, Lord Shiva.

Shakti relentlessly paints through the brush strokes of her boundless energy as she constantly creates these exhibits using three primary colors, her three modes of action called Guṇas – *Sattva, Rajas*, and *Tamas.* She is the one who veils Lord Shiva through these modes creating various portraits and themes. Through her power and potency to create various names and forms, she embodies each soul with a variation in the degree of bondage. Based on the past *Karma* profile, she encodes, engraves, and endows a mix of unique psychological and physical traits at birth. They develop unique personality, character, aptitude, and a driving force that directs the course of each life. It delivers fitting life experiences as its destiny, *Prārabdha.* Thus, she is the one who artfully veils the souls to distinguish each individual, not Lord Shiva.

As *Prāṇa* energy, she also animates the life she creates. She is the power of mind through which she constantly raises desires in which energy of our action is embedded. Moving through innumerable polarities of the inner subtle system, she defines the dimensions of our life. Thereby she directs everyone to follow a particular path and pursue a distinct career. Her authority makes poets and priests, teachers and traders, doctors and dealers, soldiers and servants. Each serves the society quite differently and leads a unique life. She also creates divisions and multiplicity, introduces norms and standards, and gives rise to class and culture in the society. However, each of the faces wearing a mask of individuality, identity, and ego has the same underlying spirit. They wander in such ignorance veiled by her powerful aspect of delusion, *Māyā*. This is how she involves and extracts our participation in the world theater. All spiritual practices are individual efforts to pierce and penetrate the layers of Guṇa coatings which reveal the common canvas and destroy the illusion of identity.

Shiva-Shakti is the core principle that forms the inner philosophy of all Tantric traditions. Shaivaits worship Lord Shiva as the source of the universe whereas Shaktas consider Shakti as the superior of the two as she plays a dominant role in the manifested world. It also forms the basis of male and female principle. Just as a woman conceives only after she receives the 'seed' from a man, Shakti creates the whole universe as she is infused with divine Consciousness of Lord Shiva. This togetherness and interdependence of the masculine and feminine energies is well represented in a reconciliatory form of '***Ardhanārishvara***', an androgynous human. A half-male and half-female figure, it embodies both principles within a single identity. It is an expression which explores the intricate relation between all existence and transcendence, the manifest and the unmanifest, the seen and the unseen, *Saṃsāra* and *Nirvāna*.

Lord Shiva is worshiped as a small pillar, a 'Linga' within the Shakti base or the pedestal, 'Yoni' in all Hindu temples. It expresses the same theme, controlled power of creation and co-existence, state of eternal love that constantly creates within the matrix of space and time. It conceptualizes the idea of infinity that manifests in nature by assuming various names and forms.

Nuggets of Wisdom

We need to follow *Dharma* and also duly protect it by giving time, energy, or money to its various causes because it is *Dharma* which saves all of humanity.

Pursuit of worldly achievements and self-gratification easily obscures awareness such that we forget our *Dharma* and compromise the rightful way of life.

3. DIVINE MOTHER CONCEPT

A female form

Divine Mother concept recognizes the Ultimate Truth in the form of an all-inclusive feminine Self called Devī.

A FEW MORE WORSHIPED ASPECTS

Mahālakshmī Devī – Represents Light energy. She is the Goddess of prosperity who gives eight different types of wealth and resources. As light travels in space, she is the consort of Lord Vishṇu. Most worshiped deity.

Mahāsaraswati Devī – Represents Sound Energy. She is the Goddess of inspiration, learning, worldly and spiritual knowledge, communication, and power of discrimination. She is the consort of Lord Brahmā.

Mahākāli Devī – Represents Heat Energy. She is the Goddess of time. Her benign form Bhadrakāli creates uniform flow of time whereas she devours it causing death and destruction. She is the consort of Lord Mahesh.

Durgā Devī – Represents the aggressive form of Divine Mother. Her active power gives protection against evil and destroys all negativities, outside as well as within us. Most worshiped deity.

Some other significant Forms

Gāyatrī Devī – Essence of the Vedas who leads to purity and light.

Lalita Devī – The most charming and charismatic form of Divine Mother.

Annapurna Devī – Provider of food and grains as the source of energy.

Nav-Durgā – The nine forms of Durgā Devī worshiped during Navrātri.

Mahāvidyas – Ten aspects of wisdom Goddesses covering ten directions.

Saptamātrika – The seven ferocious Goddesses of war and battlefield.

Gram Devī – The Goddess enshrined in a village who protects it.

Bhūdevī – The Mother Earth who is a consort of Lord Vishṇu.

DIVINE MOTHER CONCEPT

Devī as Mother of the Universe

Devī is *Sṛsti-sthiti-layātmika.*
Great Goddess creates, preserves, as well as destroys.

Whereas all other religions have traditionally conceived God predominantly in the male forms only, Hinduism emphasizes that the Ultimate Truth is beyond gender. Like the recognition of divine feminine and Goddess worship prevalent in ancient cultures of Greece, Egypt, and Babylonia, God is also quite commonly visualized, well acknowledged, and widely accepted as the female Supreme Self called Devī. Being the primal ubiquitous energy which is infinite, total, and complete, *Pūrṇa* in all aspects, she is endowed with such ontological supremacy. She expresses the Ultimate Reality as unconditional love of Divine Mother. Her all-encompassing powers and all-embracing qualities stand alone, above all, as an independent all-inclusive feminine Self. As one of the three major flourishing concepts of God, she is popularly worshipped and venerated as mother of the world, *Jagadamba.* She is also recognized and referred to as the eternal queen who effectively rules all the universes she creates that are just like dust at her feet. The classical literature on feminine philosophy and theology like the major scripture of Devī Māhātmyam reiterates her natural position of authority. It convincingly states her complete supremacy, in great depth and detail.

Being manifold and of endless aspects she radiates a multi-faceted versatile personality. An eternal champion of multi-tasking, she does it all. She wears countless designer dresses and matching masks to match her specific forms in function. Charming and charismatic, each of these amazing appearances is well recognized and revered as a deity. While portraying a composite appearance of all these underlying female deities who ultimately converge in her, she is also the source and mother of all male deities. Also, she is self-willed and self-aware. Her power is immeasurable, her compassion is limitless, her grace is boundless, and her greatness is beyond our comprehension or any comparison. Transcendent as well as fully immanent, she is constantly on the move as subtle beat of vibratory energy embodying the dynamic principle.

As female Reality, she is the only effective agency ruling the endless world of boundless energy. Ever bursting with raw power, she channels her unrestrained force in countless modes and infinite variety of ways. Also, she habitually switches the nature, strength, and direction of these streams. They enliven, as they establish countless subtle systems of the universal order. Self-organized, well interconnected, and spread out at multiple levels these synergistic systems are the roots of nature. They are present everywhere. Though imperceptible to our senses, these interpenetrating vibratory fields govern our body, mind, and the universes as perceived and known by their ultimate effects. They also impart duality to the physical plane she creates, rules, and ultimately destroys.

By condensation and conversion to 'frozen' forms, she creates all types of elements. Core of an atom confirms that all matter, though apparently different, is one. It serves as a reservoir of her stupendous energy as its ultimate particles are in constant motion. Different atoms unite to create variety of molecules that come together in countless groups to build specific societies of unique structures. Her mysterious force incorporates, organizes, and administers them so intricately and intelligently as to anatomically constitute the physical body of all organic life forms. Thus she expresses as power of life through extremely complex and ever changing mass of protoplasm materializing our existence. It is an absolutely compelling and undeniable evidence of her immanence. At each moment, the precise and inimitable action of this fundamental life substance admirably accomplishes the purpose of our life. As the primordial power of *Prāṇa* that we breathe in, she moves through the subtle system to energize and sustain all vital functions animating various aspects of our life. It creates an interface connecting the subtle mind with the physical body transferring information through vibrations. As the body fields of energy layers interact with those of the universe, she creates unique individual life patterns. They determine the nature of experiences directing the way of each particular life.

Governing all aspects of life, she operates within wide array of ranges such as gentle to harsh and cultivating to annihilating. Exercising diametrically opposite powers, she unifies or divides, creates restlessness or provides peace and quiet. She embodies the creative power of birth, growth, regeneration, and fertility. On the other hand, her anger and wrath is the power of earthquakes and volcanoes that brings about death and destruction wiping out everything in no time. Epitome of love, compassion, and care, she nestles and nurtures all earthlings, ensures their existence, and positions them to play a unique role in her creation. As the fire of life, she kindles desires and motivates us to act in particular ways. Thereby she extracts our contributions to her ongoing show in the world theater. Each individual role, carefully visualized and choreographed by her, leads us to pursue a specific course of destiny. However, within the comfort zone of her ever available attention, she also allows us the freedom to explore and enjoy her beautiful creation, in chosen ways. As we realize her enormous grace through its experience, we cannot but express our gratitude.

Devī is nescience, *Avidyā* as she binds us with delusion to the existence, *Saṃsāra*. She attaches us to the matters of the world and makes us wander in ignorance. Reciprocally she is also higher knowledge, *Vidyā* that releases and delivers us from *Saṃsāra.* Her grace imparts the true higher knowledge, elevates our being, and makes us realize the passing nature of temporal existence. As we rise above the body consciousness and all worldly attachments, she liberates the blessed few qualifying souls. Thus, she wields an enormous power, arcane in nature which is beyond our capacity to know, comprehend, or understand. As we witness its visible effects through the changes around us, she also transforms our thoughts, vision, and perception. She is beyond distinctions with which we attempt, in vain, to mentally conceive and literally conceptualize her. She is above all such mental perceptions and various philosophical constructs.

Her state before creation is *Adya* Shakti. As Shakti, in general, she personifies the energizing principle; source, essence, and substance of all creation. Being an eternal power of existence, she also supports all that she creates. She is conceptualized to operate variously as *Prāṇa*, *Prakṛti*, *Māyā*, and *Kuṇḍalinī*. As *Prāṇa*, she is the universal matrix of primal energy that catalyzes all actions and breathes life in all living beings. As formative energy of Consciousness, *Prakṛti*, she represents the finitising principle. She is the efficient and material cause that creates mind and matter in which she embodies all individual souls. As *Māyā,* she is the power of nescience. It veils individual consciousness in such ignorance that it thinks of being separate from *Brahman* and gets attached to the material world. As Devī *Kuṇḍalinī*, she is the inherent power of inner consciousness that lies dormant at the base of spine of every individual.

Energy has inter-convertible categories like kinetic and potential, electrical and chemical, nuclear and thermal, magnetic and mechanical. We study energy or harness it for use in any number of forms. Likewise, she is visualized in various portraits formalized with features and faces of deities, each associated with specific aspects in order to venerate and worship her. At times, they have a mere symbolic form in a most simple visualization. Each of the sacred portraits duly projects her associated power appropriately highlighting the underlying essence. More often than not, her inter-related forms and attributes seem to be overlapping and undistinguishable. It happens as all names and the epithets in descriptive terminology are quite interchangeable and informal. All Hinduism concepts view her from unique angles, focus on specific aspects, and achieve their own vision of her enshrined as deities in temples. Each deity provides an access to her in its own particular way. Looking at the compassionate face of the chosen deity facilitates conversation and communion in the most personal way whether approached with gratitude or in a state of despair.

Jagadamba is the mother of Lord Brahmā, Lord Vishṇu, and Lord Mahesh, the three most recognized deities of the Trinity concept. All their powers to create, sustain, and transform are derived from her. She also differentiates into three forms of *Mahāsaraswati* Devī, *Mahālakshmī* Devī, and *Mahākāli* Devī respectively to be the consorts of these deities duly assisting them in their specific functions. Worshiped as *Mahāsaraswati* Devī, she is the source of sound, music, knowledge, culture, and communication. She is also composer of the Vedas. *Mahālakshmī* Devī, her most benevolent aspect represents all kinds of wealth, peace, and prosperity. Being kind and extremely compassionate, she also provides the bounty and resources of nature. *Mahākāli* Devī, the dark and unknown power of time quite explicitly portrays the wild and terrifying aspect of her absolute force which causes death and destruction.

Pārvati Devī represents her all-encompassing powers and potencies. She is an embodiment of security and kindness, ideal of love, compassion, and comfort. Personifying Shakti, she is the consort of Lord Shiva and the mother of two virtuous and worthy sons, Lord Gaṇesha and Lord Skanda. As *Gāyatrī* Devī, a symbol of purity and light, she is called *Pārā Brahman Swarupini*, the radiance and brilliance hidden within all beings. She is called the mother of the Vedas as the sound body of her mantra encapsulates the entire knowledge of the Vedas. *Lalita* Devī is her strikingly young and beautiful face who resides as pure love and bliss in the hearts of everyone. Her tender beauty and delicate charm is the creative force of the entire cosmos. *Annapurna* Devī is her caring form who provides food, feeds, nourishes, and nurtures us. *Durgā* Devī is an active and aggressive mother who protects us from all kinds of negativities. She is the comfort for every gloom, grief, and grievance. As *Gram* Devī she assumes responsibility to protect the place and the village she is enshrined in.

Expression of Aum

As unmanifest *Brahman*, she is recognized as *Pārā* Shakti by her devotees called Shakta. In this state of slumber, her three qualities of *Sattva*, *Rajas*, and *Tamas* exist in a perfect equilibrium. Spontaneously, an impulse kindles a desire in her to create which disrupts this balance. It is the activation of *Rajas* which makes appearance as **casual** sound represented by the articulate sound Aum (Page 9). It is a soundless sound, universal and eternal, which consists of pure waves that remain the same forever. It is the first divine expression, the power of her infinite creative potential that is yet in a latent form.

The casual sound Aum is like a seed covered with a sheath. Staying dormant indefinitely, when the seed germinates under favorable conditions, the sheath is broken to establish dichotomy. Likewise, a spontaneous process known as *Sphoṭa* polarizes this sound with a burst of light into the field of electro-magnetic force called *Nāda Brahman*. It gives rise to ***Bindu*** which is an anchor, the central ground that is static. As a core, it is the concentrated point of potentialised universe. **Subtle** sound waves called ***Nāda*** emanate from *Bindu* and spread around in all directions. *Bindu* is recognized as Lord Shiva, the observer with self-illuminating awareness. Active front of *Nāda* is the power of Shakti which carries the infinite creative potential very well known as *Kāma*. It expands, evolves, and eventually actualizes the entire universe in all its beauty and harmony. Stepwise, it gives rise to various mental and material building blocks of the universe called *Tattvas*. Not limited to a particular time or a specific place in space, this process of Transcendental polarization is universal in nature.

The polarized *Nāda* waves generate vibrations, ***Spanda*** visualized as the dance of Lord Shiva and Shakti. It is a throb of blissful ocean beyond the spatial-temporal framework, a realm of their perpetual transitory state in creation. It is also the endless source of energy, life force of the universe called *Prāṇa*. These waves also carry the latent trait of ***Nāma-Rupa***. *Nāma* or *Shabda* is the energy of propagation whereas *Rupa* or *Artha* is the intelligence of a form, the body of its movement. *Nāma* is the mental vibrations of cognition, the mental plane that ultimately gives rise to the articulate sound of speech. *Rupa* is the intelligence of these waves that denotes the shape it gives rise to in the objective world, the physical plane. This trait of *Nāma-Rupa* stays as it is forever. At every stage of creation, it simultaneously gives rise to the mental and physical planes that denote the same thing; one as sound, the other as shape.

Sound and Creation

Just as white light splits into three primary colors, *Nāda* differentiates and expands into 50 root sounds that manifest at **gross** level. Each of them is unique as it carries specific power and trait of *Nāma-Rupa* and therefore, respectfully recognized as Mother, ***Mātṛkā.*** Each of these audible sounds reveals to us the vibrations that have the potential to give rise to a specific physical form. It is the power of these letters through which Devī operates, creates our mind and body, effectively holds it, and also rules all aspects of our life through their vibratory energy. All these sounds constitute the alphabets of Sanskṛit and therefore, Sanskṛit is called the language of creation. The three primary colors combine in various proportions to give rise to multitude of colors with a riot of hues and shades. Likewise, these *Mātṛkā* sounds create innumerable other sounds by innovative permutations and combinations that give rise to countless physical objects with predictable shapes and forms. These sounds are the wombs, the primary resource of the entire creation. They construct all objects of the manifested world, known as well as unknown.

Interestingly, in our subtle body there are 50 major subtle energy channels associated with six major energy centers, Chakras strung along the length of the spine. This number is exactly the same as that of *Mātṛkā* sounds which is not a mere coincidence. Each of these channels has its origin in, as it has actually evolved from the associated *Mātṛkā* power during gestation. All channels then contributed to the creation of specific physical forms around them based on their intelligence. Our entire physical body has gradually evolved from, and is duly sustained by intelligence inherent to the core matrix of these energies. These sounds are well attuned to the latent power of *Kuṇḍalinī* which resides at the base of spine in everybody. Source of all our thoughts, ideas, and speech, she rules our mental ability and expression through these sounds.

Vibrations of *Mātṛkā* sounds differentiate and combine, further differentiate and recombine in innovative ways giving rise to countless patterns of energy equations. They ultimately exhibit the enormous wave phenomenon of this marvelous universe. The fundamental nature of waves is to have a form and a pulse, harmony and resonance that expresses in cycles reaching a peak. By extension, all creation arising from waves also occurs in self repeating cycles. The entire universe is an extraordinary web of innumerable interpenetrating cycles like spring and autumn, day and night, inhalation and exhalation, full moon and new moon. It is an incomprehensibly interdependent, continuous, and repetitive phenomenon of waves, moving within other waves that further interact with more waves. Complex synergy of their casual connections weaves the fabric of all life and a stunning spectrum of cycles on display.

To enclose space and create a physical form, a minimum of three dimensions are needed as we see in a triangle. Bursting with **light,** casual sound Aum universally polarizes to establish the first vertex, *Bindu* from which appears the second as the front of propagating **sound** waves, *Nāda*. Its desire to create, *Kāma* constantly seeks the third point of limit, the vertex in creation which encloses space and creates a form. As it moves and arrives at such points at which it stops to create limits, the **heat** energy of restriction, *Nirodhikā* is released. It defines the last boundary adding that third vertex called *Kalā*. *Kāma* relentlessly moves around in all directions to discover, identify, and establish newer points of *Kalā*. It defines limits of such innovative forms so as to create unique building blocks of the universe called *Tattvas*. The human urge to create is also described in literature as *Kāma* and all forms of ensuing artistic expressions as *Kalā*. It is to be noted that the sides and vertices of this dynamic polar triangle do not have mathematical character. They refer to the specific power and potencies.

Kāma-Kalā, The Divine Desire

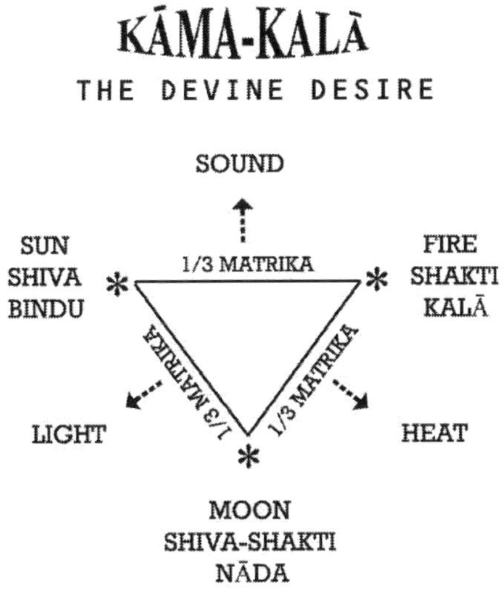

Nāda, *Bindu*, and *Kalā* define the three polar vertices that outline the first ever closed form as a triangle. Like the sprouts of a germinated seed, the radiating energies of heat, light, and sound form the three operational power lines that enclose this triangular form. It constitutes *Kāma-Kalā* triangle, the subtle body of Divine Mother who presides as the most auspicious deity called *Tripurasundari*. The emanating energies that form the sides of this triangle are her three major aspects. It is the first ever state of manifestation where reflective awareness has a form associated with self-illuminating *Ahaṃ*, I-ness of Lord Shiva enclosed within. In three groups, all *Mātṛkā* sounds reside along the sides like 'garland of letters' that together make up the subtle body of *Tripurasundari*. Hence, she is also called *mūla-mantratmika* as these sounds are the origin and source of all evolving mantras that pervade the whole universe. These three sides also represent energies of Lord Brahmā, Lord Vishṇu, and Lord Mahesh who carry out the cosmic functions of creation, preservation, and dissolution respectively. A few other major triads or triple characteristics that spiral out from the *Kāma-Kalā* triangle are -

- The power of will (*Icchā*), knowledge (*Jnāna*), and action (*Kriyā*).
- The modes of goodness (*Sattva*), passion (*Rajas*), and ignorance (*Tamas*).
- The observer, the process of observation, and the object of observation.
- The casual spirit, subtle mind, and gross body

Kāma-Kalā triangle is the first subtle expression of Divine Mother quivering with an intense desire of creation. Its creative fervor carries the power of duality, power to veil, and power of illusion called *Māyā* that initiates the manifestation process. This dynamic template spontaneously enlarges and continuously expands eventually evolving into the entire physical phenomena. Exploiting its infinite potential, it rapidly magnifies, repeatedly multiplies, and rightly modifies to generate innumerable innovative configurations that ultimately project into universes. Precise and diligent action of *Kāma* steadily establishes a host of appropriate distinguished limits in pursuit of creation. It constitutes the order of logical evolution in which mental and material principles develop as various building blocks, *Tattvas* filling the lower ontological categories. Appearing in a cascading manner, they line up in an organized sequence to be duly incorporated. The cumulative aspects of different series of triads as well as *Mātṛkā* sounds are the sacred causes of creation. They give rise to intended physical forms as the effects continuously carrying out the divine art of creation.

Consciousness of Lord Shiva thus gets confined within the limits of *Kāma-Kalā* triangle. Hence, he is also known as *Sakalā* meaning 'with a shape'. Enclosed within and so united with *Tripurasundari*, he observes and enjoys her supremely lovely form. Though his presence supports, inspires, and blossoms her power, he does not actively contribute to her endeavor in creation. He establishes a base and holds her in various ways as she operates, expands, and creates with passion. As this primary triangle radiates, replicates, and recombines to develop countless configurations of other evolving triangles, he gets veiled in numerous levels of energy fields that greatly reduce his self-illuminating awareness. A Śrī Chakra very well represents this principle. All its interacting triangles appear by the expansion of *Kāma-Kalā* triangle located at the top center which runs down to create a fertile matrix, the womb from which all creation flows.

Creation is the only passion of *Kāma-Kalā*. Operating from the *Sahasrāra* Chakra, crown of the brain, she first gives rise to the mental faculty as she begins to create an individual. She then descends to create various subtle energy centers called Chakras through the power of *Mātṛkā* that further develop the subtle and the physical bodies embodying the soul. Finally she comes to rest lying dormant as *Kuṇḍalinī* at the base of spine. From here, she constantly sustains the power of *Mātṛkā* that rule various Chakras to animate human consciousness. In women, her mother-form called *Kūrūkūlla* gives rise to ova (moon) whereas in men, her father-form called *Vārāhi* gives rise to semen (sun). Ovum and semen unite and ultimately give rise to new physical form of an individual (fire) in which Lord Shiva, the consciousness enters through orgasm. Ovum is the source of five fires – skin, blood, flesh, fat, and bones whereas semen is the source of four fires – individual soul, vital breath, marrow, and semen.

The principle of triads continues to operate even after our coming into being as it extends to various aspects of human life. There are three major subtle energy channels- Ida, Pingala, and Sushumna that create the primary axis of energy flow in the subtle body. Each channel represents the energies of moon, sun, and fire respectively. Our existence is an expression of the triad of the physical, the subtle, and the casual bodies. Also, each body experiences in one of the three states of waking, dreaming, or deep sleep respectively at any given time. We think of the past, act in the present, and plan for the future. All actions and experiences of our life are governed by the law of cause and effect, *Karma* encompassing the past, the present, and the future lives. Lastly, the physical body is made of three bodily humors, Vāta (air), Pitta (fire), and Kapha (water) which determines the individual constitution, unique to everyone.

Transcendental polarization of Aum occurs through *Sphoṭa* which releases the self-illuminating light of Consciousness, Lord Shiva as *Bindu* having ability to experience. He does so through the vibratory field of *Spanda* created by *Nāda* waves moving away from *Bindu*. Shakti is the creative front of *Nāda* who moves forward to reach various limiting points actualizing all forms of matter that he explores, enjoys, and experiences. Thus, the light of awareness experiences the ever changing physical plane, the outer world through the sound vibrations of *Spanda* which rules the mental plane. It defines the way for all embodied souls to have all worldly experiences; through mental vibrations.

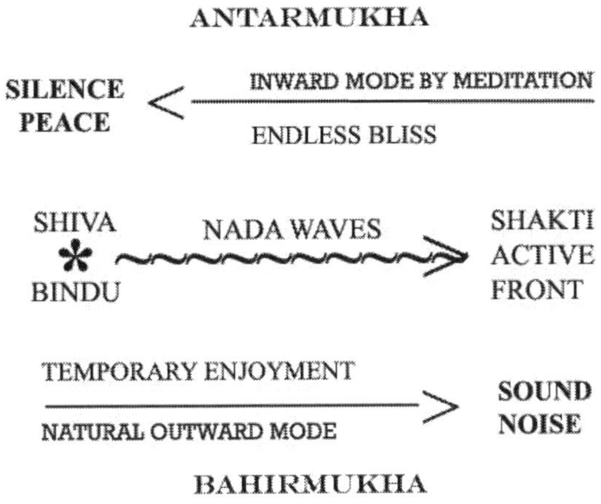

It can be seen that *Nāda* not only creates matter with limited boundaries but also connects it to the unbound Consciousness of *Bindu*. Our awareness is constantly drawn outward as it causally rides the vibratory force of *Spanda* ruling the mind. It is a direction that goes away from the self sinking us deeply in the material world and covering us in the darkness of ignorance. In this outward facing, *Bahirmukha* mode, we actively seek endless points of pleasure and power in the outer world so as to satisfy our never-ending desires, *Kāma*. But then, even those that translate successfully into the desired experiences prove to be temporary and limited. Also, light of human consciousness is the casualty as all worldly attachment and sensual acts of self-gratification scatters and reduces the level of awareness taking us away from the source.

Fortunately, we are also blessed with the unique ability to realize the potential of exploiting *Nāda* waves so as to reach *Bindu*. Meditation redirects our awareness such that it rides opposing the vibratory mode of *Spanda*, like swimming against the water flow. It is the most superior game of spiritual athletics where we swim and search within to win the most coveted prize of reaching the origin. By turning our awareness into inwards facing, *Antarmukha* mode, the conditioned human soul can trace back *Nāda* waves to gradually move towards *Bindu*. It is the eternal light of Consciousness, source of endless peace and silence. Here all our *Kāma* is satisfied, forever, providing never ending pleasure and bliss. With sound vibrations of mantra chanting, feeling of self-surrender, and energy of intense devotion to the divine, we gather power and potency to trace back the *Nāda* waves. Practice of meditation calms the vibratory field of thoughts and stills the mind facilitating the inward journey to explore our inner self. The intuitional practice of *Nāda Yoga* is aimed at achieving integration with the divine by going from sound, the chaos of the outer world to silence, the blissful source within by riding back the waves of primordial sound Aum. Such contemplative experience of *Spanda* allows us to realize the true nature of eternal Self engaged in all-encompassing activities of the universe. As *Nāda* gets absorbed in the eternal source, *Bindu*, material boundaries dissolve, awareness expands, and a state of endless bliss and peace, *Turīya* is attained.

The entire universe is an artistic expression of just one distinguished designer, Devī. Like an art gallery which exclusively features ever changing creations of just one artist, it duly projects her constantly evolving vision. She quietly conceives, quickly designs, deftly moves, and diligently weaves her energies to create countless qualities of life fabric having an incredible variety of colors, patterns, and forms. Unbeaten to date, she has always been a winner. Those who consider her to be The Supreme, *Para* Shakti and worship her as Divine Mother, *Jagadamba* are called Shakta. Her abode in the heavens is the island of jewels, **Maṇidvipa**. In their belief, she is the Ultimate Reality from whom all other forms of divinity, whether male or female emerge as deities.

One of the triads spiraling out of *Kāma-Kalā* triangle develops as three deities of the Trinity Concept of God. Therefore, she is the mother of these deities. Lord Brahmā, the creator personifies the creative aspect of *Kāma* who, in relentless pursuit of creation constantly seeks various limits. He arises out of her and encloses space to create the building blocks guided by her intelligence, wish, and command. She is also the origin of Lord Vishṇu as she differentiates into the waveform plane of ether. It subsequently gives rise to evolute elements encompassing all aspects of protection and preservation of life. Lord Shiva is the *Bindu* that comes into being after the polarization of Aum that arises from her. He makes the time manifest which is ruled by Lord Mahesh.

Her additional aspects are portrayed as the consorts of deities in other concepts

DIVINE MOTHER

▼ GIVES RISE TO

CASUAL SOUND AUM

TRANSCENDENTALLY ▼ POLARIZES

SUBTLE SOUND AUM - *NĀDA-BRAHMAN*

▼ GIVES RISE TO

NĀDA AND *BINDU* BIPOLAR FUNCTINAL REALITY
SHIVA-SHAKTI CONCEPT

NĀDA SPREAD AROUND ▼ AND CREATES *KALĀ*

TRIADS OF *NĀDA, BINDU,* AND *KALĀ*

ASSOCIATED WITH TRIAD OF BRAHMĀ, VISHNU, MAHESH
TRINITY CONCEPT

of God. In Shiva-Shakti concept, she is in an eternal union with the spirit, Lord Shiva as his active energy, Shakti. This primordial couple personifies the primary principles of polarity behind all creation. She is the active force of manifestation that constantly moves to create physical forms for Lord Shiva to enjoy and have finite experiences. The three rays emanating as the sides of *Kāma-Kalā* triangle are the light energy, sound energy, and heat energy that assume the forms and faces of consorts of the three deities of Trinity concept. They are recognized as *Mahāsaraswati* Devī, *Mahālakshmī* Devī, and *Mahākāli* Devī.

Devī brings about changes in all her manifestation either through the expansion or the withdrawal mode. The waxing phase of moon visibly illustrates her expansion mode. Each full moon night beautifully represents the extremely auspicious and ever benevolent form of *Lalitā* Devī. It is the most delightful and ravishing appearance of Divine Mother who portrays the entire manifestation as bright and beautiful, full and flawless. It is the radiation of her pure love and soothing power that creates and cares, grows and nurtures. She is the presiding deity of the entire creation as represented in her geometric abode of Śrī Chakra. Followers of ***Śrīkulā*** tradition generally pursue the path of action, *Karma* and worship this blissful form which is recognized as Śrī Vidyā.

At the time of dissolution, she destroys the countless universes she creates with the withdrawal mode. It is symbolized by the waning phase of moon and portrayed by the most ferocious form of *Mahākāli* Devī. The iconography portrays her having a black naked body with a terrifying face as blood drips from her protruding tongue. She holds various weapons and her eyes are rolling as she dances in rage. The garland of 50 skulls she wears represents the root powers of creation, *Mātṛkā* that she annihilates to destroy life. Followers of ***Kālikulā*** tradition pursue the path of knowledge, *Jnāna* and worship her in this terrible form. It signifies that it is necessary to transcend transitory manifestation in order to reach the Ultimate Reality.

Mantras written in thirteen chapters of the Holy Scripture Devī Māhātmyam, also known as Durgā Saptashati or **Chaṇḍi Pāth** articulate her glory, in details. It is the most sacred text for Shaktas. Devī Bhāgavat Purāṇa and Devī Gītā are other holy texts that enunciate her magnificence. Every year, it is a popular practice to worship Divine Mother at home during nine days of the Navrātri festival. It is a grand occasion heartily celebrated by everyone that culminates on the tenth day called Dassera, the most auspicious day of Hindu calendar. It symbolizes the ultimate victory of good over evil. A fire ceremony called Chaṇḍi Homa, where Devī is offered oblations is also customarily carried out. Spread throughout the Indian subcontinent, there are 51 major temples called Shakti Peethas, the energy centers of Devī. Each of these places is associated with different physical body parts of Devī and therefore, very powerful energy centers. These are the common places of pilgrimage for her devotees.

Nuggets of Wisdom

Fighting in the name of religion is the most profound state of ignorance.

Each religion is a path conceived by human mind to pursue spirituality.

Maya or illusion is the force that gives false credibility to things like money and power as the ultimate goal of human life and a true measure of intelligence and success.

Love is the universal force that sustains all of humanity.

Spirituality gives us strength to face the challenges of life. It also helps us to see things in their proper perspective.

Experience of duality is inherent to existence as the positive of pleasure, happiness, and joy inevitably, equally, and simultaneously exist with the negative of misery, pain, and grief in the world.

Every situation we face has two sides. Exploit the positive to harvest and enjoy its fruits.

DEITIES

GAṆESHA

God of Wisdom and Prosperity

Lord Gaṇesha is an enormously popular and well-known, the most worshiped deity of all the Hindu deities. Recognized since the Vedic period, he acquired a wide appeal and really came to prominence in 4th-5th century AD. As the lord of new beginnings, he is always invoked at the start of undertaking of all descriptions. His grace removes obstacles, marks orderly progress, and ensures successful completion of any task undertaken by a devotee. Reigning over decisions that determine the direction, he regulates the course of life consistent with the doctrine of *Karma*. He stands for an innate power within us embodying the spiritual essence that sustains our life. Followers of all different Hindu sects and traditions, regardless of their affiliation, equally revere and worship him. As the lord of categories, he rules over everything that the mind comprehends by classifying and categorizing. Also known as Gaṇapati, lord of multitudes, he transcends the sectarian and regional limits, connects with everybody, and unifies them. He is considered to be '***Aumkāra Swarūpa***' meaning that he personifies the impersonal sound representation of God, Aum.

Iconography

He is quite intriguing in appearance having the plump body of a human but the head of an elephant. With one broken tusk, large ears, and a corpulent pot-bellied figure, he is truly adorable and very easy to identify. Typically he is portrayed to have four hands - holding a goad in one, a noose in the second, a delicacy called laddu in the third, and the fourth raised in a gesture of granting boons blessing the devotees. Enigmatic yet endearing, he is the lovable God of prudence and benevolence who has a very charming, unique, and captivating appearance. Equally interesting is his ride, a mouse, especially considering his size.

But why does this Lord of good fortune have such an unusual form? There are different mythological stories surrounding his creation. What is remarkable is that every part of the body in this iconography carries special significance. It compels all rational minds to look beyond outer appearances and unusual forms to seek, uncover, recognize, and appreciate the underlying subtle reality.

Whereas the elephant head symbolizes strength and longevity, gentle nature and loyalty, the trunk symbolizes power of discrimination. He supposedly contains all the past, present, and future universes within his huge pot-belly. The noose and the goad in his hands control, command, and guide an individual to follow the right path. As a reward, he offers delicacy called laddu that he relishes. The tiny mouse, his vehicle, symbolizes the human mind and ego. While avoiding spiritual light, it constantly explores the darkest places, in sneaky ways, striving to satisfy worldly desires that eat away good merits. Guiding power of Gaṇesha riding the mouse gives it the right direction with a force that finds a way through the smallest spiritual opening. Gaṇesha on a mouse symbolizes unity of the divine and an individual soul, the big and the small within nature, reconciliation of the opposites and unity in diversity.

Hinduism is a religion rife with symbolism. Each symbol or icon stands for an aspect of divine and conveys a meaning. The awe-inspiring iconography of Gaṇesha represents the aspect of cosmic intelligence that primarily operates as the force of gravity and inertia. Shakti is creative energy of the Absolute who, with her ever evolving potencies assumes names and forms of all animate and inanimate objects. Her various aspects like heat, light, and sound combines and transforms in multitude of ways to make matter. Matter has weight, which is at all times associated with gravity. Shakti in the benign form is personified as **Pārvati** Devī and obviously, she is the mother of Lord Gaṇesha. He eternally dwells in her womb and always emerges as the 'first born', *Jyeshtharaja* with all her creation. Naturally, he is very close to her and they share a very tender and loving relationship. They reside in *Mulādhāra* Chakra of subtle body at the base of spine in every individual where the mother lies dormant in the form of *Kuṇḍalinī* energy. While enthralling and entertaining, guarding and caring for her, he draws on her immense energy, at will, whenever necessary.

Gaṇesha and gravity

Force of gravity is the most potent, invisible, and unidirectional force in the universe. It is the aspect of cosmic intelligence that projects the power behind formation of matter, spontaneously becomes operative, and starts exerting its influence. Therefore, Gaṇesha is also considered to be self-born, ***Swayambhū***. All the stars, planets, and satellites move about and position themselves in an orderly fashion under the influence of this mysterious but predictable force. It is mysterious because a change in position of one instantaneously affects all others who move, adjust, and accommodate to maintain balance and order. And the pattern of this realignment is quite smooth, orderly, and predictable. It influences everything, pulls on everyone however remotely placed, and does so all the time, transcending the limitations of time and space. As ruler of the entire universe which is considered to be contained inside his huge belly, Gaṇesha ensures an orderly existence of all entities, small and large.

In our subtle body, the flow of energy is regulated by numerous psycho energy centers called Chakras. *Mulādhāra*, the first Chakra located at the base of spine is associated with solids and the basic nature of our existence. It represents the physical or earthly plane which is naturally associated with inertia and gravity. Therefore, Lord Gaṇesha is always present there, supporting and guiding other Chakras above along the spine. As the principle primordial force, he anchors, amplifies, and allows the outward expansion of other diverse forces, all geared to operate inner wheels of life. By regulating forces operating through all other Chakras throughout the body, he directs our awareness. All energy channels of our physical and subtle bodies arise from here. While governing time, matter, and memory, he exerts his influence through them.

All our thoughts, decisions, and actions are memory driven and, often times, instinctive responses guided by Gaṇesha, subconscious aspect of our being. Fully aware of our past *Karma*, he ensures that it bears fitting and timely fruits consistent with our destiny. As we make a crucial choice every time we reach crossroads in our life, he is the guiding force who leads us to 'gravitate' in a particular direction. He is the scribe, always awake and ready, who readily knows our thoughts and witnesses all our actions. He continuously records them with his broken tusk to update our profile, grade our spiritual status, and chart the future direction of life accordingly. Just a pause to seek his grace before we proceed to do anything highlights a choice that guides our path.

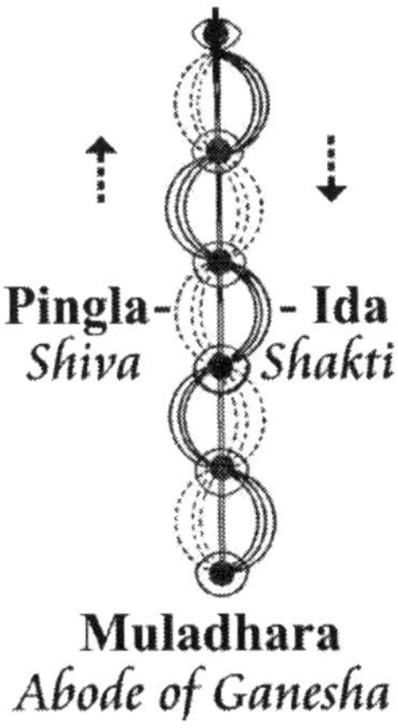

Son of Lord Shiva and Shakti

There is an intricate network of innumerable invisible channels in our subtle body through which the vital life energy flows. Of these, the two primary channels, Ida and Pingala run along the spine and meet in *Mulādhāra* Chakra. They carry the two contrasting yet complementing energies of Lord Shiva and Shakti personifying two opposite forces of the same divine source. Their union here provides an opportunity of having life to our soul as it creates the physical form of a body grounded, supported, and guarded by Gaṇesha. As their divine child, he embodies boundless consciousness of Lord Shiva unified with the primordial power of Shakti. So empowered, he is entrusted to rule all beings on the earthly plane created by his parents. He dwells in this permanent abode in *Mulādhāra* Chakra sharing a powerful and passionate relation with them. Lord Shiva usually stays away, spending most of his time meditating in the crown of brain, *Sahasrāra* Chakra. As Gaṇesha resides close to Shakti, the *Kuṇḍalinī* energy lying dormant in *Mulādhāra* Chakra, he protects and provides endless joy to her. Always available and willing to assist, he is also our constant companion on the physical plane, ready to listen to our problems and guide us.

Due to his constant presence at this gate, in mythological stories he is shown as guarding the door of the palace of Pārvati Devī and Lord Shiva. His job is to prevent intruders from entering the sacred chambers of the union of his parents. He prevents, checks, and qualifies spiritual status of everyone before granting entry with access to successively higher and more subtle planes of consciousness. They exist and operate above the physical plane of *Mulādhāra* Chakra where he resides. Gaṇesha ensures that only the truly deserving person, with right *Karma*, worthy of meeting his parents enters this realm.

Principle of Unity

As in *Mulādhāra*, Gaṇesha embodies the principle of unity within all systems of manifestation; large or small, animate or inanimate. His appearance is assured where two or more separate entities come together so as to create a new one of which they become a part. For example, he facilitates the formation of atom of Hydrogen, a new entity created by his bringing two quite different particles - an electron and a proton closer. His influence equally extends from tiny atoms, to the gigantic solar system, to all heavenly galaxies of the entire universe. He integrates individual consciousness of units to make sense for the set they belong to without which there would be utter chaos in the system. He is the unifying power of collective consciousness of cells that function as an organ, organs that function as a system, and all systems that function as a body. He monitors, organizes, and coordinates their actions at each level.

Just as he rules the physical plane by his power to incorporate consciousness in various overlays of sets and sub-sets, he also governs our psychic realm. All members in a group act in an organized way to impart a unique identity to it as it operates under his command and intelligence. Examples are an orchestra performing on stage, a cricket team contesting for world cup, or a company where people come to work every day. Working through different segments, disparate realities, and diverse planes of consciousness, he cleverly knits together the fabric of a society, class, culture, or country. As Gaṇapati, a group leader, he threads people together by the string of same family, similar background, special relation, shared interest, social event, specific purpose, or simply due to a situation just as pull of gravity ties all matter together.

The Brother, Kārtikeya

Lord Gaṇesha has an older brother named Lord **Kārtikeya.** He personifies the force of electromagnetism which holds all sub-atomic particles together. If Gaṇesha makes matter gravitate to each other, power of Kārtikeya binds and keeps them together. He is also known as Murugan, Subramanya, or Skanda. His force manifests as the power of will, direct cognition, and energy of heat and fire at the level of *Manipura* Chakra. It is the third Chakra located above *Mulādhāra.* Skanda is usually depicted having a peacock as his vehicle. He wields a lance like weapon indicative of deep knowledge, discrimination, and spiritual insight. As commander of celestial army, he is an invincible warrior holding impeccable record of destroying evil forces. He has a more direct, strong, and an electrifying approach of a soldier compared to a typically intelligent, prudent, and diplomatic handling of Gaṇesha. In contests between the two, all powerful Skanda always loses out against the wit and wisdom of Gaṇesha. His force is much stronger than the pull of gravity but it operates on a higher, deeper, and subtler level. Therefore, he is less recognized and worshiped compared to Lord Gaṇesha. We need to get spiritually empowered and duly elevated to reach his level above the physical plane at which we live. Gaṇesha, our companion and guide in this phenomenal world qualifies our spiritual status. Then he proceeds to introduce us to this divine preceptor of religion. Reaching him is the highest honor one can achieve while retaining ones identity. His domain is closest to the vibrations of sentient energy operating at nuclear level where matter and energy constantly transforms with fission and fusion of discrete particles. It is the eternal play of Ultimate Reality visualized as the power of Lord Shiva and Shakti.

Gaṇesha in our daily life

Whether it is marriage, getting a new home or business, or starting a tour, grace of Gaṇesha is always invoked at the beginning of an auspicious occasion for smooth operation and successful completion. Having an ability to mediate between disparate realities, transmute perception, and synthesize a satisfactory solution, he exhibits an amazing power of transformation. He has the strength and the skill to break existing bonds and established molds making way for new associations that initiate fresh life patterns. His grace effectively bridges transitions as incomprehensible events are not only made possible but meaningful and memorable. He brings about order to chaos as he reorients, realigns, and repositions us to create new links that restructures our life. By catalyzing a relation like that between the families of newlyweds or couple having a newborn, he adds new dimensions to the life of everyone involved. In ever evolving equations of relations and affiliations, he always figures out a formula that either facilitates or forces change in order to maintain the balance.

Some of our lower natures are selfishness and pride, anger and jealousy. These manifest and take control when our awareness is flowing through the Chakras of lower consciousness operating below *Mulādhāra* Chakra (Page 142). To protect us from such negative traits, we first pray Lord Gaṇesha before the beginning of any event. He listens and considers. His power can influence, seal off these Chakras, and direct our awareness to the other six major Chakras of higher consciousness above his abode (Page 140). As ***Vighneshwara***, creator as well as remover of obstacles, he evaluates appropriateness of the planned event before deciding whether to prevent or permit it. Having a positive as well as negative aspect, he first qualifies and then either grants success or blocks it with a barrier. To deny or to time the event, he closes the doors to success and waits for an opportune moment to open them. It ensures that we work through our *Karmic* destiny and follow the right path. In a planned and prudent manner, he proceeds with care and caution, in a sure and steady gait, to take our soul through different stages of evolution. With his grace, intelligence, and wisdom we easily overcome any dissent, disturbance, or disorder during the progress of an event. Successful end of the endeavor is our aim and the achievement we seek for. By granting success, he ultimately gives us peace and prosperity.

Lord of the threshold

Gaṇesha is called Lord of the threshold due to his unique position having an equal insight, involvement, and influence in both, the earthly and heavenly realms. Usually Gaṇesha statues are found near the entrance of all temples. It signifies that due to his proximity to the material plane of consciousness, he appears first in our spiritual journey. It is necessary to propitiate him before we proceed any further. He guides and facilitates a meeting between the humans and the divine. For the purpose, he also leads us to a Guru, at an appropriate time in our life, who directs us in our quest to reach the source.

This position at the entrance has a special significance for Shaktas, worshipers of Divine Mother. Their spiritual practices aim to awaken the latent *Kuṇḍalinī* energy residing at the base of spine. She awakens when the divine grace descends on the practitioner in an approval and acceptance of his pursuits. It is a rare achievement attained by blessed few. When awakened, she breaks the knot *Brahmagranthi* in *Mulādhāra* Chakra embracing Gaṇesha before starting her ascent up the spine. It is a time of cosmic union for the mother and the son, a moment of exhilaration and ecstasy that resonates throughout the universe of the entire body. It is only through the blessings of Gaṇesha at this gate that the adept can succeed in achieving this ultimate goal of life. Gaṇesha therefore, assumes a prominent position in all Shakta and Tantra traditions.

As *Varada*, boon giver and *Siddhidātā*, achiever of accomplishments, Gaṇesha gives general abundance and good fortune in life. He also bestows two great powers, sometimes referred to as his consorts. They are '**Siddhi**' meaning special powers of clairvoyance, psychic, healing and the like and '**Buddhi**' meaning intelligence to act appropriately at any moment. He is also known by names like *Vināyaka* (prominent leader), *Ekdantā* (having one tusk), *Lambodara* (pendant-bellied), *Vakratūnda* (curved trunk), *Gajānana* (elephant faced), *Mahodara* (big belly), *Bhālchandra* (moon over head), *Vighneshvara* (controller of obstacles), *Dhūmravarna* (smoke colored) etc.

Those worshipers of Gaṇesha who consider him to be the Supreme are known as Gaṇapatya. Gaṇapati Atharvashirsa, Gaṇesha Purāṇa, and Mudgala Purāṇa are the major Holy Scriptures dedicated to him. Gaṇapati Atharvashirsa describes him as an all–encompassing deity -

O Gaṇapati, You are the Trimurti – Brahmā, Vishṇu, and Shiva. You are Indra, the God of Devas. You are the God of fire, Agni and air, Vāyu. You are the Sun and the Moon. Embodiment and essence of sound, You are the Brahman, Consciousness. You are beyond the three qualities of Sattva, Rajas, and Tamas. You embody the three powers of Will, Knowledge, and Action. You are the three worlds – Bhuloka or Earth, Antariksha-loka or Space, and Swargaloka or Heaven. You are the past, present, and future. You are Aum.

As a patron of all forms of arts and sciences, he is often portrayed being engaged in such activities as dancing, playing musical instruments, writing etc. He is worshiped on Tuesdays and the fourth day of any fortnight of lunar calendar, four being his favorite number. His seed letter, 'Gam' used in mantra recitation invokes energy of the entire universe that breaks down disharmonious patterns. Therefore, he is also called *Vishwaroopa*. Coconut, raw white rice, jaggery, fresh grass blades, sweets, fruits, sandal paste, red flowers etc. are offered while praying him followed by Aarti, offering of flame. Lord Gaṇesha showers his grace upon the worshiper, the offerings get blessed. The fourth day of the waxing moon period in the month of *Bhādrapada* of Hindu calendar is celebrated as **Gaṇesha Catūrthi**. Starting this day, his image is installed in homes to worship for ten days. On Anant Chaturdashi day, it is carried out in a procession to immerse in sea or river water ending the festival.

BRAHMĀ

The Creator

In Trinity concept, Lord Brahmā is the aspect of God associated with the cosmic function of creation. As lord of creatures and father of the universe, he symbolizes creative intelligence of the cosmic mind. An embodiment of mode of movement and action, *Rajas*, he represents the universal passion, potency, and power of creation. In iconography, he is seen sitting on a lotus arising from the navel of reposing Lord Vishṇu who represents an imperishable principle of purity called *Sattva*. It is a neutral plane in which breath of Brahmā generates excitement by appearing as subtle sound waves, *Nāda*. Emanating as an ever-expanding field of force, they spread around to create the subtle vibratory field of living cosmic intelligence. Lord Vishṇu facilitates their arising, sustains their movement, and gives them direction. He visualizes different worlds conceived by the inner causes and directs this breath of vibratory energy to unfold and create accordingly.

The creative potential of *Nāda* inherently carries a pair of inextricable traits that it imparts to all creation. The energy that 'activates' and propagates these waves also sustains their shape. Thus, the shape and the underlying energy are two independent yet interdependent and inseparable properties personified by Lord Brahmā and Mahāsaraswati Devī, his consort. *Nāda* waves are not audible and therefore, do not create visible form. But upon differentiation, each of its gross sounds called *Mātrika* carries the prime power and potency to create unique physical forms. As Lord Brahmā passionately creates through the wave forms of these sounds, it simultaneously gives rise to the physical and mental planes. Lord Brahmā creates various shapes and structures, the material plane that Devī knows by the sound of underlying energy which is heard through the mental plane that she rules. Each object they create is the meaning, *Artha* recognized by the name heard as its sound, *Shabda*. All things of creation are of it and in it.

Brahman expresses as creation through the creative potency of Lord Brahmā. Breath of Brahmā is the unified field of vibrations that pervade the cosmos eternally animating its consciousness. The collective microcosmic and life sustaining breath of everyone is attuned to this macrocosmic and universal breath of divine. Breathing is the manifestation of basic Life Principle as we constantly draw on its energy to sustain our life. It is the power of growth that develops and maintains our physical body. It is also the power of incessant thoughts that emanate as subtle sound vibrations in our mind, always attuned to the cosmic intelligence of Lord Brahmā. It constantly raises desires that shape our will. Will articulates our speech and directs our deeds that imparts us a unique personality and character. They project the state of our inner self and appropriately position us in the society. Thus, the mental creative aspect of Lord Brahmā is the source of such forces that creates the countenance of our life. We act with intent to have fruit, in some way, in this objective world consistent with our goals. Inspired by Lord Brahmā, we embrace life enjoying it to the fullest by enactment of *Karma* that constantly renews and redraws the boundaries of our world.

Being a part of the world, our awareness is externalized and constantly directed outwards. Generally, it is led by the lower passion for survival, pleasure, and power as people enact *Karma* surrounding the I-ness directed by individual ego. By casually surrendering to such *Karmic* compulsion they participate in the rosy allurements of self-gratification ensuring their stay in the cycle of birth and death. But when the cosmic compulsion to excel prevails in some, they realize the futility of temporal enjoyment, material achievements, and entanglements of existence. As higher passion evolves and takes hold, love for others sprouts. It leads them to think beyond self, pursue spirituality, and perform self-less service. In this mode, they move towards the source, lotus feet of Lord Vishṇu who eventually offers them a release from the bondage of *Saṃsāra*.

Creation of cosmic dimension

The entire creation follows through the divine sound-codes Devī composes by combining the *Mātṛkā* sounds. Many of these were revealed to the ancient sages who compiled them as the Vedas. These codes are infinite and only Lord Brahmā knows them in their entirety. He constantly creates through these vibrations, in evolutionary steps that ultimately reaches the limits of its potency and exists for specific periods. It occurs in inconceivably immense and continuous cycles of creation and dissolution that start from, and return to the same source, Lord Vishṇu. Like the waves in an ocean that arise one after the other, each wave of creation is shaped in time, space, and causation. The vast wave of our universe called *Brahmanda* so created consists of innumerable solar systems, stars, and galaxies that manifest within unfathomable boundaries. There are myriad of such waves of universes that simultaneously exist, each created by its own Lord Brahmā. All *Brahmandas* originate from the extension of endless ocean of ethereal energy of Lord Vishṇu, recognized as *Mahā* Vishṇu.

Our Lord Brahmā is currently past his middle age. Each cycle of his creation is made up of 1000 successive and repeating phases called ***Mahā* Yugas,** each of which lasts a definite period of 4.32 million years. Also, each *Mahā* Yuga consists of four smaller phases known as Yugas. At present, we are in the last and the most difficult period, a Dark Age of Kali Yuga that started in the year 3102 BC. Lord Brahmā has a life span of a hundred years, but his one day equals 4,320,000,000 earthly years which is followed by night of an equal duration. Such period of his life is explained by the fact that the time dimension of our experience in the physical world is unlike the one in other higher planes where life spans are of cosmic dimension. It can be understood and appreciated from the fact that though Earth takes 365 days to complete a round of its year around the Sun, the planet Saturn takes 30 earthly years to complete a round of its year. Therefore, the time units of measurement we use are not extendable standard to other realms of existence. Surprisingly, they are flexible and quite variable.

Yugas in Mahā Yuga of 4.32 m years

1. Satya Yuga – 1,728,000 years
2. Treta Yuga – 1,296,000 years
3. Dwapara Yuga – 864,000 years
4. Kali Yuga – 432,000 years

Thus, during his one day of work, Lord Brahmā oversees a change of 1000 *Mahā* Yugas to complete a cycle known as ***Kalpa***. Also, within each *Kalpa*, at the end of a temporal period known as interval of Manu, ***Manvantara***, a deluge occurs with universal floods. It happens fourteen times during a *Kalpa* in which, however, the sounds of creation, the Vedas are not destroyed. This deluge is different from, and not to be confused with, the annihilation of the universe that takes place at the end of a *Kalpa*. At the end of his day's work, this manifestation is completely annihilated and a void exists during his night time sleep. The dawn of a new day marks the beginning of a new cycle when Lord Brahmā, once again, starts the creation from scratch.

1 Day of Brahmā = 1 Kalpa = 4,320,000,000 Earthly years = 1000 Mahā Yuga
Each Kalpa has 14 Manvantaras, a temporal period.

After he completes his life span of a hundred years, he dissolves back in Lord Vishṇu, another Lord Brahmā emerges who takes over, and the process continues. Lord Vishṇu is eternal and therefore, transcends all the dissolutions that occur at the end of these cycles. These incomprehensible cycles of creation having cosmic time dimension make us realize how insignificant our daily problems are and relatively how ordinary the human existence is.

For creation, the rank and role of our Lord Brahmā was assigned to a perfect yogi of the previous cycle in which he achieved supreme enlightenment through fervent austerities. Thereby, he established full control over self and all the powers of the universe. An already grown up, highly learned, and mature man, he personifies the primordial mind. When he first appeared in the midst of darkness sitting on a lotus, he viewed four directions with his four heads. All by himself and mystified by dark surroundings, he was anxious to know his origin. He first explored the lotus petals and then went down the stem in search, but in vain. Tired and with a great disappointment, he finally gave up. As he sat down, he heard a sound '*Tapas*' – meaning meditation.

Taking the cue, he started meditation. After a thousand years, Lord Vishṇu appeared in all splendors inspiring him to initiate creation. The seed of such a desire was thus sawn in the cosmic mind. As it sprouted, Lord Brahmā first created primeval waters. In it came forth an egg that contained lower twenty four *Tattvas*, building blocks of the universe left over from the previous cycle. To impart consciousness, an aggregate of all souls, Lord Vishṇu entered and activated it. It was the primordial egg, ***Hiranyagarbha***, the cosmic womb which now contained latent names and forms. Then it broke into two; the upper golden part formed the heaven and the lower silver one formed the earth.

After setting in motion abstract cosmic laws, Lord Brahmā gave rise to four sages named Sanaka, Sanandana, Sanātana, and Sanatkumāra to assist him in populating the earth. But instead, these devout souls started meditation and worship of their Lord Vishṇu. This outcome frustrated and infuriated Lord Brahmā consequently his anger giving rise to Rūdra, the lord of destruction. As he calmed down, he then gave rise to seven great sages, **Saptarishis** from his mind followed by ten sons from his body called **Prajāpati**s who are supposed to be the lords of the creatures. To speed up populating process, finally he gave rise to a male called Manu and a female called Shatrupa, the first self-born, *Swayambhū* couple of the humans. Their progeny is the entire human race.

This creation is a zero sum entity; it comes into being from a void to appear, evolve, and exist only to ultimately end in it. At the end of Lord Brahmā's day, as he prepares to retire, the world he had so painfully created, dissolves. With the sleep of consciousness, *nimesa* there is reversal of direction and withdrawal of energies. As the entire universe is absorbed into him, Lord Brahmā goes to sleep; a period of deep stillness and long pause. At dawn, he reappears on the scene to resume the next day's work and create yet another universe.

Iconography

Lord Brahmā has four heads, a beard, and four hands. In each of his hands he holds a rosary, the holy scripture of four Vedas, a bowl containing holy water, and a lotus flower. His mount is a swan. The four Vedas in his hand indicates that he is the source of all true knowledge. With each head he continually recites each of the Veda all the time. A rosary and the bowl of holy water show his supreme spirituality while swan, his mount represents his extra-ordinary powers of discrimination. This appearance of Lord Brahmā describes his serenity, enlightened state, and the mode of goodness. In the present world he manifests as tutelary pious people like preachers and priests, sages and saints. They guide people to rise above the modes of lower passion, ignorance, and material attachment to elevate values and create spiritual awareness.

Lord Brahmā appears more to be an abstract principle than a human figure. He epitomizes the unified field of all creative energy encompassing such diverse potencies as those of vibration, radiation, and differentiation. An omnipresent embodiment of supreme creative intelligence, he is the force of movement and energy of action, power of evolution and principle of growth. All material forms, contained in the seed of Lord Brahmā, duly sprout as the germs of creation. His ingenious expertise develops specific chemical codes of life mysteriously concealing them in the base combinations of DNA. Choosing the length of the ladder and the number of codes, he evolves various types of plant and animal species. As he confers them the ability to transmit that information in different ways, they continue to live through their offspring.

However, he is absolutely avoided by spiritual seekers as he carries the power of disturbance, *Vikshepa* through which the creation is affected. Consciousness moves away from the domain of Lord Vishnu, *Sattva* by his power of *Rajas* which confines it in a physical body, *Tamas* to create life and brings it to the world. He is the cause that moves our self away from Reality and veils the very Truth we seek. And then, gratitude is less ardent as for this cycle of creation he is past. Therefore, less is said and sung about his creative powers in literature and worship as if, by intent, to reduced him into obscurity. Another reason may be that though amazingly long by our standards, he has a limited life span. He is truly dependent upon the ethereal energy and the eternal aspect of Lord Vishṇu. Therefore, practically there are no temples dedicated to him.

Mahāsaraswati Devī, consort of Lord Brahmā is the goddess of inspiration, communication, knowledge, art, music, and culture worshiped for success in all types of learning. Her grace bestows purity of character which leads the individual passion to evolve and express at higher level. Therefore, she is a symbol of spiritual knowledge, wisdom, and power of discrimination. Inspired by her, Lord Brahmā became the primordial poet who has composed hymns to all other deities. Having an impulse to act and urge to create, he continuously carries out his cosmic role with her intelligent and efficient support.

VISHṆU

The Eternal Preserver

Trinity concept visualizes Lord Vishṇu as the aspect of *Brahman* associated with the cosmic function of preservation and protection. He is one of the Vedic deities in whom several other deities merged over time eventually exalting him as an all-inclusive Supreme Being. Today he enjoys the unique status of being the most recognized and worshiped of all the deities of Hindu pantheon. He personifies the all-pervading Reality beyond the past, present, and future who gives rise to Lord Brahmā for creation that he will-fully supports and shelters. An ocean well exemplifies him from which, time and again, endless waves of creation arise, exist for a period while reaching a peak only to eventually subside in it. Typically he has an ever benevolent, liberal, and generous character who is involved in every aspect of our life and always willing to bestow favors to his followers. Though usually seen standing upright in most of the temples, in pictures and paintings he is also portrayed reposing on a bed of coiled snake that floats on cosmic ocean. At times, he is artfully depicted riding the back of an eagle, Garūda. Many of his incarnations and images are very popular deities widely worshiped by people. Innumerable temples can be found all over the world dedicated to the sacred forms and faces of Lord Kṛṣṇa, Lord Rāma, Lord Jagannāth, Lord Venkateshwara, and Lord Satyanārāyaṇa.

Lord Vishṇu is an anthropomorphic representation of Ether of Consciousness. As all-pervading esoteric element ether, it occupies all apparently empty space, substratum of the cosmos. Boundless and attributeless in nature, it is a neutral and quiescent plenum, *Ākāśa* that exists beyond space and time potentially containing all other elements. The ever changing world order of all objective reality, made of various names and forms appears from this unchanging Reality that duly interpenetrates it. Its static background provides continuity and unity within which the dynamic play of materially moving world, *Jagat* takes place. The entire physical phenomenon made of mind and matter lives and exists in all its motion and shapes in this static ethereal continuum. Hence, Lord Vishṇu is invariably depicted being light blue in color to indicate his vast, endless, and infinite aspect. The cosmic breath of Lord Brahmā spontaneously arises in it as an impulse, initiates the process of creation, and continuously operates with passion to sustain its growth and development. According to the holy text of Vishṇu Purāṇa, ever expanding vibrations of Lord Brahmā create the material universe and its different life forms as per the wish, command, and direction of Lord Vishṇu. It occurs in evolutionary steps that take place in cosmic time cycles.

Ether and Panchamahābhuta

Our life is the manifestation of our soul, the casual body localized within an area of ultrasonic container, the subtle body which holds, as it penetrates the gross body made of five elements, ***Panchamahābhuta***. They are ether, air, fire, water, and the grossest of all, the earth. They sustain five phases of evolution that started with the subtlest stem substance, ether to successive grosser elements of air, fire, water, and the solids. The primal cosmic energy, *Prāṇa* catalyzed these material transformations. Holy Scriptures *Chandogya* and *Taittiriya* Upaniṣads describe their genesis in details. Most simply stated, the primary substrate ether, on condensation gave rise to grosser air. Air in motion produced heat and light which then gave rise to fire. Fire burning ether and air formed water which, on crystallization resulted in solids. These material building blocks variously combined to affect the entire physical phenomena.

All kinds of life forms then gradually evolved through the creative intelligence of cosmic mind, Lord Brahmā. His intuitive insight, inventive genius, and ingenious moves inexplicably configured variety of universal chemical codes within the molecular sequences of DNA in which unique life expressions were duly embedded. Discrete ethereal templates of consciousness, afforded by Lord Vishṇu acquired appropriate physical forms through them. By incorporating all material elements in typical combinations, they formed such body as to decide thc nature of species. Breath of Brahmā is also the source of *Prāṇa* energy which attunes these five archetypal elements to exhibit the harmonic of life resonance in everybody. Earth predominantly provides fields of force that have quality of solid structure like the skull and bones. Flow of water, in cycles, such as circulatory system is the medium that sustains life. Fire vitalizes all tissues, organs, and systems under the intelligent and integrating influence of air executed through the nervous system. Ether is the uniform field which pervades all intracellular and intercellular space of the body. A non-obstructive medium, it unites all material elements through various air movements like the upward move of expansion, *Tejas* and the downward move of contraction, *Ap*.

An element controls the other grosser one it forms in which the flow of energy gets restricted. Therefore, earth, at the bottom of the lineage is the most controlled, whereas the precursor of all, ether controls the most, in fact all other elements. This makes Lord Vishṇu, the subtlest, purest, and all-pervading element ether master of *Panchamahābhuta*. He is the starting point that provides the area of space. Also, as lord of the elements, he provides other elements for the ever evolving creation of the universe, including our physical self to come into being. As a physical counterpart of Consciousness, he acts as a conduit to connect the unmanifest casual and subtle world to the manifest material world giving way to all physical forms. He not only facilitates all forms of creation but duly supports and protects them as well.

Ether, the subtle force

Of all our aspirations, to extend life is our most potent desire, our creative ability being the most powerful force bestowed upon us by Lord Brahmā. By making the sexual engagement our most pleasant experience, he formulates fresh set of DNA as sperm fertilizes the ovum. Each imminent entity thus appears as zygote within his domain for further development. Its casual body of consciousness steps down through the neutral plane of *Sattva* by the grace of Lord Vishṇu which activates his power of *Rajas* to begin differentiation and give it an appropriate form. He now sets in motion the successive creation of mind and the subtle elements, *tanmatras* of its subtle body. *Tanmatras* are the subtle essences associated with the senses that connect with other gross elements. Then the material elements are incorporated to mark the passive and returning phase, *Tamas* ruled by Lord Mahesh which completes the formation of the physical body. Solids, the grossest element are created the last that provide the boundary within which all other elements operate while ether retains the ultimate control.

All the cavities and hollow spaces of each and every organ, tissue, and cell are contained with the homogeneous vibratory field of ether which envelopes and penetrates, connects and unifies them. It is a subtle core which encircles and permeates being outside yet within our physical body. Through its presence in, and control over all other evolute elements, it exerts its regulatory influence. *Prāṇa* of each breath duly integrates all body-mind functions through this supernatural medium of Lord Vishṇu which holds our life force. It not only supports all the vital functions of our physical self but also allows us to deal with the others routinely facilitating our receptions and responses. Countless energy fields, operating inside and outside the body, constantly interact through the interconnecting plenum of ether. Also, it readily transmits the veritable energy of sunrays and sonic pulses of sacred mantra chanting. Their influence on the rhythm and harmony of elemental movement transmutes the nature of our thoughts and feelings, perception and vision, decisions and activities.

Lord Vishṇu is the inner cause who provides, holds, and governs the limits of sonic environment, wireless energy field of our body. As a cohesive force that radiates from the central cerebrospinal system, he forms the most subtle core of our body. Through its centripetal tendency, he also holds it together. Always present everywhere and yet nowhere ever to be found, he not only controls and regulates our life but also connects us with others being the subtle substratum of the entire universe. The whole universe evolves through gradual transformation of ether but it still retains its original characteristics. The creation of material world does not change the essential nature of Lord Vishṇu. With a neutral stance, he acts as a material placeholder and transcends all cycles of manifestation. He regulates and maintains the timeless order of nature that continuously shifts and transforms thereby ensuring continuity of existence.

Lord Vishṇu allows our soul to manifest by supporting our body on a physical plane. Governing all realms of existence, he also quietly observes all our deeds. He regularly reviews them based on his ruling principles to ratify and resolve the ongoing state of our life. Therefore, he is worshiped not only for protection but also for nurturing, growth, direction, and support. He never dictates or interferes with what we do, though, at times, in hour of need, we seek his grace, direction, and help. *Mahālakshmī* Devī, his consort is generous, kind, and compassionate mother who rewards a variety of resources as the nature's bounty. She complements his effort by showering us with various necessities of life. As luminiferous ether, they not only sustain our life but give it a true meaning. Through their grace we succeed in our endeavors to earn and prosper, support our families, and enjoy life. They help us to establish our 'space' in the society.

Iconography

At times, Lord Vishṇu is seen reposing on coiled snake having a thousand hoods that floats in the cosmic ocean. Therefore, he is also well known as the one who floats on the waters, *Nārāyaṇa. Mahālakshmī* Devī, his consort is relaxing at his feet whereas Lord Brahmā, the creator is sitting on a lotus that issue out of his navel. This view conveys that he is the Ultimate Reality. It is his state of rest, *Yoga-Nidra* in the infinite ocean of primeval waters. It is a passive phase of unmanifest period, a casual interval that prevails between successive eras of existence. The coiled snake, ***Ādisesha*** represents the aggregate of residual consciousness left at the end of each cycle of existence. Lord Vishṇu preserves it in order to serve as progenitor of life forms in the new cycle. Anyone seeking grace of *Mahālakshmī* Devī in order to acquire wealth and prosperity can easily find her, at his feet, by worshiping him.

Lord Vishṇu in this portrait also represents the existence of an individual being supported by the coiled *Kuṇḍalinī* energy that floats in the sea of Cosmic

Consciousness. Lord Brahmā arising from his navel shows that each individual creates the patterns of his life by the *Karma* of his thoughts and actions, past and present, sustained by fire of the belly. *Mahālakshmī* Devī represents the wealth, power, and glory that lie at the feet of those who follow their duty, *Dharma* and lead a virtuous life. With her grace and compassion, an individual can relax to have a comfortable life and enjoy the world.

In temples, we usually see him standing upright wearing a crown and holding a conch, a chakra, a mace, and a lotus flower in each of his four hands. He wears garlands of flowers, magnificent silk dresses, jewelry, and a large jewel, *Kaustūbha* on his chest. The crown shows his supreme authority, four arms signify his all-powerful and all-pervasive nature, conch shell shows his power to create and uphold the universe, and chakra indicates destruction of ego to awaken the soul. The mace signifies his physical and mental strength and lotus shows spiritual perfection. His abode is above the three manifested worlds of Bhūh (earth), Bhūvah (sky), and Sūvaha (heaven). His mount is an eagle called **Garūda**. Bhūdevī, the goddess of earth is also his consort.

Peace and Release

Being a part of the depth of Cosmic Consciousness, etheric energy is directly related to and connected with it. The quintessence of ether is neutrality, purity, equilibrium, and freedom. It liberates us from such diametrically opposite experiences as pleasure and pain due to the polarities and dualities of nature that create the drama of life. Our life energy is duly held by the polar axis of an ultrasonic core within the central subtle energy channel, Sushumna that runs through the spinal cord. It is attuned to the ground state of universal life field, Lord Vishṇu. As an embodiment of *Sattva*, mode of goodness, he encourages the harmonic of faith, compassion, *Dharma*, and truth. Their integration in thought and action balances the flow of ether that fosters honesty and humility, contentment and clarity leading us to the light and purity.

Lord Vishṇu appreciates, as he invariably responds to the pure vibrations of love, devotion, and righteousness of his devotees. Our dedication to the path he advocates allows us to establish a lasting relation with him. His grace cleans mental impurities and clears all material impediments facilitating the course of our life. As we continue to follow the right path, it illuminates us to higher Truth and Reality. A gradual shift in the way we think, relate with people, and respond to the events takes place. Over time, as the relationship matures, it grants us a release from the lower passions of *Rajas* and unties all personal attachments. It breaks the material bondages and takes us away from the chaos of the world to his lotus feet. It is a serene state of ultimate freedom, a realm of true peace with the sense of safety, security, and sanctity.

Those who primarily worship him or any of his incarnations are known as Vaishṇavas. They readily accept other deities, personification of additional attributes of the Absolute as visualized by other theistic orders. However, they contend that Lord Vishṇu is the first principle and therefore, the most profound aspect of existence. In their view, for example, creation by Lord Brahmā and transformation by Lord Mahesh occurs in the domain of Lord Vishṇu who holds the phenomenal world. Lord Brahmā not only originates from him but also depends on him for his creative powers. And in absence of his creation, Lord Mahesh would not have anything to work upon. Hence, Lord Vishṇu is the dominating and determinative force ruling the entire manifestation.

There are five major schools, lineages of Vaishṇavas, each of which was established by spiritual leaders Śrī Mādhva, Nimbārka, Vallabha, Rāmānuja, and Caitanya. They all advocate the same path, the path of utmost devotion and complete surrender while worshiping his image. They mark their forehead with two vertical lines joined below in curve to make the figure U with a dot inside. A variety of ***Sāligram*** stones having spiral grooves that resemble the chakra held by Lord Vishṇu are also offered prayers and worshiped as his emblem. They are the fossilized, river-worn, smooth, rounded, and predominantly black colored ammonite shells. The basil plant, ***Tūlsi*** (Ocimum tenuiflorum) is considered to be holy as it is a symbol of devotion and purity. It is usually found near the entrance of their homes as well as near the deity.

Vishṇu *Sahasranāma* is one of the most popular, sacred, and commonly chanted stotra of his one thousand names. Each name eulogizes one of his countless attributes. Chanting these names calms the mind, absolves sins, and grants relief from all sufferings by elevating the spirit. Similarly, chanting of *Puruśa Sūktam*, a Vedic hymn of adoration to Lord Vishṇu brings great merit to devotees. He is considered to be *Paramātma*, the supreme soul in whom all other souls merge upon death. He is also very well known by many such epithets as Acyutah, Bālāji, Hari, Janārdan, Jagannāth, Trivikrama, Vāmana, Śridhara, Padmanābha, Purushottama etc. It is an extremely popular and a widely followed practice to worship him as ***Satyanārāyaṇa***, lord of good health, wealth, and prosperity on full moon days in homes as well as temples.

Whenever the human values go down and humanity decays in the world, Lord Vishṇu incarnates to restore *Dharma*. Thus, in addition to preservation, he also provides protection, restores order, and maintains the rhythm of righteousness.

So far, there have been nine such incarnations in the animal, animal-human, or human forms. Of these, the last three - Lord Rāma, Lord Kṛṣṇa, and Lord Buddha are the most known, revered, and worshiped. His tenth and the last incarnation, Lord Kalaki is yet to appear which will mark end of the present Dark Age, Kali Yuga. Vishṇu Purāṇa is the sacred text that provides all the details about these incarnations and also includes the two most famous epics, Rāmāyaṇa and Mahābhārat. References to his glory can also be found in the first Veda, *Ṛgveda*. Deep within the recesses of our own being lies the Ultimate Truth, his abode above the heavens called ***Vaikūntha***.

Lord Rāma

Lord Rāma is one of the most popular and famous deities considered to be the solar aspect and seventh incarnation of Lord Vishṇu. Rāmāyaṇa is the ancient holy epic, first written by sage Vālmiki which describes all the events that surround his life. Having the harmonic of well-balanced ethereal energy, he lived a life of righteousness, discipline, and virtue exemplifying purity, *Sattva* Guṇa. He led an illustrious life demonstrating the highest moral and ethical values of an ideal man. During his entire life, not even once did he indicate being God or expect others to worship him. His aim was to be a role model of conduct and set an example for others. His entire life story is a very well-known and common household tale even known by small children.

Of all the events of his life, two are the most remarkable. To honor and respect his father's promise, he voluntarily gave up the throne of his kingdom and accepted to live in exile for 14 years. The other is that he slayed demon king Rāvaṇa with the help of an army of monkeys as Rāvaṇa had abducted his wife, Sita Devī while they lived in exile. A few other major events of his life are his lifting and breaking the divine bow to win Sita Devī, helping the king of monkeys, Sugriva in regaining his kingdom by killing his elder brother Vali, and coronation of Vibhishaṇa after the killing of Rāvaṇa.

More often than not he is seen in the temples with Sita Devī, his brother Lakshmaṇ, and his devotee Hanuman. Lakshmaṇ, an incarnation of *Ādisesha* on which Lord Vishṇu rests duly assisted him during his earthly role. **Rāmanavami**, his birthday is the ninth day of the waxing fortnight in the month of *Caitra* of Hindu lunar calendar. The time of his birth, exactly at noon is celebrated with funfair. When anybody dies, it is customary to chant the name of Lord Rāma while other rituals are performed and until the body is cremated. 'Haré Rāma Haré Kṛṣṇa' mantra chanting is considered to be the simplest and the easiest, most effective and appropriate method of worship.

TEN INCARNATIONS OF VISHṆU

(DASHAVATARA - DESCENT ON EARTH)

1. **MATSYA** - THE FISH FORM. He saved saint Vaivaswata, Manu, and Vedas from flood during deluge in Satya Yuga.

2. **KURMA** - THE TURTLE FORM. He supported Mt Mandara during churning of the ocean by Devas and Danavas in search of the Nectar of immortality in Satya Yuga.

3. **VARĀHA** - THE BOAR FORM. He fought and killed demon Hiranyaksha, saved the earth, and restored it in its place.

4. **NARASIMHA** – THE HUMAN-LION FORM. He appeared from a hot column in this unique form to kill demon king Hiranyakashyapu and saved his devotee Prahalad.

5. **VĀMANA** - THE DWARF FORM. Appearing as a dwarf holy man, he requested land covered by his three strides from demon king Bali and then humbled him.

6. **PARASURĀMA** - THE ANGRY MAN. He was the first Brahmin-warrior who killed king Kartavirya and other Kshatriya rulers twenty-one times over.

7. **RĀMA** - THE PERFECT MAN. He lived the life of an ideal human being to set an example in society. He also killed demon king Rāvana with the help of an army of monkeys.

8. **KṚṢṆA** - THE STATESMAN. The most charming incarnation. He killed demon king Kaṃsa and helped Pāndava to win their war against Kaurava cousins.

9. **BUDDHA** - THE SAINT. Achieving enlightenment, he removed suffering of people and showed path to liberation.

10. KALKI – THE LAST INCARNATION. Yet to come.

Lord Kṛṣṇa

Lord Kṛṣṇa is considered to be the lunar aspect of Lord Vishṇu. He was the eighth and the most charming incarnation, a reservoir of pleasure. Born around the year 3200 BC, his entire early childhood is the story of divine love and play. He also carried out innumerable spectacular feats throughout his lifetime. In an absolute contrast to his previous incarnation as Lord Rāma, through his awesome acts and deeds, he directed everyone to recognize him as the Supreme incarnate, surrender to him, and worship him. Bhāgavat Purāṇa is the ancient sacred text which provides all the details about his life.

Before his birth, his uncle, king Kaṃsa put his parents, Vasudev and Devaki behind bars due to a prophecy that their eighth child would kill Kaṃsa. Hence, after the birth of Lord Kṛṣṇa in the jail, he was switched with another child, secretly taken away, and raised by a cowherd family in a remote village. As a child, he used to steal butter and throw stones at water pots carried by village maidens called Gopis. It was a playful act to tease them. He was a trickster and a lover who used to seduce them by playing his flute. These favorite past-times known as *Leelas* were beyond the physical and material nature. His work and deeds were full of awe and inspiration and has had a tremendous influence on the arts, music, dance, drama, and literature.

A few of his well-known feats are his conquest of the deadly snake Kālināga, lifting the mountain Govardhan to provide shelter to his devotees, killing of his uncle, king Kaṃsa, and protecting Draupadi in the court of Hastinapur in her hour of need. He also played a major role in guiding Pāndava brothers in the fight for their rights and led them to victory in the war against their cousins, Kaurava. His discourse given to Arjuna in the middle of a battlefield is now known as the Bhāgvad Gītā. It is one of the most sacred texts of Hinduism. At that time, he also showed Arjuna his universal form, *Vishwaroopa* that is beyond the perception of ordinary human vision.

Lord Kṛṣṇa is usually seen holding a flute, having a cow in the background, and his consort, Rādha by his side. In some temples he is worshiped as Jagannāth, Lord of the world along with his brother Balarāma and sister Subhadra. Balarāma is considered to be an incarnation of the thousand hooded snake on which Lord Vishṇu rests who always stayed by his side. He is also known by many other names like Vāsudev, Keshav, Muralidhar, Nandlāl, Mādhav, Madhusudan, Murāri, Govind, Ranchhod, Bānke Bihari, Gopal etc. His birthday, **Janmāshtami** is joyously celebrated at midnight on the eighth day of the waning moon fortnight of the month *Shrāvan* of Hindu calendar.

SHIVA AND MAHESH

The Eternal Liberator

The word Shiva means friendly, kind, pure, and auspicious. Just like Lord Vishṇu, he is one of the most worshiped deities of Hinduism. In the oldest and the most revered Hindu scripture *Ṛgveda*, he is referred to by the name Rūdra having a roaring, fierce, and terrible form associated with death and destruction. Well known as ***Paśupati***, he is recognized as the lord of every living being; animals and humans, spiritually elevated as well as the ignorant. As conqueror of death, he is also known as ***Mṛtyuṇjaya***. He is very commonly called Mahādeva, the Lord of all other deities and higher celestial beings. He is very merciful, an ocean of compassion and therefore, very easy to please. In all temples dedicated to Lord Shiva, his eternal and formless aspect is venerated in the form of a smooth cylindrical pillar called Linga. While representing the essence of 'void', it also indicates his limitless spiritual energy. His votaries and dedicated worshipers are called Shaivaits who hold him to be the Supreme.

Lord Shiva is primarily a deity of Shiva-Shakti concept. However, he acquires a place in two concepts as Lord Mahesh, a deity of Trimurti concept is also commonly called Lord Shiva though there is a subtle ontological difference between them. This makes it a bit difficult deity to know and understand. They slightly differ in their attributes and so their cosmic roles are also perceived differently in these concepts. But there was a unique genre of popular mythological literature known as Purāṇas composed during the classical age. After that, their overlapping character and marked similarity obliterated the thin boundary separating the two in the minds of average people. Since then, Lord Mahesh is also usually known by his higher form, Lord Shiva who is essentially a liberating force. But Trimurti concept recognizes his aspect knit with the power of time that constantly changes the material nature.

In **Shiva-Shakti concept**, Lord Shiva is the unitive field of eternal Self who personifies the first primary principle of Consciousness. He is the source and the spirit which is universal, unchanging, and unbound in nature. He is always associated with the other primary principle of energy, his inseparable spouse called Shakti. As a silent and passive observer, he witnesses the play of his ever active partner who assumes various names and forms that constantly transform with time. The concept emphasizes him to be this attributeless and endless self-illuminating awareness that pervades everything and every being. He is visualized as a Yogi in a state of deep contemplation.

As he desires for creation, he steps down as Sadāshiva stressing his 'I'ness. Then, descending further as Maheshvara, also called Mahesh or Īshvara he visualizes the details of creation and sets the stage by making vehicles like the power of time manifest. **Trinity concept** emphasizes this aspect of Lord Mahesh who rules time. It provides the fourth temporal dimension in which, as matter takes shape, the objective world appears. Between each passing moment, it also acquires duration in which all matter undergoes changes under the influence of other causes that show an order of succession. Our awareness also shifts from one perception to the other creating a sense of conversion and transformation. While sharing the portrait of Lord Shiva, Lord Mahesh assumes the majestic form of cosmic dancer well known as Natarāja. Moments are his ceaseless moves that continually renew everything that exists. His entry and exit in the world theatre mark the determined period of our life. It is an opportunity to learn spiritual lessons taught by his moves that create life changing events and circumstances.

Lord Mahesh in Trinity Concept

Trinity concept visualizes Lord Mahesh as the aspect of God who carries out the cosmic function of transformation. He rules the steady stream of Consciousness which measures constant phenomenon of change in terms of time. Therefore, as master of time, he is also known as ***Mahākāla*** ruling the past, the present, and the future. His consort, in the benign form is recognized as *Bhadrakāli* who quietly operates to create the smooth flow of time. However, when ferocious, she assumes the terrible form of *Mahākāli* and devours it like a black hole causing ultimate death and destruction. Lord Mahesh is an embodiment of *Tamas*, mode of passivity and darkness. He marks the rhythm and periodicity between which all life forms exist and the inherent tendency of all that exist to disintegrate, dissolve, decay, and die. His invisible influence continuously recreates and purifies by perishing everything that is not life sustaining eventually completing lifecycles. He, therefore, is also the Lord of generation and regeneration.

Constant conversion of energy and mass is the inherent nature of this entire physical phenomenon. Our body is also in a metabolic state of change through anabolic and catabolic processes as power of time regulates our internal clocks.

Natarāja is the very well-known posture of Lord Mahesh, the dancer in cosmic theatre who represents these changes. Its conception artfully blends the scientific facts with religious vision giving the image of Reality an expression that has an instant appeal and universal acceptance. It signifies the dynamic matrix of nature that relentlessly transforms with time. With a drum in one hand and a fire in the other, his ceaseless moves create vibrations that carry out conversion of all forms of matter. It symbolizes the dance of discreet particles at the nuclear level, the emission and re-absorption of virtual particles that continually changes the material nature. Dance routine of his rhythmic moves is the streaming moments of time which makes changes that drives the world. Lasya, his gentle and smooth steps represent the power of creation whereas Tāndava, his violent and aggressive steps represent dissolution.

Time orders changes in the outer objective world simultaneously synchronizing our consciousness, the subjective experiences to align and adjust to the same order. Division of time and space in our consciousness mirrors the state, series, and sequence established in the outer world. The dynamic dimension of time is the rhythm of life through which we coordinate our activities and plan for the future. At each arriving moment, we face odds of the unknown brought upon us by the unfolding of our *Karma*. We constantly plant its new seeds, screened and selected through the power of volition, and harvest the fruits of those sawn earlier. Passage of time catalyzes all transitory experiences through our intent, purpose, and expectation ridden actions. They precipitate fitting effects in the outer objective world, in correspondence with those of the past.

All spiritual aspirants are aware that the body is a temporal abode of the soul. It is a vehicle for the journey through life that rides the flow of existential moments of time. So carried by its **linear** dimension, we dwell in thc past, deal with the present, and drive for the future. To break free from this temporality, part of the very essence of our existence is possible only after our soul leaves the body. However, upon death, linear time ceases to exist in the vista of the soul as such dimension exists only in the physical creation. The soul then dwells in eternity merged with infinity. But such state of its release proves to be just a pause as time, like a **circular** wheel**,** *Kāla-chakra*, takes it through self-repeating cycles of birth, death, and rebirth. It is duly fueled by its book of *Karma*. Therefore, all spiritual aspirants are really wary of their *Karma*. They realize that the present life in the linear dimension offers an incredible opportunity to get an eventual release from this endless cycle. They exploit this lifelong period by pursuing spiritual practices to eliminate *Karma* load, elevate, and eventually liberate.

Our existence is our 'being' at any given instant, the static aspect of time. Its dynamic aspect is the interval that acts like an unseen catalyst, a period of our 'becoming'. It is a relation between changes that happen within us marking the difference in our thoughts, emotions, perception, and awareness before and after. It also relates to the shift in material nature that happen in the outer phenomenal world that is often linked with the changes within. As life moves forward, we also witness unfolding of various events, some planned and others quite unexpected that we constantly strive to see through. Treating favorable as opportunities and unfavorable as challenges, we duly respond to the changing situations in all circumstances. Therefore, Lord Mahesh has an auspicious and positive as well as a fearful, unknown, and negative side to him.

These life experiences carry out an inner transformation within us by raising our awareness. Each incident is meant to teach us a lesson in serenity; enjoy life with detachment and recognize the futility of physical phenomenon. Thus, cosmic dancer Natarāja also portrays the role of a Guru. We believe he assumes the posture of a dancer on the world stage to entertain. But his intent is to teach us subtle spiritual lessons for inner growth and ultimate enlightenment through the experiences of his each spontaneous move in moment. The moves of his repertoire reflect our everyday experiences straddled with a steady stream of such spiritual lessons that ceaselessly flows along the path of our lives.

A spiritual aspirant constantly strives to rise with an aim to 'become' so that he ultimately unites with him. By bending down with humility, his 'being' constantly fetches pails from this stream and learns new spiritual lessons thereby elevating his self. Often times, due to distraction, he also spills and loses what was collected earlier only to prolong the quest. Over several lifetimes, by spiral process of growth and change, his persistent pursuit penetrates various layers of subtle realities raising him to newer heights. By successfully acquiring the utmost expanded state of consciousness, *Samadhi*, he finally graduates to conquer and establish his position at the peak. At this supreme summit with the Absolute, all future potentialities of 'becoming' collapse and coalesce into the blissful experience of the present that, forever, ends his pursuit.

Whatever exists has a definite life span and a time comes when the old needs to make way for the new to appear. Lord Mahesh as ***Kāla***, the centrifugal force of dispersion and the time of disintegration is unwavering, uncompromising, and deadly. With his power to determine life span, Lord Mahesh rules the age as well as destiny. This aspect of Lord Mahesh associated with death and destruction is recognized as the ferocious Rūdra. Therefore, he is thought to be ruthless. But in fact, he is very compassionate. With age, our physical body gets weak, impaired, and dysfunctional. His grace provides a gateway that ultimately releases the soul from the old body granting it an opportunity to reincarnate into a new one at an appropriate time. Known as ***Tripurari***, ruler of the three cities – physical, astral, and casual body, he is thus actually a liberator. Hence he smears his body with what is left, the ash, which is the symbol of the soul.

Lord Shiva in Shiva-Shakti Concept

In Shiva-Shakti concept, Lord Shiva and Shakti are the faces that personify two functional forms of God, *Brahman*. God is the abstract principle of unmanifest Ultimate Reality. Impersonal, infinite, and indivisible, it is omnipotent, omniscience, and omnipresent. Sublime in nature, it is beyond all types of dualities, devoid of qualities, and past relativities. As supreme Godhead, it is also known as *Pārā* Shiva by Shaivaits. As the immutable infinite intelligence that exists beyond time, space, and causation, it permeates all forms, whether animate or inanimate. It is both immanent as well as utterly transcendental. The whole universe is considered to be its ever changing expression.

Pārā Shiva, the Supreme Reality first appears as the casual sound Aum which transcendentally polarizes to assume the primary identity of Lord Shiva as *Bindu*. It is the center of spirit and principle of Consciousness whose creative potential simultaneously appears as subtle sound waves, *Nāda*. The active front of these *Nāda* waves represents the other identity of Shakti who embodies the principle of primal energy always connected with him. They represent the two interdependent yet quite opposite functional forms assumed by the Absolute in order to create. As Shakti gradually moves away from Lord Shiva, the movement of these waves generates subtle vibrations called *Spanda*. These spontaneous moves have an infinite potential that gradually fills in the details of the entire cosmic expansion. Lord Shiva enjoys each of these pulsations created by Shakti, going forward in cycles. Progression of these waves establishes the inexhaustible source of primal energy called *Prāṇa* which is the life force of the universe.

Consciousness of Lord Shiva is the cause and source of 'I', the observer with self-illuminating awareness who observes himself through the reflective awareness of Shakti. Shakti imparts vision and ability of experience to Lord Shiva who begins to see and feel his infinite Self through her. *Spanda* is their cosmic dance of delight, in rhythm where extrovert Shakti always leads and directs its course. However, she acts with a singular aim to satisfy and please Lord Shiva. Lord Shiva is the inner ground who holds Shakti in various ways to view her at different angles, like in a mirror, to observe his reflected image. Shakti is the outer movement who stops at innovative limiting points to create various articles and objects for him to look at, entertain, and enjoy. He is truly amused by her inventive ability as she constantly comes up with new shapes and structures.

The transcendental polarized vibrations, *Spanda* create the throbbing field of force of the Absolute from which successive emanations of creation takes place. The Shaivait School elaborates a model of orderly evolution in which the Absolute descends through thirty six ontological states. As per the model, this bipolar Reality is the primary pair of two pure universal principles, key source of all other metaphysical categories of existence. Lord Shiva embodies the first pure universal principle as absolutely static *Cidākāśa*, the seed containing the entire universe in a potentialised state. Shakti is the second pure universal principle that exploits this source through her infinite potential to expand. He contains within, subsequently gives rise to thirty four other principles emerging through the initiative of Shakti. These are known as the building blocks of the universe, *Tattvas*. Of these thirty four principles, first three evolve as pure universal

BUILDING BLOCKS OF THE UNIVERSE

36 *TATTVAS*

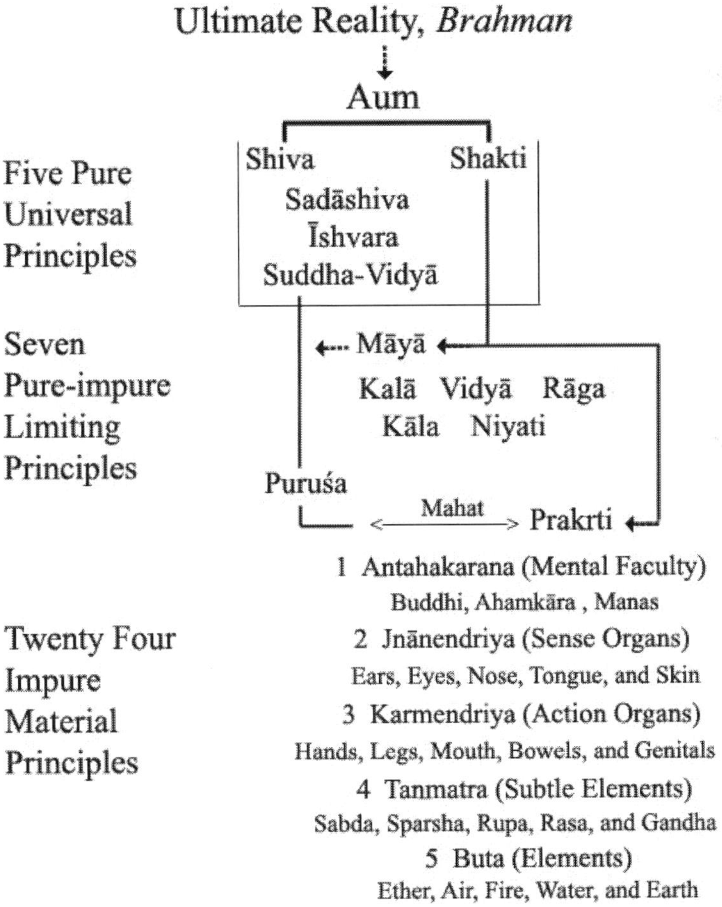

principles, next seven in the middle as pure-impure limiting principles, and the remaining twenty four as the lowest being impure material principles.

Lord Shiva evolves into three pure universal principles variously recognized as Sadāshiva, Īshvara, and Suddha-Vidyā associated with his specific state and quality as he descends to be many. Consciousness of Lord Shiva, *Cit* begins the descent as Sadāshiva who now expresses his transcendental will, *Icchā*. This is his ever-benevolent state which stresses his 'I'-ness as he assumes five faces looking in five directions. Each face is variously recognized as Isāna, Tatpurusha, Vāmdeva, Aghora and Sadyojata that later associates with one of the material elements. Isāna faces the sky it represents. Tatpurusha faces east and represents air. Aghora that faces the south direction represents fire. Vāmdeva faces north direction and represents water. The last face, Sadyojata looks to the west and represents the element earth. It is believed that all the Shiva Āgama scriptures emanated from these five faces of Lord Shiva.

Sadāshiva then steps down as Īshvara to express his subjective mind having the divine knowledge, *Jnāna* which is total and complete. In this state, he conceives the details of the universe and sets the stage for cosmic expansion by making various vehicles like the time manifest. Descending further as Suddha-Vidyā, he distinguishes the subject and the object acknowledging the relation of two sides. His acknowledgment activates Shakti who now takes the initiative to create such dualities. Thereby he experiences her action, *Kriyā* initiated by *Māyā*, the power of delusion she rule. Sharing his ability of knowledge, *Jnāna*, she already knows his desire, *Icchā* which she executes by taking him through the first step using five kinds of powers called the limiting principles. Acting in stages, she diligently divides Consciousness into discreet parts variously confining and conditioning each of them to reduce their awareness. It effectively individualizes them into different souls that eventually manifest as various entities.

Leading the pure-impure state, she acts on non-discreet Consciousness through the first limiting principle, *Kalā*. It limits the power of Consciousness in a discreet part called *Ātman* which now forgets its omnipotent nature. It is destined to act in its limited state reaping and enjoying the fruits of *Karma* during its existence. Then, power of *Vidyā* finites and constricts its infinite knowledge, omniscience whereby it loses its state of completeness, *pūrṇatva* and therefore, contentment. So it acquires *Rāga*, the power of attachment which develops numerous desires in order to experience the original state of fulfillment. Such an experience however, is now always going to be temporary and partial in nature. The time of its manifestation, *Kāla* reduces it to the temporal confinement of physical existence eliminating the state of its eternity. *Niyati* is the limitation of cause by which it comes to manifest with a particular form losing its omnipresence. These five limiting principles of *Kalā, Vidyā, Rāga, Kāla,* and *Niyati* are also known as *Kaṅcukas* through which the power of *Māyā* operates as a restrictive force.

Ātman so bound by these veils is the individual soul, *Puruśa* which is the

individuation principle of spirit. It now dwells in this pure-impure state, the middle ground between the pure state of the Absolute and the lower objective world. *Puruśa* so bound by *Māyā* is known as *Paśu* when it finally manifests as an entity whose master, *Pati* is always Lord Shiva. Therefore, Lord Shiva is also called ***Paśupati,*** Lord of all the embodied souls.

Like *Māyā*, *Prakṛti* is another aspect of Shakti, the other **individuation principle of matter.** She rules all the lower impure principles necessary for the physical manifestation of *Puruśa*. Contact of *Puruśa* agitates *Prakṛti* when the time is ripe for its manifestation. It activates her three modes of action that operate in tandem to evolve all the mental and material elements called *Tattvas*. As creation of the intellect, ego, sensorial mind, and then the body with senses and organs of action follows through, it variously covers *Puruśa*, in a step down manner to create an individual (Page 144). As power of *Prakṛti* embodies *Puruśa*, he exhibits the character of a quiet observer who stays idle and watches it rather than participate in this process of his finitising. He is aware of her action and enjoys her moves but does not interfere or intervene, involve or inquire. He stays passive as the versatile performance of Shakti prevails dominating all physical creation. He becomes a part of all manifestation through her various modes of action. Motivated, encouraged, and duly inspired by his presence, Shakti orchestrates the entire show of creation, maintenance, and dissolution.

Thus our soul is the casual body of *Ātman*, a part of the boundless Consciousness of Lord Shiva. Veiled by the limiting principles, it acquires identity and ego to take birth as an entity. The so embodied soul then inevitably enacts *Karma* as it enjoys and experiences life. Shrouded in ignorance, it also believes to be a part of the world and develops various attachments. Its unfulfilled desires and *Karma* impressions become a part of its profile that it carries upon death. With such renewed burden of causes of confinement, it takes yet another birth. It then becomes a perpetual cycle in which it constantly undergoes birth, life, death, and rebirth. The law of cause and effect, *Karma* governs his endless wandering. Its release from this cycle is possible only when it gradually eliminates its *Karma* load. Only by exercising power of volition and following the spiritual path, it can get a release from the bondage of *Saṃsāra*.

Lord Shiva is usually depicted as an ascetic, a yogi engrossed in meditation and enfolded in perfect enlightenment. Disembodied from the worldly matters created by *Māyā*, he values nothing of material nature. He wisely stays away from the all entanglements, his abode being the snowcapped mountain, Kailāsa. He easily embraces death, the ultimate fate of life. He often lives in crematory where everything eventually turns into ashes with which he happily covers his body.

Crematory is the place where he not only burns the body, but the individual ego, darkness of illusion, and the fetters binding the soul. He offers release from the bondage of *Saṃsāra* to the blessed few enlightened souls.

However, he cannot be separated from Shakti. Determined to have a home, a family, and enjoy worldly life, she leads and dominates the world of objective reality. She successfully domesticates him but it is not easy for him to leave peace and meditation, come home, and face the realities and responsibilities of a householder. The house that Shakti loves to decorate, live in, and enjoy is too confining and stifling for him. He prefers to dwell in the openness of mountain tops close to the universe that he considers his home. All attempts and endeavors of Shakti to make him happy and enjoy as an entity, without exception, proves to be a restrictive experience. It is only out of his love for Shakti that he fulfills his duty as a spouse, but reluctantly and with detachment.

Lord Shiva is totally focused to pursue the ascetic ideal. Preoccupied in austere meditation, he is usually away from home where Shakti is all alone. She is the creative energy of Consciousness and yet, lonely and therefore, frustrated. Desperate for action and company, she gives rise to a son, Lord Gaṇesha from her body for love and protection without involving Lord Shiva. Can there be any greater example of his passive character? This story signifies that as solids are formed by her energy, the mysterious force of gravity spontaneously comes into being. As depicted in mythological tales, Lord Gaṇesha guards the palace, place of the union of Lord Shiva and Shakti in *Mulādhāra* Chakra. When Lord Shiva returns home, he doesn't recognize his own father.

In temples, form of a phallus that symbolizes Lord Shiva is worshiped. Even though represented as an erotic ascetic, he is the master, a supreme yogi who truly has no worldly desires. Phallus represents creative power but its pointing upwards symbolizes his control over sexual urges. He is a true yogi, *Urdhva-reta* who redirects the energy for spiritual elevation and Self-Realization. It is a symbol of celibacy and austerities, higher values and virtues, strength and stability.

Iconography

Lord Shiva is seen as a yogi in deep state of meditation. He is sitting on a tiger skin holding a rosary completely oblivious of his surroundings. He carries a trident and a drum, his body smeared with holy ashes. A snake around his neck, the third eye, a crescent moon on the forehead, and a river flowing of his matted hair stands out and catches our eye. The mount by his side is a bull, **Nandi**. This image reflects inert nature of Lord Shiva. His body smeared with ashes signifies that he transcends the physical phenomenon. Just as everything eventually turns to ashes, he reminds us of the transitory nature of things. The crescent moon represents the cycles of time; Lord Shiva transcends time. His matted hair is indicative of him being the supreme yogi. The snake around his neck is the '*Kuṇḍalinī*' power, an emblem of eternity. The third eye shows his spiritual knowledge and divine powers. The tiger represents an ever-active mind; his sitting on tiger skin represents his conquering the mind. The trident represents three modes of human nature: *Sattva*, *Rajas*, and *Tamas*. The bull embodies sexual energy that is powerful but ignorant. Riding on his back, Lord Shiva is in control of these powerful impulses.

The names Rūdra and Bhairava reflect his fearful aspects. His form facing the south called ***Dakshināmurti*** is recognized and worshiped as the archetypal spiritual master who is the First Teacher of the Vedas, *Yoga*, dance, drama, and music. He imparts esoteric knowledge to all the yogis and siddhas. He is also known by many other epithets like Mahādeva, Shankara, Chandrasekhar, Neelkantha, Shambhū, Āshutosh, Gangādhar, Tryambakaṃ etc. Five is a sacred number for Lord Shiva. Shiva Purāṇa is the ancient text that describes his life. A stotra from Yajurveda, *Śrī Rūdram* is used to worship him and invoke his grace. Mount **Kailāsa** in the Himalayas is his abode.

He is very easy to please and when pleased gives powers to everybody without any reservations. A simple offering of lotus flowers, trifoliate leaves of the Bilva tree (Aegle marmelos), and bathing with water and milk called Abhishek makes him happy. Mondays and new moon days are the days of his worship. Dark berries, **Rudrāksha** of the tree (Elaeocarpus ganitrus) are his favorite. Most commonly, he is worshiped in temples in an aniconic, unborn, infinite, and invisible form represented by a small pillar known as Linga. It is the axis of the universe, an eternal column of Consciousness that supports the cosmos within the window of space and time. There are twelve shrines of Lord Shiva spread throughout the Indian continent called Linga of light, *Jyotirlinga*. They are supposed to have materialized spontaneously in a radiant form and then the temples were built around them. The 14th night of the waning moon of the month of *Māgha* of Hindu calendar is considered very auspicious and celebrated every year as **Shivarātri**, night of Lord Shiva. People observe day long fast and he is worshiped the whole night while chanting mantra '*Aum Namaḥ Shivāya*' to attain spiritual emancipation.

SHAKTI

Various Deities with aspects

Shakti personifies the self-igniting spark, the energizing principle that moves the whole universe. She powers mind, all movements in nature, and the entire material manifestation as she constantly creates variety of material names and forms, including limitless life forms. An unfathomable force of beauty and delight, care and comfort, she sustains the breath of life she creates like a kind and compassionate mother. And her ultimate exit or occasional outburst which develops like hurricanes marks an end of all that she passionately creates. Eternally pulsating within the sea of Consciousness, she is the primeval cosmic energy, cause of determined life and source of all objective reality. All her activities are transient in nature giving her dynamic character.

Acting in multitude of ways, her infinite qualities constitute an extensive palette of countless colors, hues, and shades with which she relentlessly paints and creates. Self-willed and self-aware, she appropriates her boundless energy by splitting it into specialized channels for ease of operation, effective action, and efficient execution. Each stream carries a level of responsibility aimed to accomplish a particular function in manifestation. Therefore, she is visualized by various faces, each symbolizing a specific form and function worshiped as a deity. Her different forms personify her various acts in manifestation each of which highlights her particular area of operational domain. They efficiently manage innumerable titles and tasks, offices and portfolios she simultaneously carries to exalt her as the eternal champion of multi-tasking.

Such phenomenon of her differentiation into different states, each associated with specific attributes was Realized by ancient seers in their deep meditative state. Blessed with micro-clairvoyant vision, they had the exclusive inspirational view, *Darśana* of these magnificent goddesses who made a breathtaking appearance before them. The characteristic features and forms of these legendary deities were identified with appropriate names and then described and related to people. Therefore, she is sensually celebrated, warmly venerated, and sincerely worshiped by her devotees with unflinching faith and absolute conviction. Being extremely kind and compassionate and just as available to all her devotees, she duly appears before us in the preferred form of worship. It is very assuring that she can be reached through any of her sacred expressions.

The all-encompassing power of Shakti is primarily visualized and commonly depicted in the benign form of a fair and beautiful woman called **Pārvati** Devī without having superfluity of limbs. A portrait of grace and elegance, she personifies the warmth, charm, beauty, and compassion of womanhood. She is the picture of piety and penance, purity and love, duty and dedication. She embodies within all types of immeasurable energy of the universe, source and cause of ever changing forms of matter. She also rules sanctity of life being the mother of countless variety of life forms. Her power is visually evident in the rain and lightning, gushing streams and waterfalls, breeze and the blowing winds, flora and fauna of nature, and various species of the world. Her cosmic dance of delight, spontaneous in nature is her eternal expression in creation. It is the source of unrestrained flow of energy which powers our passion for life.

In mythological stories, she is described being daughter of the great mountain Himalayas. Even though she was an incarnation of the primal energy, she had to perform severe austerities in order to win over ascetic Lord Shiva. It was only after a period of long austerities, *tapas* that she qualified herself and ultimately succeeded in marrying him. She is the mother of Lord Gaṇesha, who always stays very close to her and Lord Skanda, also known as Kārtikeya. However, she did not bear both as each was born in unconventional ways and under unique circumstances. Having honorable and noble character, they deservedly achieved immortality like their parents. Gaṇesha acquired name and fame as the lord of prosperity, Kārtikeya as the invincible leader of celestial army.

Happy to be with Lord Shiva and enjoying each moment of her association with him, she presents a role model to women expressing loyalty and devotion to the spouse. She is worshiped by unmarried girls to fulfill their desire of having a worthy spouse as well as by married women for getting marital felicity and fertility. Sati, Kamākshi, Kalyāni, Bhavāni, Vindhyavāsini, Girijā, Amba, Uma, Meenākshi, and Gaurī are just a few of her other very well-known names. It is evident that she is affectionately visualized and joyfully celebrated in innumerable ways not only as these sacred temple deities but also having various characters in performing arts and literature, poetry and painting. *Saundarya Laharī* is a classical literary work that attempts to describe her charming face and lovely features, in detail, eulogizing her infinite power and enormous grace.

Durgā or Chaṇḍi is her aggressive form portrayed astride a tiger or a lion where, dissociated from Lord Shiva, she assumes quite an independent status. In this portrait, she also carries an array of weapons, in multiple arms to show her extraordinary strength and enormous might. This battle form and warrior aspect of Shakti, as Supreme Self, embodies her invincible power. She fights to eliminate the demons ruling the universe from time to time. While destroying such negative forces, she also dispels the darkness of ignorance of her devotees as she takes care and protects them in all circumstances. Therefore, she is one of the most popular deities widely remembered and heartily rejoiced every year during Durgā Puja. It duly commemorates her boundless force with feast, fervor, and festivities while seeking her shelter, boons, and blessings.

Lalitā Devī and ***Gāyatri*** Devī

As Shakti undertakes the process of creation, she appears in peculiar forms at various stages of her evolutionary enterprise. *Kāma-Kalā* triangle is her subtle body, the first ever form through which Consciousness manifests carrying the divine desire, intensity, and purpose of creation (Page 57). The presiding deity of this quivering triangle is visualized as beautiful ***Lalitā*** Devī. Her name means 'she who plays'. She portrays the primordial energy in a dazzling and glamorous form of a perfect sixteen year old beauty, *Sodashi*. Also well known as *Tripurasūndari*, *Tripuréshi*, and *Kāmesvarī*, she encompasses various arrays of triads that spiral out by the sides of *Kāma-Kalā* triangle. In iconography, she holds five flowery arrows which symbolizes five senses, a sugarcane bow which represents the mind, a noose, and a goad. Fully immanent as the creative matrix of the universe, she carries infinite scope of expression through which diverse names and forms constantly appear. Creation is her deep desire and the only intent, her artful act and a powerful play. Her amazing face, attractive figure, and alluring form truly portrays the most blissful and auspicious state of Shakti. The strength of her pure love sustains everyone as it connects their hearts.

Kāmesvarī has a rosy complexion who wears a crescent moon as the crown. Governing all creation with complete autonomy and absolute authority, she takes it to the peak of perfection. With supreme sovereignty, her majesty relaxes over lying deity Sadāshiva who makes the bed of a unique throne called *Paṇchabrahmāsana*. It is supported by legs of inert and inactive elements known, when active, as Brahmā, Vishṇu, Rūdra, and Isāna. These deities are supplicant figures, subsidiary, subordinate, and secondary in nature. They remain still like statue and immobile like dead body, unable to move, operate, and carry out their function until activated by her. Whereas she is commonly venerated in her widely recognized and well represented geometric abode, Śrī Chakra, the worship of her anthropomorphic image is less common. Her grace confers overall peace and prosperity allowing enjoyment of life to the fullest while also leading to the release from its constraints, fetters, and bondages. Therefore, she is extolled as bestower of material enjoyment as well as spiritual liberation and fittingly called to be *bhūkti-mūkti pradāyinī.*

All *Mātṛkā* sounds, the fifty primeval root powers that appear through differentiation of the primordial sound Aum reside in three groups like a 'garland of letters' along the three sides of *Kāma-Kalā* triangle. As *Tripurasūndari* delights in wearing these gemlike sound energies, their vibrations pervade the entire cosmos carried by the power of her radiating energies. These are the rays of incomprehensible brilliance that make the light of all the suns, stars, and galaxies. During their course of prolong propagation, these sound energies combine in typical patterns to compose the divine sound-codes of creation. Their vibrations and the ensuing mantras so created pervade the entire cosmos. Many of these were revealed to ancient sages who classified them into four comprehensive categories compiled as the sacred scripture, the Vedas.

The abstract of their entire knowledge is well encapsulated in 24 seed letters arranged in a specific order of a sacred formula. It is known as *Gāyatri* mantra that constitutes the body of ***Gāyatri*** Devī. This mantra contains pure nectar as it is the essence of the Vedas and therefore, she is called the mother of the Vedas. She represents the radiance and brilliance of sun, giver of all life, the light of consciousness. Her power relates the glow of our individual self, encased in various sheaths of material existence to the origin of universal effulgence. Chanting of her mantra penetrates and obscures the mental and material envelopes of our soul to reveal the light of the Supreme hidden within all of us.

She is visualized having five faces as she protects the five types of *Prāṇa* movements in our body that sustains our life. Her mantra is the source of supreme knowledge and therefore, most sacred and powerful in which all other mantras converge. Glory of *Gāyatri* Devī has been widely accepted as chanting her mantra imparts intuition, sharpens intellect, confers devotion, and develops detachment. Also, it bestows power of speech and sanctifies life by dispelling the darkness of all kinds of negativities. Her worship is of the highest nature as her power has infinite potential to purify, illuminate, and elevate. While leading us from the darkness of ignorance to the light of true knowledge, it also fulfills all the material, mental, and spiritual aspirations.

The Three Goddesses

Kāma-Kalā triangle is the subtle body of *Lalitā* Devī. As the three rays of heat, light, and sound that form the sides of this polar triangle radiate and expand, each of them develops a form with prominent personality. As they evolve, they acquire a truly distinct identity known as *Mahākāli* Devī, *Mahālakshmī* Devī, and *Mahāsaraswati* Devī respectively. Thus, it can be seen that *Lalitā* Devī primarily differentiates in these three major forms that grow to be the consorts and power behind the three deities of Trinity concept. They are the most recognized, revered, and respected of all the other Goddesses. As they continue to spread out and differentiate further, they proliferate into innumerable appearances and aspects. Each of these radiating forms is variously envisioned as a deity, embodied and enshrined in the temples, and befittingly worshiped by people.

The first of these three figures that evolves from heat energy is recognized as ***Mahākāli*** Devī, the consort of Lord Mahesh. Her benign form, *Bhadrakāli* creates the uniform flow of time providing the dynamic dimension to our life and all that exists in space. A mere glimpse of *Mahākāli* Devī, the power of time grants release from the limitations of life, paradoxically created by her, within which we all live. Her power is immense and absolutely incomprehensible which oscillates between two diametrically opposite extremes; the positive, creative, benevolent, tender, and auspicious aspect on one hand and the negative, destructive, aggressive, malevolent, and inauspicious aspect on the other. Her extremely terrifying appearance shows her ultimate destructive power. In this form, *Mahākāli* Devī has intoxicated eyes and a protruding tongue as blood drips from her mouth. A garland of skulls around her neck and an expression of ugliness show her ferocity. This is the formidable form she takes, in wrath, to battle demonic forces ruling the universe from time to time. The sacred text of Devī Māhātmyam contains all historical accounts and describes many such episodes in details. Each incident is a metaphor for such battles against negativities that ensue at different times in the life of everybody.

Consciousness is her ever guiding force. Only the constraint of consciousness can contain her colossal power. Without such restraint, she would spin out of control, become dangerous and harmful, and cause indiscriminate death and destruction as seen by her trampling of Lord Shiva in many portraits. Such is the case when her aspect of *Kuṇḍalinī* gets improperly awakened unleashing her immense force. However, Durgā Devī is her aggressive state, under control which provides strength and protection against evil, destroys negativities, and helps to overcome mode of ignorance, *Tamas* in a devotee. Her power on our side can turn dark into light and beautify ugliness of the world around us. It transforms our life to the desired dream state. Tuesdays are the days of her worship and 'Hrim' is the mantra seed letter which invokes her energy.

The second major expression evolving from light energy is ***Mahālakshmī*** Devī, the most popular and propitiated aspect of the three. Her image is usually seated, or sometimes standing, but always on a lotus in bloom. As her energy stream of photons travels through ether, she is always associated with Lord Vishṇu, her consort, the master of space. Royal by authority and loyal by nature, she invariably accompanies him in all his earthly incarnations. Being kind and caring, she is quite easy to approach. She is an embodiment of love and compassion from which the devotion flows. She lets the feelings of devotion flow freely towards Lord Vishṇu bringing the devotee closer to him. Willingly playing the role of a mediator, she also advocates the cause of a devotee. She is the central figure in second Caritra of Devī Māhātmyam which describes the well-known episode of her slaying the demon king Mahishasura.

She symbolizes the sparkle and shine of life. Whereas her grace gives luster and glory, she brings beauty and bounty with her presence. She dwells in truth, austerity, virtue, and strength which provides marital bliss and establishes domestic order. As a protector and approver of married life, she is one of the most respected, revered, and worshiped deities widely invoked in song and ceremony. Her majestic power grants physical health and sense of well-being. Personifying the principle of illumination, auspiciousness, and abundance she showers all kinds of resources; money and prosperity, food and grains, wealth and assets, knowledge and children, fame and victory. It accommodates, as it allows, our mode of passion, *Rajas* to achieve, accomplish, and fulfill desires leading to happiness. **Diwali** is the new moon night of *Āso* month of Hindu calendar. Householders and businessmen worship her alike, especially on this day for her plentiful grace during the New Year starting the next day.

She is also known by many other names like Kamalā, Padmā, Padmapriyā, Padmākshi etc. All of these show her association with lotus, a symbol of growth and fertility that blossoms various aspects of life. Often she is seen flanked by showering elephants, a symbol of royal consecration. Her portrait also signifies the treasures and resources of nature. However, she is fickle as she constantly shifts and relocates. Like the 'mobile' ray of light that 'flows' continuously, she is very 'active' and 'restless' as she comes and goes. Therefore, the material wealth and assets, fame and fortune that one acquires never remain the same but always fluctuate, passing over time. A prefix '*Śrī*' is used to represent her when describing anything auspicious or affluent. *Śrī Sūktam* is a hymn from *Ṛgveda* in her praise that is very sacred and popular. Fridays are the days of her worship, red is her color of choice. The seed letter 'Śrim' used in mantra recitation and chanting invokes her grace.

The third major aspect, sound energy is portrayed as ***Mahāsaraswati*** Devī. In Vedic literature, she is recognized as the Goddess of speech, *Vāc* who is associated with the river Saraswati. Sound is the first cause of creation, *Nāda Brahman* being the first universal manifestation of the Absolute. Therefore, she inherently carries the sacred knowledge of creation playing an active and indispensable role by the side of her consort, Lord Brahmā. Whereas she embodies spiritual essence, her favor reveals its mysteries while her compassion renders it useful through the potency of all mantra sounds that shower her grace. With her blessings comes *Sattva* Guṇa, mode of goodness leading to purity. She is the mother of inspiration, thoughts, and intellect empowering all mental pursuits and creativity. Also, she is the chief patron of all forms of fine arts, music, and knowledge; worldly as well as spiritual. She represents all forms of speech and communication, whether verbal or literary. All of these develop the totality of art, culture, and civilization which is her domain.

For students, writers, poets, and singers as well as the philosophers, priests, preachers, and philanthropists she is the deity of choice for worship. Goddess of eloquence, water, and fertility, she is usually seen near a river to show her association with anything that flows. Always appearing very graceful and serene, she is usually resplendent in white sari which shows her purity. A white swan by her side indicates her discriminative powers and the wisdom. She holds the knowledge of creation, the Vedas, a rosary representing her spiritual nature, and a stringed musical instrument called Veena. It signifies her association with sounds of seven major notes, the artful combination of which constitutes all forms of music. **Vasant Panchami** festival on the 5th day of *Māgha* month of Hindu calendar is the special day of her worship. She represents knowledge in nature and white is her preferred color. The seed letter 'Ayim' is used in mantra recitation and chanting to invoke her energy and get her blessings.

Shakti pervades the three forms of *Mahākāli* Devī, *Mahālakshmī* Devī, and *Mahāsaraswati* Devī. These are her colorful shades in creation, preservation, and dissolution, the power behind the three faces of God in Trinity concept. Besides these, she also has two more, quite contrasting shades concealed in her palette that perform two more functions. These five functions together are known as her *Paṇchakṛtya*. As *Mahāmāyā*, she entangles us by creating a strong attachment in our minds to this world. This is her power of ***Māyā*-Shakti** which binds us with the mode of ignorance, worldly knowledge, and lower passion called *Avidyā*. We live with an identity and ego limited to the time-space of our existence. But

TEN MAHĀVIDYAS
(WISDOM GODDESSES)

KĀLI, the dark and destructive goddess is the enigmatic flow of time. Her mysterious power gives life, sustains and transforms it through the breath, whereas her terrifying power takes it away.

TĀRĀ is a compassionate goddess characterized as a savior. She represents the fire of cremation ground having purifying and transformative power through which she severs all attachments.

TRIPURASŪNDARI is the sixteen year old beauty also known as Lalitā Devī. She represents love and bliss, light and totality in all manifestation creating everything perfect, complete, and beautiful.

BHŪVANESVARI is the ruler of the universe. As space she is complementary to Kāli. Her rhythm creates, maintains, and destroys the phenomenal world as she controls all aspects of existence.

BHAIRAVI is the energetic goddess of heat and radiance as seen in the fire, lightening, and sun. Her anger burns impurities, guides us, and protects us from all negativities. She is also known as Rūdrani.

CHINNAMASTA is the goddess who severs her own head signifying dissolution of mind into complete awareness. It also represents the truth of all manifested reality as life, sex, and the ultimate death.

DHŪMAVATI is widow, an old goddess. Her smoky appearance represents ignorance which obscures, embodies all the unsatisfied desires, and signifies everything inauspicious.

BAGALAMUKHI is the tongue seizing goddess of speech. She seizes the tongue that conceals thoughts and perpetrates evil. She represents the power of speech that effectively pronounces truth.

MĀTANGI is the goddess of pollution. She reverses the protocol and embraces the lowest by associating with all that is dirty, left-over, and unacceptable by normal standards.

KAMALĀ is the most worshiped Mahālakshmī Devī by herself. She is the goddess of good luck, fortune, and delight who brings wealth and prosperity. She is the most auspicious Mahāvidya.

***Cit*-Shakti** is her inner guiding power that lies dormant at the base of spine of every individual as *Kuṇḍalinī* energy. Its grace allures few fortunate ones who lose interest in the transient experiences of the world and senses. By realizing the futility of physical phenomena and temporality of material existence, they seek higher knowledge called *Vidyā*. Taking them into her fold, she reveals the mystery of life, teaches the subtle secrets of eternity-infinity, and releases them from the bondage of body and mind.

Ten *Mahāvidyas*

Besides the three most venerated forms of energy triads, Shakti is also worshiped as **Ten *Mahāvidyas***. Here she exhibits her power of multiplicity in a unique set of abstract images and identities. Each *Mahāvidya* covers, as it seals, one of the ten directions to completely cover Consciousness so that it is absolutely enveloped by her. The nexus of these wisdom goddesses represents her many contradictory powers. It encompasses several principles, diverse levels of energies, and a number of faculties of the universe. These forms are very unconventional in nature having one-of-a-kind depictions. Most of these goddesses appear to be mysterious and thought provoking, disturbing and challenging, disgusting and repulsive, or awe inspiring and ambiguous.

But there is logic behind each of the bizarre forms of this diverse portfolio that reveals a spiritual truth when understood in a proper context. Their eccentric, unorthodox, and exceptional appearances compel us to dig deeper to know the subtle underlying principles. They break away from all that is forbidden by customs, norms, and established social orders of caste, class, color, and creed. They offer choice for the liberating experience of spirituality to everybody, socially accepted or marginalized. Independent and powerful goddesses in their own right, they are usually worshiped with the associated form of Lord Shiva, each identified as Bhairava, except for *Dhūmavati* who is a widow.

Kāli, the first *Mahāvidya* is dark as night who personifies the power of time from which everything duly appears, and then, eventually disappears. She is the primary aspect of primordial wisdom that ultimately grants liberation. *Tārā* is a savior and a star, dark blue in color who is recognized even by the Buddhists. She was duly appropriated by them and given a prominent position. From the truly frightening face of *Kāli* to the destructive natured *Bhairavi*, to gorgeous looking *Lalitā*, to the social outcast *Mātangi*, to instantly inspiring *Kamalā* are all different expressions of the same Goddess who enjoys appearing in various forms to suit the spirit of devotee worshiping her. *Kamalā* appropriated as a *Mahāvidya* is no other than *Mahālakshmī* Devī who is not associated with Lord Vishṇu. She

Nav–Durgā

Shailpūtri – Another name of Pārvati Devi. She is worshiped on the first day. Shaila means mountains (Himalayas) and pūtri means daughter. She is visualized holding a trident and a lotus riding on a bull.

Brahmachārini – Represents devotion, penance, loyalty, dispassion, and restraint. She is worshiped on the second day of Navrātri. She is visualized wearing Rudrāksha holding a kumbha and a rosary.

Chandraghantā – Radiant like cool and bright moon-light, she showers supreme bliss and peace. She is worshiped on the third day. She is visualized having ten arms, three eyes, and riding on a tiger.

Kushmāndā – Representing effulgence and splendor, she imparts knowledge of cosmic intricacies. She is worshiped on the fourth day. She is visualized having eight arms holding weapons and riding a tiger.

Skandamātā – Mother of Lord Skanda, she is worshiped on the fifth day. She personifies wisdom and knowledge. She is visualized having four arms, three eyes, and sitting on a lion with Skanda on her lap.

Kātyāyani – Daughter of sage Kātyāyan, she is worshiped on the sixth day. She represents power that imparts success and salvation. She is visualized riding a lion and holding a shining sword that slays demons.

Kālrātri – Provides protection by the destruction of ignorance, evil, and darkness. She is worshiped on the seventh day. She is visualized having black skin and four arms sitting on a donkey.

Mahā Gaurī – Represents destruction of sins and mental agonies. She is worshiped on the eighth day. She is visualized having a fair complexion having four arms, holding a trident and a drum riding on a bull.

Siddhidātri – Grantor of wealth, occult powers, and adeptness. She gives 26 kinds of divine powers known as Siddhis to devotees and worshiped on the ninth day. She is visualized having four arms sitting on a lotus.

is the most revered and desired of all *Mahāvidya.* Her auspiciousness is in an absolute contrast to that of the old emaciated widow, *Dhūmavati* who stands for unfulfilled desires, all that is inauspicious, and the ultimate destruction. Also, it is really unusual and quite significant that *Tārā* and *Bagalamukhi* are depicted as seated on a corpse.

Bhūvaneshvari projects the power of space and consciousness. *Bagalamukhi* is a tongue seizing goddess who stops the sins perpetrated by speech that conceals the truth. She also portrays the veiling power of illusion. *Bhairavi* carries the unavoidable power of death and decay that rules the life of all individuals. *Mātangi* is unique in nature as she stands for domination and justice. *Chinnamasta*, who severs her own head, portrays the state devoid of mental distraction, but not death in which one experiences eternal bliss. The entire extraordinary ensemble encompasses wide spectrum of feminine divinity in which conspicuously young and beautiful, queen of queens *Lalitā* projects the most gorgeous form. She symbolizes the original impulse of divine love, the central motivating force of cosmos that radiates from a pure heart. *Lalitā Sahasranāma*, a stotra of her one thousand names which describes as many aspects is very popular. The power of her creation is in absolute contrast with the destructive power of the other *Mahāvidya, Kāli.*

Various energies of our body responsible for our digestion, excretion, movement, vision, and speech are different aspects of Shakti. *Panchamahābhuta* - the five elements that make our body, the breath of *Prāṇa* that sustains our life, and the power of sex and reproduction are all due to her. The power of will, knowledge, and action are also her manifestation. Our desires and decisions, thoughts and actions, reasoning and emotions, involvements and achievements are all a part of her play. We show divine qualities of compassion, forgiveness, kindness, love, and charity only due to her grace. Thus all our physical, spiritual, mental, intellectual, and biological powers are due to her.

Nine special days of the year in the month of *Āso* of Hindu calendar called Navrātri are the most auspicious days for the worship of Shakti. It is celebrated as a grand community festival eulogizing her enormous powers and absolute grace. The three major well known forms - *Mahākāli* Devī, *Mahālakshmī* Devī, and *Mahāsaraswati* Devī are commonly worshiped for three days each, in that order, during these nine days in homes and temples. The fact that Shakti is worshiped in innumerable forms and aspects is evident as, in some traditions, she is worshiped in nine different forms called Nav-Durgā. Each form represents a day of the Navrātri, a plane of the Śrī Chakra, and a level of consciousness corresponding to an energy plane of the universe.

HANUMAN

God of Strength and Devotion

Lord Hanuman, also known as Anjaneya is an extremely popular deity well recognized in the western world as the monkey God of Hinduism. An incarnation of Lord Shiva, he personifies virtues like strength, service, and sacrifice. He assisted Lord Rāma in his earthly mission to kill the demon king Rāvaṇa. An embodiment of supreme power, intelligence, higher knowledge, and humility, he exemplified the character of a true friend and an ideal devotee. He is widely revered and worshiped, especially on Saturdays for getting strength and courage, protection and power. A mace was his weapon of choice.

His father was the God of winds, Vāyu who imparted him the unique ability to fly. When he was a child, an incredible incident occurred. He mistook sun for a fruit and leaped for it. As he was getting close, to stop him, Indra, the ruler of Devas, threw his weapon, a thunderbolt at him. It struck him on the face, left a permanent mark, and made him unconscious. His father, the god of winds was so angry that he stopped functioning. To appease him, Hanuman was revived and all Gods granted him various boons that gave him legendary powers.

He was very playful and mischievous in his childhood. He would tease sages engrossed in meditation, distract them, and steal their belongings. Frustrated, as a sage cursed him, he forgot his powers. He would remember and regain them only when someone reminded him about them at an appropriate time. He later learned scriptures and received higher knowledge through sun God.

He saw Lord Rāma and his brother Lakshmaṇ for the first time when they were searching Sita Devī abducted by the demon king Rāvaṇa. He approached them under a disguise with intent to seek their true identity. Once he realized who they were, he was gratified that his long-cherished wish to meet them had materialized. He revealed his true identity and then led them to meet his friend Sugriva, a monkey king living in exile. Lord Rāma, knowing the plight of Sugriva, helped him to reclaim his kingdom from his brother Bāli.

Ever since Hanuman met Lord Rāma, he dedicated himself to serve the Lord. His life story of devotion to Lord Rāma is very well read, known, and appreciated by people all over the world. A life-long bachelor, he carried out many extraordinary feats during his lifetime. The most awesome was his mission to find Sita Devī on behalf of Lord Rāma. When his team was looking for a way to cross over the vast ocean and search for her on the island of Lanka, he was reminded of his extraordinary powers, including his ability to fly. Regaining his powers at this crucial moment, he made a colossal leap to Lanka and luckily succeeded in locating Sita Devī as a prisoner of Rāvaṇa. He met her, gave solace, and reassured her that Lord Rāma will soon come to her rescue. Then, acting as an envoy of Lord Rāma, he met and warned Rāvaṇa to release Sita Devī or face the consequences of a war. Before leaving Lanka, he went around the kingdom wreaking havoc by causing a lot of destruction and damage.

Another great feat of Lord Hanuman was his timely and thoughtful action that revived unconscious Lakshmaṇ during the war between Lord Rāma and Rāvana. Lakshmaṇ got hurt, became unconscious, and the only cure lied in a specific life-restoring herb that grew on a remote mountain in the Himalayas. Hanuman volunteered to fetch it and flew there but after reaching he was unable to identify that herb. Realizing urgency of the situation, he lifted and carried the whole mountain in his bare hands and flew back! His extraordinary physical power, intelligence, and timely action saved the life of Lakshmaṇ.

In yet another incident during the war, two demon associates of Rāvaṇa named Ahirāvaṇa and Mahirāvaṇa, expert in black magic and spells, abducted Lord Rāma and Lakshmaṇ. They took them to the netherworld and hold them as prisoners. Once again, Hanuman, in yet another search mission, started looking for them and ultimately succeeded in finding them. However, to release them, it was necessary to kill those two demons. In the battle that ensued, no matter how hard he tried, he could not succeed. He soon realized that the demons must have a secret to their life. Searching for clue, he eventually got lucky and stumbled upon that secret; they would die only if five lamps, lighting in five different directions were extinguished at the same time. This was truly an impossible task but he assumed a five faced form, blew them simultaneously, killed the demons, and then rescued Lord Rāma and Lakshmaṇ.

Along with Gaṇesha, his image smeared with vermilion can be seen at the entrance of most temples. It signifies that pure devotion, complete surrender, and an absence of ego are the qualities one needs to have before one approaches the divine. Students, wrestlers, and fighters seek the grace of Hanuman for getting strength and courage as well as success and victory. On Saturdays, he is worshiped in temples with an offering of coconut, oil, black sesame seed, fruits etc. Sixteenth century poet Tūlsidas has written a poem in his praise called Hanuman Chalisa; with 40 verses, it is a very well-known and the most popular prayer to him. It provides inner strength and helps fight troubles, especially the afflictions caused by planet Saturn.

THE SUBTLE SYSTEM

TANTRA, YANTRA, AND MANTRA

Universal Spiritual Practice

Tantra is an unorthodox system of belief and practices, developed in antiquity but well known to be within the fold of Hinduism for over fifteen centuries. A spiritual core without limitations of tenets of religion, it is practiced in a variety of forms. Many other cultures of south Asian countries and the religious tradition of Buddhism, *Vajrayana* also recognize, accept, and extensively practice it. Not being a system of dogma based on creed or authority and often practiced with a veil of secrecy, it has not acquired the status of a mainstream religion. It remained ambiguous over centuries due to the intended format of its obscure texts and use of diagrams called yantras that depict cosmic energies with complex symbolism. It is radical in its approach, often going against the social standards, accepted norms, and the moral grain. Secretive initiation rituals, many unconventional methods, and several sexually oriented practices tainted its image as it fell into disrepute and was coined as morally corrupt path. Therefore, it is commonly misrepresented and misconceived as always associated with sex and black magic. In fact, everybody can pursue these practical, energy, action, and devotion driven methods for Self-discovery while keeping their faith.

The fast pace and ever shifting paradigm of life in the current Dark Age, Kali Yuga makes traditional Vedic rituals and practices quite obsolete as they are difficult to perform. Also, they are not conducive to spiritual growth due to comparative lack of purity and character of the people. Hence, the period of renaissance saw a decline in such ritualistic practices and rise of devotional stream. Esoteric system of Tantra, which harnesses universal energies and emphasizes intuitive realization of *Brahman* also gained ground and came into prominence. By having a really powerful impact on the Vedas, it revamped, reconfigured, and reconstructed some of the traditional methods such that they are effective even today and therefore, suit and satisfy the needs of everyone. Its influence is quite evident in the last Veda, *Atharvaveda* which is hallmark of their spiritual synthesis. By combining the Vedic and Tantric principles, it describes esoteric formulas and techniques that all individuals can use.

The culture of orthodox Vedic system and distinct tradition of innovative Tantric schools, almost like twins, tread the same spiritual path. Also, they learn from, and lean on each other every step of the way. However, they avoid looking eye to eye as they lack warmth and cordiality. This antagonism stems from the fact that Tantra is a scientific cult whereas Hinduism is a religion based on the Vedic philosophy. Radical in approach, Tantra views life 'as it is', with an open vision, totally avoiding interference of the mind. Mind is a worldly tool that qualifies and judges, classifies and categorizes, accepts or rejects. It discriminates races and divides people by the class, culture, society, and religion. An ally of the world, it is the primary cause that veils our consciousness. Also, it is constantly drawn outwards having unending desires and numerous attachments. Hence, it is a weak tool to seek the higher Self. And yet, ironically all world religions, including Hinduism are various ways of the mind in spiritual pursuit. Religions create misbelief that it is the only right path thereby giving rise to religious conflicts. Also, their ways are often in variance with the strong worldly aspirations of the followers which causes a lifelong battle within them.

Tantra accepts the Reality of *Brahman* as taught by *Vedānta*, the crown jewel of Hindu philosophy. But to perceive the Reality, it actively engages with its manifesting power and duly exploits it. By such direct involvement with ubiquitous energy, it offers an exposure to, and a journey through the subtle realms of existence giving ultimate spiritual experience. For the purpose, it avoids mind that analyzes, assesses, and approves thoughts and emotions, acts and attitudes based on religious, moral, or social norms. It accepts human nature, as it is, equally embracing its worldly ways and spiritual aspirations. It celebrates the power of life that enlivens individual consciousness, human body being a living temple. Hence it accepts everyone, without exception, respecting their position in the cosmos and power of their existence. It has human approach and universal appeal. Instead of preaching asceticism, suggesting suppression of desires, or postulating codes of conduct, it accepts all ways of life.

It truly understands the human psyche which, though very diverse, always surrounds the I-ness and seeks self-gratification. Considering it to be natural, it effectively reconciles such desires with spiritual elevation. By employing one or more methods, it rechanells psychic energy towards the positive outlets gradually raising awareness. Yantra worship and mantra chanting use these drives as fuel carrying out their sublimation and transformation by purification and elevation. Employing many powerful, eccentric, and at times disconcerting techniques, it achieves a break through the attachments, inertia, and ignorance. These practices ultimately optimize the energy flow in the subtle channels by cleaning up their energy centers. It eliminates illusions, opens up vision, and reinvigorates the spiritual dimension to experience non-dualistic bliss.

All thoughts and actions, good or bad, right or wrong are driven by passion propelled by the power of energies. Rather than viewing as an obstacle, Tantra regards even the negative streams as welcome source of untapped opportunity.

For Tantra, the flow of energy is an indispensable resource that enlivens the path to spirituality as it carries the potential to transform all worldly actions into the transcendental experience of fulfillment. All Tantric thought, wisdom, and practice revolves around harnessing the universal energy called Shakti. Her power is immanent, present here and now, around us, constantly flowing within us that animates our life enlivening our consciousness. Tantra taps this ever existing energy of polarity that links matter with spirit to acquire paranormal powers, experience divinity, and ultimately attain enlightenment. Hence, Shaktism and Tantrism are two overlapping systems like two isomers. All Hindu concepts like Shiva-Shakti and Divine Mother are at the core of Tantrism.

In the eyes of Tantra, life is a powerful play of energy. It is an intricate game of handling the polarities and dualities of nature, outside and within us, that constantly give rise to challenging and life ruling experiences. For example, our breathing constitutes the harmonic of polar opposites, inhalation and exhalation as we live in the dual states, either waking or sleeping. We are inevitably exposed to dualities of nature like heat and cold, day and night. Normally good natured, we often pass through periods of negativities like jealousy, anger, and greed. Also, we routinely pass through dichotomy of experiences like gain and loss, pleasure and pain. We constantly live through such diametrically opposite experiences. In the process, we oscillate between these extremes like a pendulum periodically and quite invariably swinging through adverse weather pattern of stress, emotions, anxiety, and suffering. Tantra aims at neutralizing all polarities of our nature by transforming, centering, and aligning these energies to establish a state of transcendental unitary consciousness. In such an elevated state of equanimity, we acquire immunity to all kinds of dualities that influence our life. They become meaningless rendering all experiences blissful.

To acquire such control over cognition and perception, it targets main subtle energy centers, Chakras strung along the spine. They regulate the energy flow of *Prāṇa* via other smaller Chakras spread throughout the body. These psycho-energy centers are governed and regulated by the dormant energy, *Kuṇḍalinī* residing at the base of spine of every human being. As Divine Mother, she controls all aspects of our existence through these centers. Ideally all these Chakras should be bright and vibrant vortices that operate in harmony, at an optimum level to create an extremely efficient energy flow. Such an orderly function translates into perfect attunement with the nature. It imparts a state of absolute awareness as one dwells in one's essential nature.

Unfortunately, it is not so due to the past *Karma* acquired and accumulated over numerous previous lives. In most people, they are often covered with layers of impurities and conditioned with impressions, ***Saṃskāra***. It causes Chakras to be dull and lusterless, partially or fully blocked so that they underperform or overact. Such imbalance and malfunction manifest as problems of ignorance, illusion, apprehension, and attachment. As they taint awareness, we easily get caught up in the worldly show of outer appearances, sensory pleasures, and material needs. We often seek happiness outside ourselves in inappropriate ways. Driven by desires to become, achieve, and enjoy, we fail to make right choices and follow the right path. Instead of living a happy life meant to be full of bliss and peace, we constantly face failure and heartache, misery and grief.

Tantra believes that the omnipresent cosmic energies constantly correspond, interact, and influence the energy flow of our subtle system. Specific rituals and practices can gather, bind, and direct these higher, purer, and stronger energies from outside into the subtle channels. Directed to the Chakras, their powerful frequencies clean, stimulate, and activate them to renew, revitalize, and rejuvenate. As mental and material layers melt, consciousness expands to feel and enjoy the freedom of release; a state of higher unity is experienced. The conditioned human intelligence finds new dimensions, resonates with the power of being, and enjoys the blissful state of mere existence. While restoring our original self, it also awakens abilities and gives unique powers.

The primary goal of the esoteric practice of Tantra is supposed to transmute desires in order to power the path of spiritual awakening. Its ultimate aim is to awaken and raise the latent power of *Kuṇḍalinī*. An extremely difficult task, it may be realized by controlling the *Prāṇa* flow within our subtle channels and then concentrate and direct it to its location. The awakening, while leading to the state of endless bliss and peace, also gives mystical experiences and supernatural powers. Direction and grace of a Guru is absolutely essential for success in this powerful path. He is the liberated one who assesses the competency and spiritual status, *Adhikāra* of the disciple. He qualifies and coaches, trains and guides by initiating the disciple into the chosen practice by navigating him through the ritualistic steps of the sacred path. Guru tradition is the heart of spirituality that transfers such knowledge through generations.

Yantra

The two most commonly used tools by a practitioner of Tantra, besides his body are yantras and mantras. Yantras are the specific physical templates through which he transacts the universal cosmic energy. They are the hallmark of Tantric theory and practice. Just as power of a deity is visualized in human shape, yantra is a linear geometric diagram in which its vibratory pattern is engraved. It depicts the specific energy pattern of a deity using cosmic symbolism as visualized by a seer in his transcendental state. Imbued with esoteric meaning, it graphically expresses the subtle energy flow of a deity. It is subtler than the corresponding anthropomorphic image but grosser than the energy vibrations created by its mantra. Yantra may also be viewed as a physical body designed to acquire and hold the depicted pattern of energy. It acts as a vehicle for the soul of deity dwelling in its mantra. Mantra chanting during *Prāṇa Pratishthā* ceremony creates vibrations with the same pattern as engraved on its surface. As they repeatedly strike on it, the yantra gets duly energized. Then its sacred surface carries power of the deity in a vibrant state that influences the surrounding area.

The two dimensional flat yantras are most commonly drawn on the ground, paper, or engraved on metals like gold, silver, and copper. Usually geometric figures like triangles, circles, squares, and lotus petals are inscribed in different combinations to make a deity specific diagram. All yantras have a point at the center signifying the origin. The circle around is time, an expansion of the origin with the radius of desire. The upward pointing triangles represent fire and male, the downward pointing triangles represent water and female. The sides of a triangle represent the three energies – heat, sound, and light. The lotus petals show spiritual unfolding and gradual rising of the soul that takes place from the water and mud of darkness and ignorance. The entire diagram is enclosed within an outer square having two walls and a gate on each side.

Durgā Yantra

Gaṇesha Yantra

Besides the flat form of linear dimensions, some yantras have a pyramidal structure known as Meru. Potentially there can be countless yantras, each depicting a specific cosmic energy that may be propitiated for a particular purpose. Śrī Yantra is by far the most comprehensive, well recognized, and widely worshiped yantra in homes and temples for overall prosperity. It is the entire energy matrix of the cosmos which contains the individual energy patterns depicted in all other yantras. Such yantras are also extensively used in Tibetan Tantric Buddhism where they incorporate various pictorial elements beautifying the whole diagram. They are better known as Mandala.

Mantra

Mantra is a general term referring to the sound body of divine cosmic energy that simply exists in the universe. In its totality, it is encapsulated in the primal sound Aum that constantly resonates around us. It is the eternal source of all other energies operating at various sentient levels that appear through the differentiation of Aum. Each kind has its own vibrational form, well captured in its mantra which reveals to us its specific power through an audible sound. The cumulative, complementary, and creative function of these energies is the cause of all physical phenomena. The cosmic will conceives, conducts, and controls the affairs of this wonderful world enterprise through the mind of these energies. All material forms it variously creates are sustained by the power of their underlying energy. Intelligence of its vibratory patterns also initiates and sustains living processes of all life forms. Each mantra articulates the power of a particular thought from among the plenty through which the cosmic mind propitiates.

Prayers are human composition that uses words of supplication chosen from a common language of communication. Mantras are quite different from them. It is the potential of divine power that variously exists as ubiquitous vibrations of mantra sounds. They represent the subtle medium through which transcendental Truth was revealed to the ancient sages during deep state of meditation. These sounds were compiled into the collection of various scriptures, the most ancient being the Vedas. Realization of such phrases of spiritual wisdom which embeds within the energy of their conscious effect was the sweet fruit of their severe austerities and long period of *tapas*. Following esoteric tradition, they generously shared it among others. Each incantation develops typical vibratory pattern as seen engraved on its yantra. It extols certain power and potency, visualized as a deity commonly represented by its anthropomorphic image.

These mantras are in complete harmony with the principle of natural law and universal order, *Ṛta* which governs all the subtle and physical realms. Their vibrations pervade the entire cosmos. They focus on specific aspect of the Reality, capture it with true knowledge and deep insight, and provide an access to it in their own particular way. As we chant mantra, its vibrations attune the patterns of the finite individual mind to those of the infinite cosmic mind enabling us to draw on its specific power and potency. Thereby, it gathers its underlying thoughts while selectively strengthening those of ours that align with the cosmic intelligence. Thus, it gives us a glimpse of the cosmic vision which expands our awareness and guides our path. Each mantra is empowered in twofold manner; the frequency of sound vibrations and formal elements of its composition. An exquisite rendition of a mantra harnesses its potential to the fullest.

A FEW MANTRAS

GAṆESHA MANTRA

AUM VAKRATŪṆDA MAHĀKĀY KOTISŪRYA SAMAPRABHA
NIRVIGHNAṂ KŪRŪMĒ DEV SARVA KĀRYĒSHU SARVADA

GĀYATRI MANTRA

AUM BHŪR BHŪVAH SŪVAHA
TATSAVITŪRVA REṆYAṂ
BHARGO DĒVASYA DHĪMAHI
DHĪYOYO NAHA PRACHODAYĀTA

MAHĀ MṚTYŪNJAYA MANTRA

AUM TṚYAMBAKAṂ YAJĀMAHE SŪGANDHIṂ PŪSHTI VARDHANAṂ
ŪRVARŪKMIVA BANDHANAṆ MṚTYOR MŪKSHIYA MĀMṚTĀT

DEVĪ MANTRA

AUM SARVA MANGALA MĀNGALYĒ SHIVĒ SARVARTH SĀDHIKĒ
SHARANYĒ TṚYAMBAKĒ DEVĪ NĀRĀYAṆI NAMO STŪTĒ

SHIVA MANTRA

AUM KARPUR GAURAṂ KARŪṆĀVTĀRAṂ
SANSĀRSĀRAṂ BHŪJAGENDRAHĀRAṂ
SADĀ VASANTAṂ HṚIDAYĀRVINDĒ
BHAVAMBHAVĀNI SAHITAṂ NAMĀMI

VISHṆU MANTRA

AUM SHĀNTAKĀRAṂ BHŪJAGASHAYANAṂ
PADMANĀBHAṂ SURĒSHAṂ
VISHVĀDHĀRAṂ GAGANSADṚSHAṂ
MEGHAVARṆAṂ SHŪBHĀNGAṂ
LAKSHMIKĀṆTAṂ KAMALNAYANAṂ
YOGIBHIRDHYĀNA GAMYAṂ
VANDĒ VISHṆU BHAVABHAYAHARAṂ
SARVA LOKAIKANĀTHAṂ

GURU MANTRA

AUM GURU BRAHMĀ GURUṚ VISHṆU GURU DEVO MAHĒSHVARAḤ
GURU SĀKSHĀT PARA BRAHMĀN TASMAI ŚRĪ GURAVĒ NAMAḤ

A mantra is a power phrase Realized by a sage during meditation the alphabet sounds of which are typically from Sanskṛit language. It is a unique arrangement of its letters having specific pattern of a formula. Each sonic encryption encapsulates certain cosmic energy which releases upon its chanting effectively enlivening its presiding deity. By dedicated chanting, we create a bond which establishes a relation with the deity thereby getting an access to its specific powers. The grace of deity showers upon us which clarifies our thoughts, harmonizes our energies, and inspires our mind. It carries an inherent power and potency to heal, fulfill desires, illuminate, and provide protection by releasing the mind from ignorance, illusion, and evil instincts. Thereby, it guides our path truly enhancing our ability to pursue worldly as well as spiritual goals.

There is variety of mantras classified into three categories based on the era of their Realization and the purpose of their incantation. The most ancient **Vedic** mantras are kind of adoration eulogizing various elementary forces of nature. Having a form and formula that functions well during the fire ceremony, they are mostly used by the presiding priests for conducting rites and rituals. They engage in cosmic currents and participate in the function of Eternal Truth. The mantras that were Realized later during the **Purāṇic** age were made available to common man for their individual prayer and worship. These are primarily used for worldly goals and material achievements. Some of them also carry an avenging power as duly outlined in *Atharvaveda*. There are other mantras for spiritual elevation that detach us from the world, internalize our mind, and help us to concentrate on our inner self. Therefore, they are important for all types of *Yoga* and meditation practices. **Tantric** mantras are unique as they use specific seed letters that have the power to harness ubiquitous energy for empowerment of the inner self while awakening the power of higher consciousness within.

The mantra having just one concentrated syllable, with or without a meaning is called a seed letter, **Bija mantra**. It is a natural sound which reveals to us the subtle nature of a particular deity, each governing a specific psycho energy center, Chakra of our subtle body. It creates powerful vibrations that resonate with the associated Chakra effectively energizing it to have a tremendous influence on our entire system. Longer mantras with a meaning are formed in conjunction with one or more such seed letters. Aum is the most important of all seed letter as it is the mother of all mantras. All mantras can be reduced to Aum, the phonetic seed of the cosmos. Therefore, all mantras commonly begin with the recitation of Aum which potentialises them and makes them effective. A few other common Bija mantras are Ayim, Hrim, Śrim, Dum, Klim, and Gam.

Ayim is the seed letter that invokes the grace of *Mahāsaraswati* Devī for gaining knowledge and raising the power of discriminative faculty. Hrim is a very common seed letter in all Shakti mantras as it invokes the power of inexhaustible energy of the universe. Śrim is a very auspicious seed letter that invokes the power of *Mahālakshmi* Devī who fulfills all our worldly desires as she provides wealth and abundant resources. Dum is a potent seed letter of Durgā Devī who grants protection from evil and ignorance. Similarly, Klim is the seed letter of Kāma Deva and Gam that of Lord Gaṇesha.

All living beings continually chant the life giving mantra 'Soham' without having to make an effort or being aware of it. It pervades our breath with the subtle sound 'sah' on inhalation and that of 'ham' during exhalation. Breathing is the basic Life Principle, absolutely essential for existence as its power sustains our life. The mantra of each breath pervades the entire universe of our body. It not only sustains our individual self but keeps it connected with the Great Self as well. Every day it sounds 21,600 times as we constantly respire. Since it is chant-less, it is also known as **Ajapa (**unchanted**) Gāyatri** which has the same potency as Aum. Gāyatri mantra is the first long mantra that appear from Aum which is the essence of all Vedas and contains all other mantras.

There exists several major psycho energy centers, Chakras strung along the length of our spine visualized as colored lotuses. Each lotus has different number of petals, each petal representing a subtle energy channel linked to it. In all, there are 50 of these distribution pathways, each of it ruled by the specific alphabet of Sanskṛit language, also 50 in number. Their equal number, where each alphabet is paired with a channel divulges and discloses an intrinsic relation between them established at the time of our creation. Each Sanskṛit alphabet, *Mātṛkā* is a key cosmic sound endowed with the prime power to create specific physical form. Their evolutionary energy gave rise to the corresponding subtle energy channels. These channels then developed the extensive web of field that created the entire physical body around them during gestation which it penetrates, energizes, and supports throughout the life. Hence, each channel resonates with the vibrations of its specific sound source. Vibratory energy of a mantra sound tunes into specific channels, in an order that empowers them. These sound energies are essential to sustain our life. Graphic portrait of the terrifying Goddess *Mahākāli* Devī wears a garland of skulls, each symbolizing a Sanskṛit letter. It indicates that as she withdraws these energies, it causes death and destruction.

We routinely tune in to the frequency of a particular radio station or TV channel from among the plenty in atmosphere to exploit and enjoy its content. Similarly, dedicated mantra chanting generates a steady stream of vibrations that tune in to invoke the specific cosmic energy from among the plenty lying dormant in the universe. As the sacred vibratory field addresses these subtle essences and effectively communicates with them, the energy of its grace is gradually released. It is gathered and accumulated by those Chakras receptive to it which activates and energizes the associated channels. Assimilation of this energy enhances their power of operation, harmonizes the *Prāṇa* flow, and improves the efficiency of its distribution. These vibrations duly penetrate the mental and material layers, reach the spirit encased within, and connect it to the divine source. It is an auspicious force invigorating our entire system, the blessings of deity showering upon the devotee that empowers, enlightens, and elevates. As a result one gains control over senses, acquires power and knowledge, name and fame, and a release from ignorance, pain, and sin due to the past negative *Karma*.

The sacred mantra sounds, therefore, are the soul and substance of spirituality. As powerful catalyst for spiritual transformation, they are extensively used in prayers, rituals, and worship not only in Tantra but in all Hindu religious, *Yoga*, and meditative practices. They are universally applicable to every being and relevant at all times. Chanting of mantra calms the mind and creates a sense of well-being as it harmonizes individual energies with the nature. Regular repetition and chanting burns all *Karma* impurities, penetrates the layers of ignorance, and brings forth wisdom from within. It elevates consciousness and strengthens our will which allows us to pursue the path of our *Karmic* destiny.

Some mantras precede with an introduction, **Viniyoga** describing the basis upon which the associated energy is invoked. Viniyoga is an indicator of the guiding Guru who first realized the energy of the mantra, the rhythm of the composition, the name of the deity or the energy it invokes, the associated seed letter which is the key sound, and lastly the key element. Like the ripples generated in a pond when a stone in thrown, repetition of a mantra chanting called **Japa** produces waves of reinforced energy currents that repeatedly strike and stimulate the subtle energy flow. Usually Japa is carried out in cycles of an auspicious number 108 which is called *Mālā*. A rosary made with the beads of Rudrāksha, Tūlsi, Crystal, Lotus seed etc. keeps the count.

One may not know the exact meaning of the mantra one chants. Mantras being impersonal and irrational, their sounds carry energy independent of the character of chanter and his religious affiliation. A mantra is empowered by perfect rendition which unleashes the full power of the underlying element of Truth innately embedded in its structure. The key point is to focus on the pronunciation and power it carries to create such vibrations that invariably have its desired effect. However, attentiveness of the mind determines the extent of its effect as mechanical chanting without the intent to go inward, concentrate, and connect may prove to be fruitless. Mantra may be recited out loud, gently whispered, or best of all, they may be internal mental incantations. Even listening to their sound has its own benefits.

Mantras have the capacity to bind specific cosmic energy and therefore, an indispensable spiritual tool. In the most ancient Guru tradition, a Guru usually gives initiation into a specific mantra to a disciple based on his affiliation and theistic order. It becomes the pivot of his spiritual practice as he continuously chants it during the period of his worship. Empowered and sanctified by the tradition and so potentialised by Guru, it has a tremendous impact on the consciousness of disciple ultimately leading him to emancipation. Many mantras are very well known and commonly used by people during their worship at homes and other religious ceremonies. Also, there are specific mantras for the morning and evening prayers. Gāyatri mantra, essence of the Vedas is a potent mantra that destroys ignorance, bestows enlightenment, and grants liberation. All other mantras originate from, and merge into Gāyatri mantra made of 24 unique seed letters which ultimately merges into Aum.

Tantra Worship

The ultimate aim of Tantra practitioner is supposed to be the transmutation of desires so that the energy of consciousness flows in the direction of higher self. Tantra worship is also known as the other face of Shaktism. Besides the use of a yantra and a mantra, the practitioner often uses his body as well to carry out many of the rituals. They have cosmic dimension and aid in achieving the primary goal to correct and purify the energy flow in the body. At the beginning of ceremony, the most common ritual of 'placement' called ***Nyāsa*** is usually performed to sanctify the body. Different body parts are touched with fingertips in conjunction with mantra chanting to internalize, synchronize, and secure different aspects of mantra energy with those of the associated limbs.

Different symbolic hand gestures called ***Mudras*** are also commonly used during the ceremony. It is supposed to stimulate the nerve centers and purify the body by removing all types of negative energies. In some practices, the practitioner first invokes and invites the deity associated with the divine energy within his body and then transfers it to the yantra of worship. This is followed by the ritual of making orderly offerings to the yantra while concentrating on the deity and chanting its mantra. Various accessories offered to the yantra are different kinds of flowers, rice, milk, fruits, light, incense, turmeric, vermilion etc. A rosary keeps the count of mantra Japa. In general, Sun is one of the five chief Tantra deities; others are Gaṇesha, Shiva, Shakti, and Vishṇu.

The vibrations of mantra chanting invoke specific energies that slowly begin to flow like a stream having the same pattern as depicted on the yantra of worship. As the stream becomes powerful and its energy field widens, it effectively energizes yantra having the same pattern by repeatedly striking its surface. Just as software program installation brings computer to life, these divine vibrations bring the yantra to life. They also resonate with the subtle system of the worshiper to activate and amplify the latent forces within.

The practice of such sacrament leaves lasting *Karmic* effect and strong mental impression. It alters, aligns, and integrates the body, mind, and spirit having significant effect on the life of practitioner as he now has a greater awareness, capacity to pursue his worldly goals, and ability to indulge in such spiritual practices. He feels empowered and virtuous, fulfilled and flourishing. An advanced adept even acquires paranormal powers that defy the laws of nature. The energized and sanctified yantra also has a purifying effect in the place where it is kept. Regularly worshiping the yantra, especially on auspicious days, reenergizes it and consecrates the place of worship.

In Tantra worship there are innumerable traditions. According to the nature and scope of the practice, it propitiates a certain deity, uses its mantra and the corresponding yantra in the methods of initiation, consecration, and ceremonial rituals. In some practices the most potent energy source, power of aroused sexual energy is used for effecting a real inner transformation. Tantric sex is sacred, a union at the highest possible level. However, it has wrongly become the face of Tantra in many parts of the world. Therefore, this and many other practices are forbidden as they are used to indulge and gratify, create spells and acquire occult powers. It not only defies conventional social standards of ethics, morality, and purity but also leads to their excesses.

Just as a child uses stroller to learn steps, these rituals combined with other *Yoga* practices and meditation techniques initiate one into the realm of spirituality. The worship invokes and invites the deities and other higher beings within the sacred space of the self. It diverts the mind inwards. To render it quiescent is as difficult as not falling down for the child. Just as the child slowly begins baby steps, transformation of awareness begins. Ultimately one day child gives up the stroller. Similarly, at some point this external worship may not be necessary. As the envelopes of matter and mind weaken, it results in exalted consciousness, empowered character, and enhanced well-being. As spiritual evolution accelerates, mind totally melts and dissolves in awareness. Limited individual consciousness merges with unimpeded Cosmic Consciousness to achieve the state of eternal bliss, ***Satcitānanda*** (being-consciousness-bliss).

ŚRĪ CHAKRA

The Yantra for Prosperity

Śrī Chakra is a sophisticated geometric design which represents the abode of Divine Mother, all her creative energies, and the entire physical manifestation as conceived by the metaphysical vision of Shaktas. It has an intricate structural pattern which embeds within her various sentient energies that create, preserve, and dissolve this vast and variegated universe. The prefix Śrī denotes that it is very sacred and auspicious, truly worthy of worship. The entire configuration is based on a brilliant mathematical formula which artfully combines geometric figures like lines, triangles, and circles with lotus petals to create its elaborate matrix. Besides the two dimensional linear form, it also has as a three dimensional pyramidal structure called the cosmic mountain, Meru.

Human body is a universe in itself as all energies and cosmic principles of the entire universe, the macrocosm are replicated in our body, the microcosm. The beauty of Śrī Yantra blueprint, therefore, is that it simultaneously represents the energies of the entire universe as well as the human body. ***Lalitā*** Devī, the most blissful state of Divine Mother is its presiding deity who resides at the top center called *Bindu.* Starting from this uppermost level and going towards the lowermost outer square, there are nine different levels of veiling called ***Āvarnas***. Each outer level represents her successive emanation, a grosser element, and a lower plane of consciousness governed by her different aspects.

Energy patterns in a Śrī Chakra are made by the intersection of two sets of total nine dissimilar triangles. The five progressively larger and downward pointing triangles show the descending energy of creation, an aspect of Shakti. The other four progressively larger and upward pointing triangles represent the ascending energy of dissolution, an aspect of Lord Shiva. They intersect and interpenetrate at various points graphically showing the complementarity of masculine and feminine principles upholding the whole manifestation. They create the central matrix of 43 small triangles, on five different levels, each governed by a deity. It projects quite a complex structure having fourteen corners.

Bindu is the place of cosmic spiritual union of Lord Shiva and Shakti at the uppermost level. It is the source of energies for all other triangles and the point of origin for the whole universe. With Divine Mother's desire of creation, *Bindu* expands into the innermost and downward pointing first triangle called ***Kāma-Kalā*** at the second level. It carries an impulse to create and an urge to manifest

having the power to expand and the potential to multiply. This quivering form is constantly craving for creation from which four pairs of other triangles, the upward pointing Shiva and downward pointing Shakti triangles make appearance. As these triangles emanate and gradually expand, they spread out and intersect at four successively lower levels of energy fields. Each level is represented by the concentric circular pattern of 8, 10, 10, and 14 small triangles making a total of 42 other small triangles. The various points of intersection of the sides of Shakti and Shiva triangles represent a meeting of their energies. Each line, angle, triangle, and circle carries a meaning having a specific power presided over by a deity, each an aspect of *Lalitā* Devī generally recognized as Yogini.

Two levels of circles of petals, the inner circle with eight petals whereas the outer circle with sixteen petals surround these six levels that represent flowering of the human being and creation of the universe. These petals, each a seat of divinity, represent different energies within us that encompass our abilities and virtues, pleasures and desires. These eight levels are further enclosed in three concentric circles within an outermost square which is made of three parallel lines thus making a total of nine levels, *Āvarnas*. Each level of consciousness has a specific name and is associated with a particular form of Devī. The outermost square shows the physical plane of earth in the form of a temple which has openings or 'Gates' in the middle of each side. These are supposed to be closed. Mantra chanting, devotion, rituals, and meditation are the four keys to each of these gates. Any one or more may be used to enter Śrī Chakra, the realm of Divine Mother to mark the beginning of a spiritual journey.

Evolution and Involution

Starting from the top center, *Bindu*, creation takes place by moving down and out in evolutionary steps. Conscious element gradually transmutes into matter made in space and time for the soul to come in existence represented by the lotus petals. It finally manifests in the material world, the outermost square. The journey going inward, towards the top represents withdrawal of the manifested energies, dissolution, or involution where matter eventually fades into spirit. As the various obstacles represented by different *Āvarnas* are overcome with each rising step going up the spiritual ladder, it progressively raises the level of consciousness which finally merges with *Bindu* at the top.

A Śrī Chakra also represents the energies of the entire universe grounded in the physical world within each being. To put it differently, our body itself is a Śrī

Chakra. In fact, there are 43 main energy centers in our body just as the matrix of 43 small triangles of Śrī Chakra. Various subtle psycho-energy centers, Chakras along the spinal cord govern our entire subtle system. Each of them corresponds to different *Āvarnas* of Śrī Chakra. Just as *Bindu* is the origin from where energy flows down the Śrī Chakra, cosmic energy enters the crown of our head, flows down the body, and leaves through our feet to the ground. For this reason, we bow down and touch feet of a saint, a holy person, or a Guru. The feet where all nerve currents end exude their divine grace. Guru is a Realized soul who can draw divine energy at will and direct it to the crown Chakra of deserving disciple. This transmission stimulates and energizes the entire subtle system; the process is known as ***Shaktipāt*,** advent of grace.

The nine intersecting triangles represent nine basic elements called *Dhātu* that make up our physical self. The four Shiva triangles correspond to the solar energies that make marrow, semen, vital air, and soul. The five Shakti triangles are the lunar energies that make skin, blood, flesh, fat, and bone. Each of the twelve sides of four Shiva triangles represents one of the twelve Zodiac signs, the associated sidereal constellation, and a month of the solar calendar. The fifteen sides of five Shakti triangles represent the phases of moon. Thus, the entire matrix remarkably represents the exact way in which lunar and solar energies complement to constitute our body. These energies flow in opposite directions through the two subtle energy channels, Ida and Pingala in our body. They create the principle axis of energy flow which sustains our life.

Supreme Yantra

Śrī Chakra is the most comprehensive yantra as various cosmic energies represented by all other yantras are contained in this all-inclusive design. Worship of Śrī Chakra is equivalent to the worship of all other yantras together. It transforms the place of worship to a powerful energy center like the abode of Divine Mother. Therefore, it is the most auspicious yantra for overall prosperity. *Lalitā* Devī is also known by names like *Rājrājeshwari*, *Tripurasūndari*, *Tripurāmba*, *Tripuréshi* etc. At sweet sixteen, she is the perfect beauty who has a very playful nature. To venerate her in Śrī Chakra while chanting her powerful fifteen fold 'Panchadashi' mantra constitutes the highest form of worship which is known as Śrī Vidyā. It creates a bond with the flow of energy between the devotee and Divine Mother. Chanting *Lalitā Sahasranāma*, the thousand names of *Lalitā* Devī in front of a Śrī Chakra on Fridays and full moon days is very auspicious. Also, worshiping it during **Navrātri**, the nine special days of *Āso* month of Hindu calendar grants the worshiper protection, prosperity, and higher knowledge. Therefore, it is a very popular practice.

Different *Āvarnas* starting from the Outermost *Āvarna*

1 **Trailokya Mohan Chakra.** The outermost square with 3 lines is known as Bhūpūr. The outer line has eight guardians of directions, one on each side of the gate. The other two lines show the 'obvious' Yoginis: the middle line has eight Siddhi Shakti of senses, and the innermost line has eight *Mātṛkā*.

2 **Sarva Āshāpurak Chakra.** This *Āvarna* is made of sixteen petals that represent our innate desires; each is governed by a 'hidden' Shakti also known as Nitya. A Nitya also represents phase of the moon. This *Āvarna* corresponds to *Mulādhāra* Chakra in our body.

3 **Sarva Sankshobhan Chakra.** This *Āvarna* is made of eight petals that represent eight very secret Yoginis. This Chakra governs our passions; name of each petal describes the terms of loving sexuality that corresponds to energies associated with *Manipura* Chakra in our body.

4 **Sarva Saubhāgya Dāyak Chakra.** Consisting of fourteen petals, the Yoginis governing this *Āvarna* bestows good fortune in all aspects of our life. A Yogini governs each of these 14 triangles that represent the 14 chief bio-energy currents in our body.

5 **Sarva Artha Sādhak Chakra.** This Mandala is a Chakra that consists of 10 triangles, each governed by a Shakti that represents a vital breath of our body. Grace of these Shakti bestows any and all objects desired by the adept.

6 **Sarva Rakshākar Chakra.** This *Āvarna* is also made of 10 triangles governed by Shakti who are the rulers of the 10 vital fires in our body. As the name indicates, this *Āvarna* gives total protection.

7 **Sarva Roga Hara Chakra.** This *Āvarna* made of 8 triangles is governed by secret Yoginis also known as Vāsinis, each ruling one of the 8 groups of Sanskṛit language letters.

8 **Sarva Siddhiprada Chakra.** This is the *Āvarna* governed by three very secret Yoginis, each associated with Brahmā, Vishṇu, and Rūdra. They give all round success and achievements.

9 **Sarva Ānandmaya Chakra.** This is the purely blissful state and seat of the queen of queens, *Lalitā* Devī.

IDA, PINGALA, AND SUSHUMNA

Three major subtle channels

Though human existence on earth primarily depends on the sun, it is too hot to live on. The other heavenly body having the most significant effect on our life is the moon which is too cold to sustain life. Both appear to be of the same size and at the same distance, but it is an illusion as, in fact, it is not so. Earth is at such appropriate distances from them that they appear equal in size, rule equal parts of the day, and provide a happy medium of warm environment. Such balance in their energies enables our existence as it empowers all types of life harmonic on earth. Their energies not only create our physical self but also exert tremendous influence on the subtle energy flow which sustains our life, determines its rhythm, and also defines its various aspects.

There are thousands of big and small astral channels called ***Nādis*** interwoven with the physical nervous system. They constitute the subtle body, wireless flow of psychic energy current called *Prāṇa*. *Prāṇa* is the primal ubiquitous energy that we naturally breathe which animates our life. Out of the network of some 72,000 large and small *Nādis* spread throughout the body, Ida, Pingala, and Sushumna are the three main channels running along the length of the spine. *Prāṇa* flowing through them carry the energy of the moon, the sun, and the earth respectively. They are united as a knot called *Mūkta Trivéni* in the subtle energy center, *Mulādhāra* Chakra near the base of spine from where they rise navigating upwards. The only other place where they all meet again is in *Ajna* Chakra in the forehead which is recognized as *Yūkta Trivéni.*

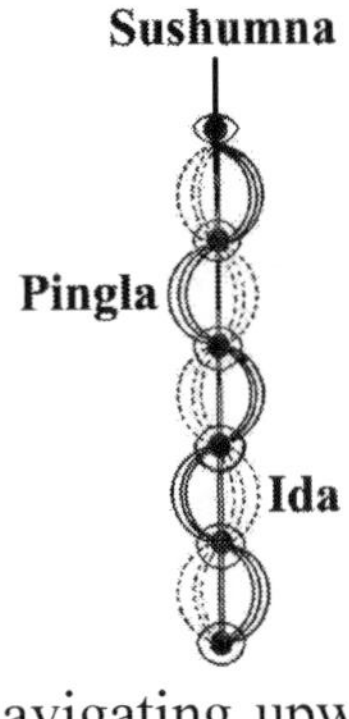

The central channel Sushumna is the path of enlightenment, neutral in nature. Attuned to the universal ethereal field, it duly holds the fire of our life. Ida and Pingala are intertwined around Sushumna in the form of a double-helical pathway all along the length of the spine. Ida moves predominantly on the left side, rules the smaller *Nādis* of the side, and then terminates into the left nostril. Pingala moves predominantly on the right side, rules the smaller *Nādis* of the side, and then terminates into the right nostril. Sushumna constantly balances the downward flowing lunar energy of Ida and the upward flowing solar energy of Pingala. The current of Ida is the manifesting power of Shakti that allows us to enjoy the world, *Bhukti*. The power of Pingala is the liberating force of Lord Shiva that ultimately releases us from the world, *Mukti*.

Prāṇa, the primordial energy of each breath sustains the energy flowing through Ida and Pingala, each connected to a nostril. Though *Prāṇa* equally energizes both the channels, it primarily flows through any one channel at any given time. This direction shifts periodically, the time and duration of which varies individually. When the flow is predominant in Pingala, we experience its activating and stimulating energy but when it mainly flows through Ida, it has the relaxing and soothing effect. When the energy flowing through them is balanced, then it creates the feeling of peace and harmony.

Ida and Pingala

The breath taken through the left nostril energizes Ida. Ida is –

- cold, feminine, pink in color, and represents moon
- energy of Shakti flowing downward, negative, and centripetal
- representing relaxation and para-sympathetic nervous system
- having influence on hypothalamus and the pituitary gland
- the flow of energy that helps in manifesting ourselves
- pull of our soul as well as our physical body
- an introvert channel that controls all the mental processes

The breath taken through the right nostril energizes Pingala. Pingala is –

- hot, masculine, blue in color, and represents sun
- energy of Shiva flowing upward, positive, and centrifugal
- representing action and sympathetic nervous system
- having influence on thalamus and hypothalamus
- responsible for seeking pleasures, doing things, and activity
- the flow of energy for the mind as well as spirit
- an extrovert channel that controls all the vital processes

Ida current is passionate in nature which nourishes and nurtures all personal emotions and raises desires. It develops strong feelings within us. It is the feminine aspects of our being, the source of love and affection, care and kindness. It also sustains the power of intuitive mind. Pingala conducts the dispassionate fuel powering the impersonal and rational mind which sustains all intellectual and logical thinking. It controls the masculine aspects of our self. Also, it carries the powerful energy of inquisitiveness, argument, and accomplishment. Whereas the power of Pingala raises metabolic rate and activates all physical systems, the calming energy of Ida lowers the same to the extent that a Yogi can stay breathless for hours by controlling its flow.

Sushumna

Sushumna is the ultrasonic core, white in color which holds our life energy. Representing the energy of earth, it is made of several layers. Starting from the base of spine, this luminous filament moves up to end in *Sahasrāra* Chakra. From the two points on it where Ida and Pingala cross over along the spine, other two points between their loop, and at the two ends where they all meet extend six major circular movements of Chakras. Within the core of Sushumna (*Tamas*) runs an adamantine channel called Vajrini (*Rajas*). Within Vajrini runs yet another channel called Chitrani (*Sattva*) within which runs the ultra-fine Brahmanādi, the conduit of awakened *Kuṇḍalinī*. *Kuṇḍalinī* is the dormant power that lies in a coiled form at the base of spine in everybody. Her rising through Sushumna is the liberating force that leads to enlightenment.

Ida, Pingala, and Sushumna are the nexus through which the creative aspect of Shakti, *Prakṛti* condenses her energy and gives rise to the physical form of a body effectively crystallizing individual consciousness. It is duly energized to life through the breath of *Prāṇa* consistent with the basic Life Principle of breathing. Whereas the axial pathway Sushumna carries the life sustaining energy of the soul, *Prāṇa* of each breath equally energizes the opposite streams of Ida and Pingala. It creates the circuit of energy which flows through their intertwined loop, animates all the psychic and spiritual realms, and co-ordinates various body-mind functions. This current also flows through the chain of Chakras extending from various points on Sushumna. These psychic centers are attuned to the latent power of *Kuṇḍalinī*. They affect the horizontal distribution of *Prāṇa* directing it through diverse systems of energy fields, each operating at different levels of consciousness. Each Chakra personalizes its flow by drawing our awareness, which is centered in Sushumna and duly externalizes it through these disparate fields. They constantly project the state of our inner self as we face the dance of dualities operating the outer world of lesser experience. Being the subtle energy receptors and responders, they rule our thought, speech, and action. They define our interaction with others as we enact and experience *Karma* while engaged in the inevitable encounter of life.

The pushing and pulling, centrifugal and centripetal energies of Ida and Pingala choreograph endless dance routines between their domains of rational and intuitional minds. We command or care, act or relax where each partner gets to lead the other at various times, one more than the other in a person. They determine individual choices and type of responses, individual nature and type of behavior. Dominating Ida gives nurturing, receptive, supportive, and caring personality who likes to introspect and prefers to stay in the background.

Dominating Pingala gives aggressive, forceful, creative, and very commanding personality who strives to achieve and stay at the forefront.

Specific breathing exercises of *Yoga* called *Prāṇayama* help us to regulate the flow of *Prāṇa* in these channels. Regular practice not only corrects the rhythm of its flow but also establishes control over its direction. These exercises are deliberate and conscious attempts to alter the way we normally breathe which organizes and vitalizes all psychic movements, *Vṛtti*. One simple yet powerful practice of alternate nostril breathing, *Nādi Shodhana* stimulates as well as equalizes its flow which synchronizes the breathing and thinking patterns. To control breath is very important for meditation, vital to success in its practices. It allows the suspension of all body-mind activities, pass beyond the state of breathlessness, and experience the superconscious realm.

Holy Scripture Devī Māhātmyam narrates a beautiful story of Lord Vishṇu who is engaged in a constant battle with two demons, Madhu and Kaitabh. Lord Vishṇu signifies the etheric energy of Sushumna who supports our existence. His fight represents the continuous struggle of our life, attempts of Sushumna to control and balance the energies of Ida and Pingala, Madhu and Kaitabh. By himself Lord Vishṇu fails to restrain or conquer them; with our life directed by mind and the senses, balancing the power of enjoyment, *Bhūkti* and spirituality, *Mūkti* so as to win the battle of life proves to be an ongoing challenge. However, finally Lord Vishṇu triumphs when he seeks the help of Divine Mother, Devī *Kuṇḍalinī*. She quietly lies coiled at the base of spine in every individual. When invoked and successfully awakened, she comes to his rescue. As she uncoils, she rises through the channel Sushumna by integrating the energies of Ida and Pingala. It leads to the state of eternal bliss, peace, and Supreme Consciousness. Thus Divine Mother helps us to achieve this ultimate goal of life.

Meeting of the energies of Ida, Pingala, and Sushumna is the union of sun, moon, and fire that signifies the ultimate liberation. Ida is associated with the river Ganga, Pingala with the river Yamuna, and Sushumna with the river Saraswati. This is the reason that taking a dip at the confluence of these, or any other three rivers, generally called Trivéni Sangam is considered holy in Hinduism. Upon death, a person's last rites are also preferably carried out at such a place by the family members. In the modern symbol of medicine, Caduceus, we see a winged staff. It represents the central channel Sushumna around which the two serpents, Ida and Pingala wind around starting from the base to the top. It signifies that these three channels are the basis of human life. Each of the two wings signifies the spiritual and the physical realm.

CHAKRAS

Subtle Energy Centers

We are always conscious about the physical body we see which allows us to transact the business of life and enjoy the lower material world. But we are usually not thoughtful of the subtle body which holds, as it duly interpenetrates this gross body. It is the flow of primal energy called *Prāṇa*, a homogeneous core that sustains all vital functions and animates our life. An etheric field with a luminous aura, it encircles and permeates, being outside yet within our physical body. As an interface which is visible only through clairvoyant vision, it integrates all the physical body functions with the emotional and mental world of the subtle mind. Thus, it vitalizes various tissues, organs, and systems while coordinating and regulating our thoughts and actions.

It consists of five different types of vital breaths, each having a specific seat in the body and associated with a particular function. They are known as ***Prāṇa*** (respiration), ***Apāna*** (excretion), ***Samāna*** (assimilation), ***Vyāna*** (distribution), and ***Udāna*** (regeneration). It flows through a wireless network of 72,000 big and small subtle energy channels called *Nādis* spread throughout the body. The strength, fluency, and harmony of the entire stream determine the overall quality, efficiency, and nature of all body-mind functions.

This energy flow is regulated through numerous big and small psycho-energy centers called Chakras spread throughout the body. They defy logic as they are also invisible, not having a physical presence. During their deep meditative state, sages and yogis inwardly perceive these noisy, bright, and colored spinning centers. They appear like vortices that float on the surface coinciding with the physical nerve ganglions. These wheel-like centers continuously process *Prāṇa* that is primarily received through the incoming breath. They assimilate, transform, and distribute the energy of this vital life force through *Nādis*. Their color, brightness, and size as well as the rhythm of their spinning are directly related to the amount of energy processed. The course of its flow connects the subtle mental realm with the gross physical body.

Of these, the group of seven Chakras beautifully strung along the length of the spine starting from the base to the top of the head constitutes the key chain of centers. The routine of their synergies continuously regulates the entire subtle system. As the core of cerebro-spinal system, they develop as the first step of our creation during gestation. *Kuṇḍalinī*, the creative energy of consciousness

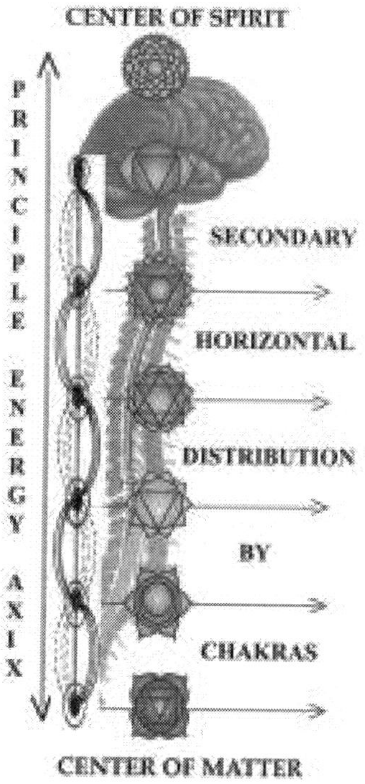

selectively allocates her specific sonic powers, in a step-down mechanism to successively establish these primary power centers as her seats. They, in turn, institute the entire subtle system of fine astral channels as the flow of *Prāṇa*. The channels then intricately incorporate various evolute elements around them to ultimately form the physical body. The upper two Chakras essentially govern the mental and the lower five the physical aspects of our being.

Of all these *Nādis*, Ida, Pingala, and Sushumna are the three major conduits running along the length of the spine. Ida and Pingala create the principle axis of energy flow in the body as we breathe in *Prāṇa*. A polar opposite of the other, they end in each nostril while running intertwined in a double helical pattern around the central channel Sushumna all along. The points on Sushumna where they cross-over encounter the pull of their opposing forces. As a result, a circular movement extends and radiates from them rotating like a fan. It assumes the shape of shining gemlike Chakras, each associated with different number of subtle channels through which the horizontal distribution of their energy takes place. Each Chakra pulsates with either centrifugal or centripetal current as it draws and balances the complementing energies of Ida and Pingala. It then organizes its stream which effects its horizontal distribution to sustain the energy field predominant at the level it governs. Each center acts as psycho-energetic screen duly 'personalizing' the flow of this universal life energy, *Prāṇa.* Vital and essential elements of our spiritual anatomy, they constantly externalize our awareness as functions of individual consciousness. Each Chakra is associated with specific powers and attributes, a positive as well as negative archetype.

Unique and one of a kind, the divine law of seven refers to the well-integrated seven universal energy planes in nature. Interestingly, they invariably underlie diverse systems of manifestation in each of which harmony of correspondence prevails. For example, the seven colors that create a brilliant spectrum and a fascinating rainbow constitute the illuminating system of visible light rays. There are seven major planet members in the family of our solar system and the same group of seven days, in the same order, makes each passing week. Also, each of these planets dominates a particular day of the week which, in turn is related to one of the seven spectral colors. Likewise, the seven key notes of music is an inexhaustible resource for all musicians to compose an endless variety of enchanting tunes. The nexus of seven Chakras, each corresponding to a particular energy plane duly conform to this intriguing pattern in nature. They team up to undertake the process of our individuation by building the distinct psycho-physical system of our being that they not only create during gestation but also operate, maintain, and administer through our life.

Creation of Chakras

The divine power of *Kuṇḍalinī* first establishes the subtlest center *Sahasrāra* Chakra attuned to the Cosmic Consciousness. It is visualized as a lotus of thousand petals located in the crown of the brain. It is the center of spirituality from which begins the finitization of each individual soul, in a body, on the earth through the cumulative function of other Chakras *Kuṇḍalinī* then creates. Creation of *Ajna* Chakra is the next step in this process associated with the development of the mental faculty. It is a lotus of just two petals located in the center of the forehead between the two eyebrows. One petal represents the transcendental world of the first Chakra above, attached at this center of clairvoyance with the other which represents the physical world ruled by all other Chakras below. Meditation helps in developing the power of intuition and light of this Chakra which constantly guides the path of our life.

Kuṇḍalinī further descends and discriminatively distributes the power of her root sounds, represented by various Sanskṛit alphabets to create five other Chakras in an increasing order of density. These centers rule the five physical elements necessary to make our gross body. The first in the line of their creation is *Vishuddhā* Chakra that rules the esoteric element ether, the subtlest of all and precursor of the other elements. A beautiful lotus with sixteen petals, each of its petals corresponds to a root sound of *Kuṇḍalinī* which contributes to the creation of associated channel. As the subtle center of expression, it connects us with others through the power of speech as we express our thoughts and communicate our views. Then, twelve grosser roots sounds of *Kuṇḍalinī* combine to create the lotus of twelve petals recognized as *Anāhata* Chakra. It is the divine center of love located near the heart which radiates endless love and bliss connecting all of humanity. Uniquely positioned between the three Chakras above and the three below, it is the center of their balance. It connects the Chakras on both sides through the element air it rules which moves in either direction.

Ten root sounds of *Kuṇḍalinī* vibrating at the same level of consciousness create the lotus of *Manipura* Chakra, the center of passion near the navel. Its fire empowers all our thoughts and actions. It directs our awareness to indulge in the

CHAKRAS		NUMBER OF PETALS	ELEMENT	SEED LETTER	LOKA
SAHASRĀRA (spirituality)		THOUSAND			SATYA
AJNA (intuition)	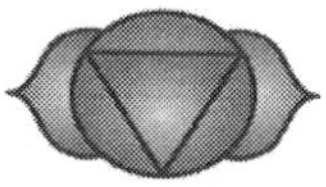	TWO	LIGHT	AUM	MAHAR
VISHUDDHĀ (expression)		SIXTEEN	ETHER	HAM	JNANA
ANĀHATA (love)	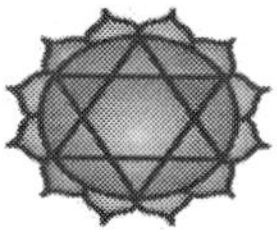	TWELVE	AIR	YAM	TAPAH
MANIPURA (power)		TEN	FIRE	RAM	SUVAHA
SWĀTHISHTHĀN (pleasure)		SIX	WATER	VAM	BHUVAHA
MULADHĀRA (survival)		FOUR	EARTH	LAM	BHUH

outer phenomenal world enabling us to enact *Karma* and experience life. Of the other remaining root powers of *Kuṇḍalinī*, six vibrate at the same level creating the lotus of *Swadhishthān* Chakra located near the sacral plexus which rules water. It is the center of emotions and sensations through which we delight in all worldly joys including the pleasure of sex. *Mulādhāra* Chakra is the center of grossest matter, solids formed by the last four root sounds of *Kuṇḍalinī* which lays the foundation and grounds our body on the earth. It is the center of survival in which now *Kuṇḍalinī* passively resides as she brings down our awareness and confines it at the level of the physical world.

Each Chakra is receptive to the vibratory energy of the related planetary field and resonates in harmony with its corresponding color. They invariably respond to the sound vibrations of those root sounds inherently linked to their subtle channels. It is a binding relation the power of *Kuṇḍalinī* establishes at the time of their creation. Operating in the universal mode, she successively establishes the series of these Chakras as active centers ruling typical principles of mind and matter called *Tattvas*. Simultaneously acting in the individuation mode, she also imparts them a unique makeup, quality, and character consistent with the latent tendencies of the embodied soul. Carrying impressions of the past traits, *Saṃskāra*, Chakras constantly translate them into the unique set of mental and physical state. It projects one of a kind personality defining the nature of character and level of awareness. The organized sequence of these subtle centers constructs seven steps of spiritual ladder, energy grid of seven planes that connects our earthly existence with heavenly realms. This colorful series shows diverse nature of sentient levels through which the same divine force operates. Synergies of these well differentiated energy planes govern all kinds of existence; the microcosm of human being as well as the macrocosm of the entire universe.

Each Chakra expresses varying combination of *Sattva* - mode of purity and balance, *Rajas* - mode of energy and action, and *Tamas* - mode of matter and inertia. The lowest Chakra, *Mulādhāra*, ruled by *Tamas* is the densest and darkest of all which grounds and establishes us in the physical world. The uppermost Chakra, *Sahasrāra* ruled by *Sattva* is the brightest and subtlest of all attuned to the universal mind. Between these two Chakras predominant in matter and spirit lie five other Chakras. Each has a gradually decreasing density, *Tamas* whereas increasing subtlety, *Sattva* as we move up. *Rajas* is predominant in *Manipura* Chakra, the center of passion located near the navel which decreases in its intensity as we move away in either direction. Each Chakra above *Mulādhāra* Chakra represents a successive higher plane of consciousness that offer an ever expanding view of Reality. As a Loka that represents spiritual subtlety, each plane has a more efficient level of vibrations than the one below. Besides these Chakras of higher consciousness, there are also seven other Chakras of lower consciousness below *Mulādhāra* Chakra known as Talas.

Characteristics of Chakras

As centers of transformation, the energy patterns of Chakras evolve throughout the life. And they eternally perpetuate through life cycles. Upon birth, they develop and function as per the accumulated *Karma* of past lives to expose and involve us in the world such that it gives fitting life experiences. Genetic inheritance and health status, upbringing and environment during early years of growth, the living conditions and surroundings have a great influence on them. Working in harmony with each other, they direct *Prāṇa* to energize, activate, and animate different aspects of our life. They constitute a unique operating system, a personalized program for everybody. As constantly updating log centers of the soul, they carry the impressions of all aspects of our current inner being. These are variously projected through our actions and expressions that orchestrate typical interactions with the others as we react and respond to the forces of the outside world. It gives rise to such situations and circumstances as to determine the paradigm of our life. Each passing experience leaves an impression on them that directs the path of life as destiny, *Prārabdha*.

Each Chakra administers, as it empowers an index of multifaceted aspects of the level it operates and governs. A few of these are the area of physical body, the kind of element, the stage of growth, the mental attitude, the aptitude for activity, and the level of consciousness. All Chakras contribute archetype patterns of attitudes and emotions that, together, define the overall dimensions of our life. Being the subtle conduits of consciousness that operate at different levels, they offer their own perspective and meanings to a particular expression, event, or experience at any given time. All inherent immeasurable traits of the soul, imperceptible to the mind and senses are actively translated by these psycho-energy portals into the variety of human experiences.

Each of them operates at its own pace and efficiency that often changes with the time, event, and circumstances. Harmony and balance between them, a measure of the degree of polarization determines their overall effectiveness. Chakras operating at optimum level are expressions of ideal state. Overactive Chakra concentrates and accumulates energy that indicates fixation, over indulgence, and predominance of the aspects it governs. A dysfunctional Chakra, by avoiding energy flow, blocks reception of stimulus that restricts the play of its characteristics. Both are undesirable extremes that manifest as chronic ailments detrimental to lead a normal and balanced life.

As an individual interacts with people and involves in everyday situations, this routine reinforces impressions. The established pattern of activities forms a habit. Our awareness is drawn to the world by those Chakras through which we habitually perceive the reality as it elevates the level of consciousness at those levels. Therefore, the levels to which all attention, endeavors of life, and energy of action gets directed dominates outlook of life. Most people spend their life stuck in habit patterns around the aspects governed by the lower three Chakras: *Mulādhāra* related to grounding, existence, memory, and survival, *Swadhishthān* governing sense gratification, pleasure, and sex, and *Manipura* associated with money, power, and control. When their awareness rises from such worldly life and ignorance at least to the level of fourth Chakra, *Anāhata*, it connects them to the realm of universal love bestowing lasting happiness.

All Chakras are interconnected relays that work like the gears in continuum supported, controlled, and administered by the power of *Kuṇḍalinī*. They receive as well as radiate vibrations of specific frequencies to the environment. It has a positive as well as negative influence on the self and surrounding. As they also effect and influence each other, they need to be in balance and operate efficiently. Inefficiency of Chakras due to blockages created by past *Karma* prevents free flow and uniform distribution of *Prāṇa* within the subtle system. Restrictions so imposed by *Karmic* dust obscure Chakras to be dull, dark, and lusterless that inhibits them from operating at optimum level. It emerges as personality patterns and also manifests as physical ailments. It is the cause of rift between thoughts, desires, and perception and the ordinary sense of reality surrounding the facts of life; the root cause of all problems. Also, persistent prevalence of stressful and unresolved situations triggers protection and defense mechanisms. They initiate contraction and establish inhibition patterns. In severe cases, they may block Chakras to cause permanent and irreversible damage.

Specific spiritual methods like breathing exercises, *Yoga* postures, mantra Japa, and meditation practices clean, energize, and activate Chakras to make them brighter, vibrant, and efficient. As we meditate upon the divine, transcendental spiritual energy gets concentrated in *Ajna* Chakra in the forehead which duly energizes all other psycho-energetic centers. Colored gemstones and crystals as well as energized yantras also influence the vibratory fields of Chakras. It harmonizes the flow of *Prāṇa* within the body to enhance the efficiency of all body-mind functions. One feels energized and exudes confidence, acquires clarity of thoughts in facing daily challenges, acts to realize the true mental and spiritual potential, and experiences an everlasting peace and harmony.

Seed letter and Bija Mantra

As repository of psychic energy, Chakras are also symbolized as colored lotuses. They blossom from Sushumna *Nādi* and have different number of petals, each representing a subtle energy channel. Each channel distributes energy of a specific root sound, the associated Sanskṛit alphabet visualized as written over it. It signifies the vibrations of specific intensity that it resonates with, revealed to us through its characteristic sound. Vibratory energy of the petals converges to build its lotus as nucleus of their active distribution center. Each lotus gently vibrates as it receives, combines, and processes these energies to organize its stream. The rhythm of its movement produces a subtle sound typical to each Chakra which is known as its seed letter. These characteristic sounds are heard by a yogi in deep state of meditation through which they identify Chakra.

The number of channels of all Chakras and the Sanskṛit alphabets are the same as each channel has evolved from the energy of the associated alphabet sound. This powerful relation, established during gestation between the alphabets and subtle channels is the basis of our creation. Therefore, Sanskṛit mantras have an instant influence and immediate impact on the energy flow of the entire subtle system. Vibrations of each manta selectively determine the subtle channels that they influence, stimulate, and empower. Rhythmic vibrations of mantra chanting resonate with these channels in an order that evokes, amplifies, and armors their positive qualities. Therefore, it is one of the most effective tools used to purify and correct the energy flow within the subtle system.

A Chakra is an expression of consciousness at a specific frequency presided over by a deity. The seed letter of Chakra is also called a Bija mantra which is the natural name of its presiding deity. Each Chakra is an extremely subtle force representing a specific seat and power of *Kuṇḍalinī* that animates the matters of the level it administers. Chain of these Chakras, together with the latent energy of consciousness which resides in *Mulādhāra* Chakra constitute the entire body of *Kuṇḍalinī*. She is the Divine Mother who holds our body in etheric matter through life and limits human experience to the physical world we live in. Therefore, we are oblivious to other realms of existence where consciousness manifests at successive higher levels. Just as the infra-red and the ultra-violet light rays having frequencies outside the visible spectrum are beyond our visual experience, though all these realms manifest simultaneously, we are not aware of them. Perception of human mind, a tool excellent for use in the physical world is limited by senses. Therefore, it fails to comprehend the other subtle realities and conceive the totality of existence at various sentient levels. Thereby, it keeps our awareness restricted to the lower physical world, *Saṃsāra*.

However, with the advancement in spiritual practices, as awareness expands, an access to these subtler realms is achieved. Spirituality is a scientific quest for the infinite and eternal, a mission to explore the metaphysical aspects of life. It is not merely intellectual. Acquiring higher knowledge does not grant an access to these realms. Mostly it is an experience of direct engagement at various levels as one rises and lives through the consciousness of each Chakra. When the chosen spiritual practices are carried out diligently and cultivated sincerely, with complete faith and self-surrender, preferably under the guidance of a Guru, one can advance, access, experience, and realize.

CHAKRAS OF HIGHER CONSCIOUSNESS

Mulādhāra Chakra: Located near the perineum between the genitals and the anus, this is the root Chakra related to memory, instinct, security, and survival. It is a lotus with four petals each symbolizing a subtle energy channel and a specific root-sound associated with this Chakra. One petal governs memories of the past lives and the other three those of the current life. It governs over body, the necessities to sustain it, and matters of everyday life locating and connecting us with a place and surroundings. Ruled by *Tamas* Guṇa and planet Saturn, it represents Bhūh Loka, earth element, and solids that ground us to the physical realm. Its malfunction causes weight problems, hemorrhoids, constipation, sciatica, and knee problems. The seed sound of this Chakra is Lam and its color is red. All the subtle energy channels originate from here. This is the abode of Lord Gaṇesha and the latent *Kuṇḍalinī* energy.

Swadhishthān Chakra: It is located in the sacrum and therefore, also known as Sacral Chakra. It is related to the base emotions, sexuality, and creativity. A six petal lotus, it symbolizes six subtle energy channels and six root-sounds associated with it. Most people live and think with reasoning and habit patterns at this level. Bhūvah Loka and water element are represented by this Chakra governed by Moon. All forces of the polarities and dualities manifesting as attraction of the opposites are experienced at this level. It rules genitals, circulatory system, kidney, and bladder. Inefficient working of it causes problems with money, power, and control issues with other people, impotence, sexual dysfunction, allergies, uterine or kidney trouble, and stiff lower back. The seed sound of this Chakra is Vam, the color is orange.

Manipura Chakra: This Chakra is located near the navel region in the solar plexus. A transition from base emotions of Swadhishthān to complex emotions occurs at this level. It governs will power and energy, digestion and assimilation, pancreas and muscles. A lotus with ten petals, it symbolizes ten subtle energy channels and ten root-sounds associated with this Chakra. Five petals that face up add power to spiritual consciousness of the two Chakras above, and five petals facing down add power to the worldly consciousness of the two Chakras below. This Chakra represents Sūvaha Loka, Fire, *Rajas* Guṇa, and is ruled by Mars. Its malfunction causes digestive disorders, ulcers, diabetes, and hypoglycemia. The seed sound of this Chakra is Ram, the color is yellow. This is the level at which the force of electromagnetism operates...

Anāhata Chakra: This is called the heart Chakra related to complex emotions, compassion, love, and equilibrium. It is the center of perception and insight that balances the pull of lower three Chakras of physical and emotional centers with that of the higher three mental and spiritual centers. Rising from self-involved thoughts and activities, at this level we begin to move outward building relationships. It is related to the thymus gland. A lotus with twelve petals symbolizes twelve subtle energy channels and twelve root sounds associated with it. Governed by Venus, it represents Tapah Loka. Asthma, bronchitis, heart and lung disease, and high blood pressure result due to its malfunctioning. The seed sound of this Chakra is Yam, the color is green.

Vishuddhā Chakra: This Chakra, governed by Mercury is located in the throat parallel to the thyroid gland. It is related to verbal communication and physical growth symbolized by a lotus with sixteen petals representing sixteen subtle energy channels and sixteen root-sounds. Universal love and kinship with the entire mankind develops at this center transcending the limitations of distance and location. The sound vibrations at this level correspond to the consciousness of Jnāna Loka. Inefficient working of the Chakra results in expression issues and inability to speak up for oneself, sore throat, hearing problems, colds, shyness, laryngitis, depression, and stiff neck. The element it rules is ether, the seed sound is Ham, and the color is bright blue.

Ajna Chakra: Located in the forehead in the middle between the two eyebrows, Ajna Chakra is also known as the third eye. It is linked to the pineal gland and related to the light and awareness. It is the center of divine insight and direct cognition. A lotus with two petals symbolizes two subtle energy channels and two root-sounds associated with it. One petal stands for the state of mind and the other for the state of consciousness. This is the center upon which we concentrate during meditation. With the opening of this Chakra, the life we experience with the mind and senses transforms as we gradually enter the transcendental world through it. It is associated with Mahar Loka. It transcends time and planet Jupiter governs it. Malfunction of this Chakra causes blindness, headache, and the nightmares. Its seed sound is Aum, the color is indigo.

Sahasrāra Chakra: This crown Chakra of consciousness is the seat of Lord Shiva which is beyond the ego of manifested world. Most subtle of all, it integrates all other Chakras of our subtle system. It is linked with the pituitary gland and thus affects hormones and central nervous system. Associated with thoughts and Satya Loka, it is a lotus with a thousand petals, arranged in 20 layers. When activated by the rising power of *Kuṇḍalinī*, these petals open up leading to the state of enlightenment. It has an aperture called Brahmarandhra through which the soul leaves the body at the time of death. Its malfunction gives rise to depression, alienation, confusion, and boredom. Violet is the color.

CHAKRAS OF LOWER CONSCIOUSNESS

Atala: It is the first lower Chakra that is located in the hips region. This Chakra governs the individual state of fear and lust.

Vitala: It is the second lower Chakra that is located in the thighs. It is a center of anger and resentment developing from despair and frustration.

Sutala: The third lower Chakra is located in the knees. It governs jealousy, inferiority, inadequacy, and helplessness.

Talātala: The fourth lower Chakra is located in the calves. It governs greed and deceit that manifest due to prolonged confusion.

Rasatala: It is the fifth lower Chakra that is located in the ankles. It is home to lower animal nature and total selfishness.

Mahatala: The sixth lower Chakra is located in the feet. Having total lack of conciseness and deep depression, it is the state which leads to stealing.

Patala: The seventh and lowest Chakra is located in the sole of the feet. It is the state of destructiveness, revenge, torture, and even murder.

Nuggets of Wisdom

All actions motivated by power, pleasure, or profit create obstacles whereas all selfless actions remove them while crossing the sea of life.

We gain worldly knowledge and imagine that we make our destiny but the fact is we wander aimlessly from birth to birth driven by desires and fears.

Living in the material world is a life in darkness. Living in the spiritual world only is a life in greater darkness..

KUṆḌALINĪ

The Dormant Power

Kuṇḍalinī is a reservoir of latent energy that resides at the base of spine of every human being. She is innately located in *Mulādhāra* Chakra, the lowest psycho-energy center of our subtle body. Lying in a coiled form of three and a half time at the mouth of central energy channel, Sushumna, she keeps it closed. Psycho-spiritual in nature and an aspect of Shakti, she is also known by names such as 'Liquid Fire' or 'Liquid Light'. Āgama and Tantric scriptures give all the details about this 'Serpent Power' that usually remains dormant throughout the life for most of the people. During gestation, she actively catalyzes formation of the mind and matter of the fetus preparing it to enter the realm of the physical world. Her creative energy is the evolutionary force responsible for our coming into being. However, once her job is done, her left over aspect becomes passive and lies peacefully, in a state of slumber, as static potential energy.

Prāṇa, the body of our breath is her dynamic aspect with which she actively maintains human existence by respiration. *Prāṇa* is the primal cosmic energy, in transcendent state that becomes immanent in an individual as it expresses as vital functions and animates all life. It consists of five different types of vital breaths essential to our life known as ***Prāṇa*** (respiration), ***Apāna*** (excretion), ***Samāna*** (assimilation), ***Vyāna*** (distribution), and ***Udāna*** (regeneration). They together represent the subtle, vital, and homogenous core that not only energizes, but regulates and co-ordinates the actions of our physical body with the mind. During meditation, the focus of our awareness on the pause between inhalation and exhalation gives the ultimate experience of the Absolute. If *Prāṇa* leaves the body and does not come back, it marks the end of life.

In fact it is *Prāṇa* that initiates the creation of our body at the completion of which its residual aspect assumes the dormant form of *Kuṇḍalinī*. The subtle sound Aum is the source of *Prāṇa* energy. It differentiates into vibrations of various sound frequencies in ethereal continuum, *Ākāśa* each carrying specific power and potency to create a physical form. They give rise to several subtle energy centers, Chakras, each operating at different levels of consciousness. Each center then incorporates the corresponding evolute element to form our physical body. At the end of this individuation enterprise, the remaining energy resides as *Kuṇḍalinī* in the lowest center, *Mulādhāra* which governs the solid matter. It is her divine power that holds our body during lifetime, the anchor that grounds us on earth and directs our awareness on the physical plane.

Kuṇḍalinī energy is also the source of unmanifest form of speech known as ***Pārā***. When it develops an impulse to manifest, it is known as ***Pashyanti***. *Pārā* and *Pashyanti* are too subtle to know and understand. As such an instinct to express rises and gradually moves upward, it selectively gathers the typical sound energies left with the Chakras during their creation. Each of these is a root sound, a deity with specific powers that holds our body and energizes our life on the material plane. Therefore, they all are respectfully called Mother, *Mātṛkā*. Their vibrations serve as the sound source of all kinds of languages. The impulse of *Pashyanti* ultimately transforms to the successive grosser levels known as ***Madhyamā***, the mental sounds of thought that finally expresses as ***Vaikhari***, the articulate speech. All mental powers originate from *Kuṇḍalinī* and operate through the body of these sound energies. It is this incessant flow of her energy that, as *Mahāsaraswati* Devi is the giver of ideas and intuition, higher knowledge and thoughts, ability to communicate and speak.

Thus, *Kuṇḍalinī* begins as the universal kinetic energy, *Prāṇa*. After she creates mind and matter of the baby in a mother's womb, her residual power resides as the static potential energy at the base of spine. *Prāṇa* of each breath animates the sound energies of each Chakra she holds which sustains our life. These sounds govern the psychic and spiritual realms that direct the path of our life. Upon death, with the last breath of *Prāṇa*, she leaves with these sounds to end the life she had so intricately created and efficiently maintained. Thus, she is *Sṛsti-sthiti-layātmika*, the compassionate mother who creates, sustains, and dissolves the life and body of every human being. She is the divine force that transcends the entire universe. In fact, she is the mother of the universe.

Puruśa and *Prakṛti*

Transcendental polarization of the casual sound Aum is the self-igniting spark that creates *Nāda Brahman*, functional bipolar Reality of two aspects, that of static 'I' ness, *Ahaṃ* and the active 'This', *Idaṃ*. *Ahaṃ* is also recognized as Lord Shiva whereas the spark behind the polarization that develops everything else, *Idaṃ* is the primal energy, Shakti. This primordial couple constitutes the first pair of ontological category, cause of subsequent development of 34 other lower categories in creation, all characterized as *Tattvas*. These 36 principles are the cosmic planes, building blocks of the universe that represent order of logical evolution. They are classified into three groups: five pure universal, seven pure-impure limiting, and twenty-four impure material principles.

Shaivait School explicates the making of discrete spirit, ***Puruśa***, an individual soul as the first individuation principle. A part of non-discrete Lord Shiva,

36 TATTVAS

(Building Blocks of The Universe)

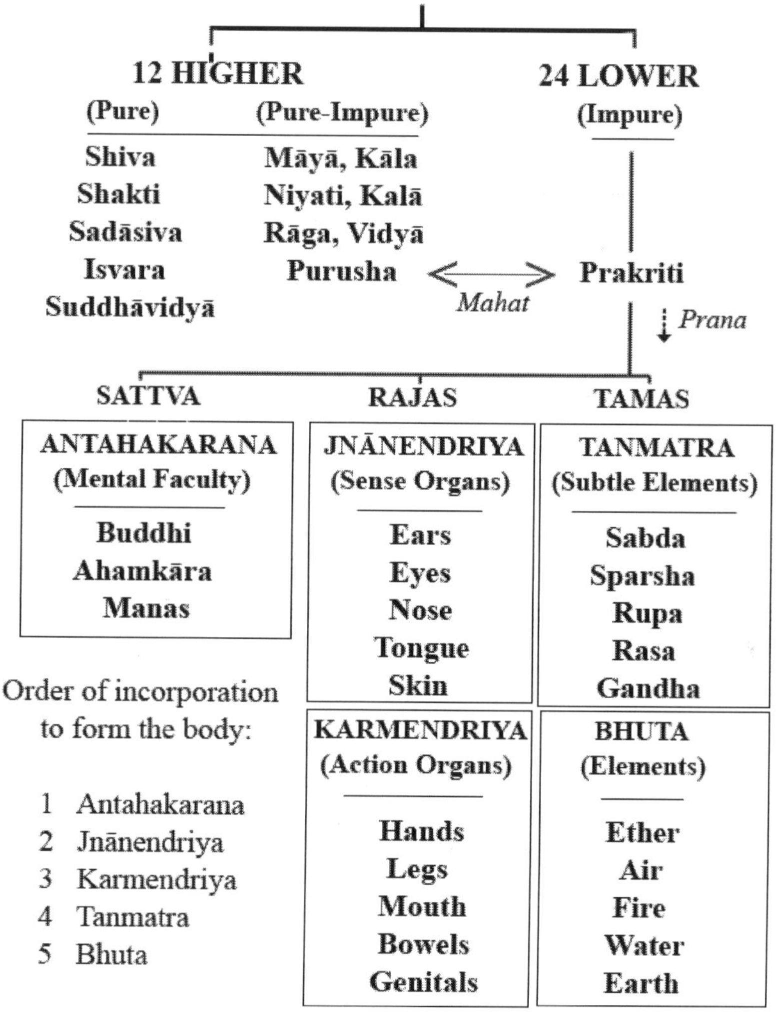

Atman achieves the distinct state of *Puruśa* as it gets conditioned by *Māyā* through other pure-impure limiting principles she rules as explained on Page 90. The second principle of individuation is the finitising aspect of Shakti, ***Prakṛti*** who governs the lowest impure material level. She rules the 23 impure material principles, *Tattvas* in the plane. She exhibits two kinds of powers, the power to veil, *Āvarna* as she covers *Puruśa* in various ways and the power to project, *Vikshepa* through which she brings it in the material plane.

Puruśa and *Prakṛti* are the two individuation principles of spirit and matter.

Prakṛti, the substratum of universal primordial energy is one whereas *Puruśa*, presupposition of individual consciousness are many. Only when *Puruśa* activates her, it ensues in physical creation. During the classical age, doctrine of *Sānkhya* enumerated the steps through which *Puruśa* of latent tendencies, *Saṃskāra* positions with *Prakṛti* towards its finite manifestation. Whereas the casual body of *Puruśa* is unmanifest and formless, when it activates *Prakṛti*, it breathes life into matter. *Prakṛti* is the source of all the mental and material principles who operates through three fundamental modes - *Sattva*, *Rajas*, and *Tamas*. In her state of rest, these are inactive having a perfect equilibrium.

At the time of conception, time element of *Puruśa* in contact with inactive *Prakṛti* gently agitates and stimulates her. It disturbs the equilibrium of her three modes effectively activating her. As these two individuation principles come together, they primarily establish the consciousness-matter field of creative cosmic intelligence, ***Mahat*** as the seed of individuation. It is an implicit center of operation setting the stage of its individualization. All implicitly contained particulars brought in by *Puruśa* are made explicit by *Prakṛti* from here as per the blue print of its destined life experience, *Prārabdha* it carries. Its manifestation process is catalyzed by *Prāṇa*, the primordial force. *Prakṛti* and *Prāṇa* are different aspects of Shakti. Specific combination of her three modes, *Sattva*, *Rajas*, and *Tamas* creates to provide the other 23 subtle and gross elements necessary for physical manifestation of *Puruśa*. Thus, the pure and unbound individual soul now begins to have the limits and boundary of a body by incorporating various elements through *Prāṇa*.

In a step-down mechanism from spirit to matter, *Prāṇa* that ultimately resides as *Kuṇḍalinī* initiates the process of creation. Starting with the mental faculty, three principle *Tattvas* of **Buddhi** (intelligence), ***Ahamkāra*** (personal ego), and ***Manas*** (mind) are first incorporated, in that order, to create the ***Antahakarana*** (mental faculty). *Antahakarana* is the primary agent that effectively veils and conditions consciousness. Its revealing power is based on the inherent tendencies, *Saṃskāra* of *Puruśa* that operates in various degrees during the life. Brain is its physical organ, encased in a solid skull and yet, its active force radiates through senses like a ray of light which experiences the characteristics of outer objects. Its creation is followed by assimilation of the *Tattvas* of subtle organs; ***Jnānendriya*** (sense organs) and ***Karmendriya*** (action organs) that associate with *Manas*. *Manas* is the chief controller of all senses, perception, and action.

Then, to create the subtle body, *Kuṇḍalinī* descends further to create various energy centers called Chakras by distributing different root powers, *Mātṛkā* among them. At each level, as she leaves her specific powers with a Chakra, she loses that level of her energy as well as subtlety progressively becoming grosser. The Chakras, as subtle psycho-energy centers, in turn, use these powers to create subtle energy channels, incorporate various ***Tanmatras*** (subtle elements), and associate them with *Jnānendriya. Tanmatras* are the essences, five subtle energies of the senses whose action relates the consciousness of sense organs to the gross forms of matter it then recognizes. Vibration of *Prāṇa* in *Tanmatras* produces the other four material *Tattvas* of air, fire, water, and earth. They originate from the subtlest substrate, esoteric element Ether, precursor of all sensible matter. These five elements, ***Panchamahābhuta*** which are necessary for manifestation on the physical plane are incorporated at last. As the densest *Tattva*, earth is finally created and incorporated, this self-restricting process confines the residual power of *Prāṇa* to the extent of static *Kuṇḍalinī.*

The corporeal energy of Devī *Kuṇḍalinī* rests at the perineum near the base of spine in *Mulādhāra* Chakra, the subtle center of her location. Holding the ground and lying quietly, here she is inactive. The group of Chakras she created along the spinal column appear like a series of colored flowers on a string. She always stays connected with them, supporting and filling them with her psychic energy. She is also a repository of the past and present memories and experiences. Exerting her influence from the sacral plexus of her sacred location, she controls their power and regulates their action governing different planes of consciousness through them. Source of all kinds of thoughts and ideas, she determines the nature and extent to which they energize and animate various aspects of our life. They together form the entire body of *Kuṇḍalinī.*

The return journey

The awakening of dormant *Kuṇḍalinī*, followed by its ascent up the central pathway, Sushumna marks the return journey. Sacred path of enlightenment, it grants us release from the impurities and bondages of the world, *Saṃsāra.* It is her binding power which encases our soul to bring us in this world, whereas the grace of her releasing force grants us the ultimate liberation. *Kuṇḍalinī* meditation is a magnificent practice, well perfected for the adepts to pursue this path. But to awaken her is the biggest hurdle to overcome, a deeply involving and an extremely challenging task. Even an entire lifetime of spiritual pursuits and practices, *Sādhana* may not be enough to reach this prime objective.

To stimulate and activate her, external pressure is applied on the center of her location by exoteric practices like many *Hatha Yoga* postures. Many Tantric practices tap the most powerful source of energy in the body, aroused sexual energy, in their esoteric attempt to awaken her. Usually the grace and guidance of a Guru is needed to awaken as well as to control her once awakened. Her awakening triggers dramatic physical, emotional, and mental changes in the body that may have an adverse effect. Ferocious goddess *Mahākāli* Devī portrays the wild, deadly, and destructive power of improperly awakened *Kuṇḍalinī* that creates restlessness, conflict, and violence spinning out of control. In iconography, she is seen trampling consciousness, Lord Shiva. Goddess Durgā also represents her active power, but properly awakened and under control which destroys negativity and ignorance. It also imparts devotion and bliss spiritually elevating and benefiting the practitioner.

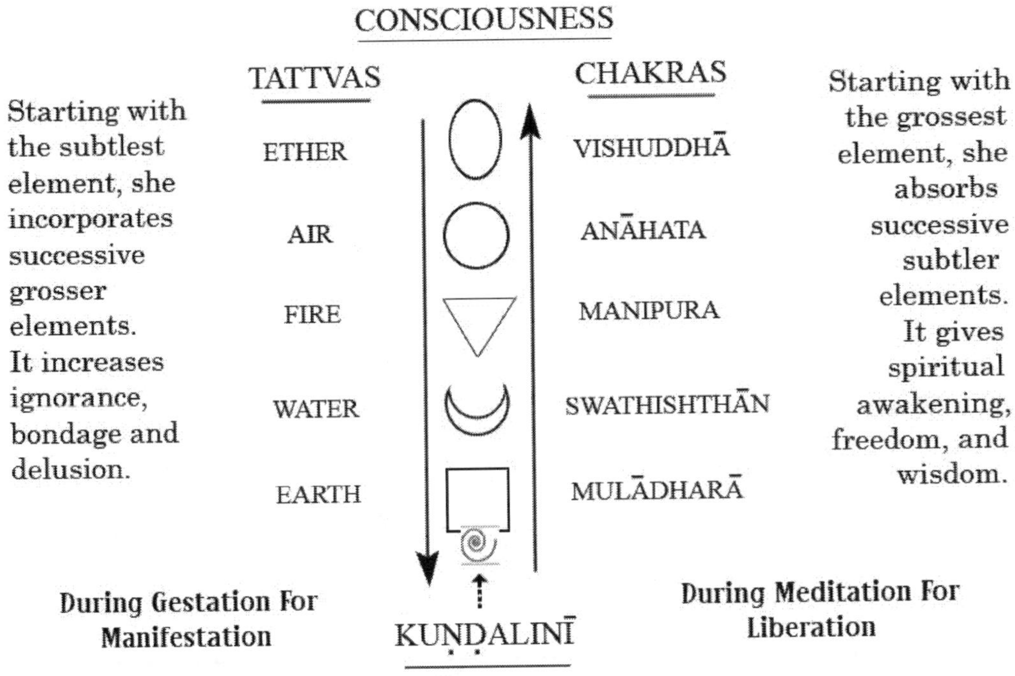

THE ACTION OF KUṆḌALINĪ

Ida and Pingala are the two major channels through which *Prāṇa* energy flows in the subtle body to sustain our life. This dynamic aspect of *Kuṇḍalinī* is duly exploited to activate the Goddess power of inactive *Kuṇḍalinī* at the base of the spine. Various *Yoga* practices, breath control, mantra chanting, and meditation techniques help us to control, concentrate, and direct the flow of *Prāṇa* in the body as desired. The accumulated power of *Prāṇa* is made to stop at the mouth of Sushumna which acts like a spark. As it ignites and awakens *Kuṇḍalinī*, she uncoils and opens up the mouth of Sushumna. By integrating the *Prāṇa* energy, she rises up through this subtle channel. Some people in the spiritual path experience this happening spontaneously.

There are three knots that *Kuṇḍalinī* needs to break to complete her ascent up the spine. These are the specific blockages, at different levels that attach us to this world. The first of these, *Brahmagranthi* is located in the densest psycho energy center, *Mulādhāra* Chakra. Predominant in the *Tamas* Guṇa and related to the physical body, it heavily obscures consciousness as it attaches us to the material world. The awakening of *Kuṇḍalinī* breaks this most difficult knot. The second knot, *Vishṇugranthi* is predominant in *Rajas* Guṇa and relates to the subtle body. It is located in *Anāhata* Chakra, near the heart. It is the seat of all passions, desires, and emotional attachments. The last knot, *Rūdragranthi* is located in *Ājna* Chakra which is in the forehead between the two eyebrows. It relates to the casual body where *Sattva* Guṇa prevails. It attaches us to the mind creating bondage of thoughts and mental powers. As *Kuṇḍalinī* rises up the spine, she successively breaks these other two knots to ultimately reach the subtlest psycho energy center, *Sahasrāra* Chakra, her ultimate destination.

Self Realization

When awakened, starting with the energies of four root powers of *Mulādhāra* Chakra, she successively gathers those of all other Chakras as she moves up. These are the specific energies that she had left behind at the time of their creation. By recollecting these powers, she effectively absorbs the energies of their presiding deities. Thereby, she dissolves the associated elements, *Tattvas* and overcomes these material obstacles. Each of her rising step leads to higher level of awakening often associated with mystical experiences. As impurities and pollutants blocking subtle pathways are removed, each gross element gets progressively absorbed into the higher subtler element. As a result, Chakras get purified, fully energized, and vivified. They become bright and radiant, get well integrated and harmonious which heightens their activities and expands their abilities. At each level, to the extent this mission is accomplished, the bondage and impurity of mind and matter is reduced and the level of consciousness is proportionally raised resulting in rejuvenation.

This process of Self-discovery reverses the conditioning of individual soul, *Puruśa* that occurred during its embodiment. As the gross matter dissolves in subtle mind, the mind then gets absorbed in the casual consciousness that finally dissolves in *Mahā Bindu* in *Sahasrāra* Chakra. Rising of *Kuṇḍalinī* gradually weakens various sheaths of the soul which consequently expands awareness. It also effectively erases all types of *Karmic* impressions from the subconscious thereby transmuting perception. It is a state of resolution of all dualities leading to the attainment of a state of equanimity. The adept is suffused with extraordinary powers as the body radiates superhuman energies.

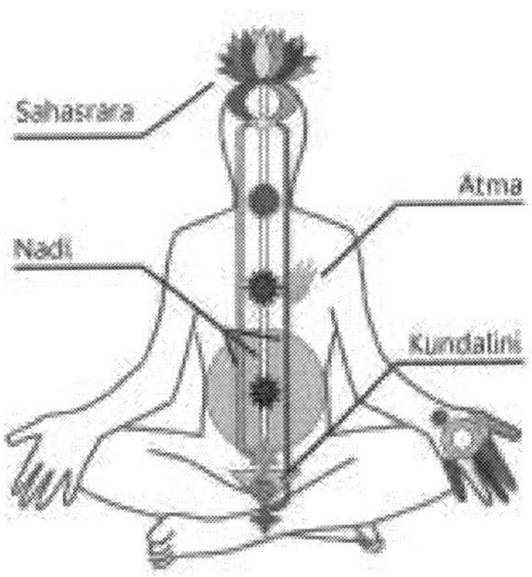

With her rising, heavenly nectar in the head melts and trickles down in drops. As she ultimately reaches the crown of the brain after gathering the energy of all 50 root sounds, the nectar falling down reaches the base of the spine. It duly permeates and drenches the whole body. The blessed adept is completely immersed in non-dualistic bliss by attaining this most coveted state of *Samadhi*. In this supreme state, the universal vision of being one with all, *Sarvaṃ Khalvidaṃ Brahman* is experienced.

Every spiritual experience has the power to blossom Devī *Kuṇḍalinī*. As we focus and contemplate on the Supreme, we try to awaken and raise her with the inner peace of silent meditative mind. We need her favor in our spiritual quest constantly in search of the divine. It eventually consumes every other inferior interest as it progressively becomes our most profound aspiration. But only when the divine grace descends through the crown of head, it awakens Devī *Kuṇḍalinī*. It is the sacred power of a liberating force. Her rising is the fire which engulfs, breaks, and burns down all kinds of negativities and impurities into ashes. Thereby, she ultimately grants us a release, *Moksha*. When so awakened, her creative energy endows power, health, wealth, and success. For artists, singers, and poets awakening of *Kuṇḍalinī* is a boon, boosting their imagination and all types of creativity. She unleashes the unlimited potential that exists in all human beings. She is the source of all knowledge and bliss.

Devī *Kuṇḍalinī* is the divine energy of human consciousness, *Cit*-Shakti and therefore, possesses the power to transform it. Her energy connects our physical body with our inner self, our soul. Her flow, when directed towards the body is the all-powerful sexual energy that is meant for procreation. Its immense driving force, temporary power of her intensity, and the ultimate experience of ecstatic illumination during sexual orgasm is common to everyone. When this flow is controlled and redirected inwards, towards our soul, this transmigration results in spiritual elevation. We rediscover our true nature beyond the confinement of space-time we live in. As the awakened *Kuṇḍalinī* rises, she pierces and crosses all Chakras one at a time. But even then, she returns again and again to be at her place of resting. When she finally reaches the crown of the brain to unite with Lord Shiva, she still remains connected to her base in *Mulādhāra* Chakra. In this state, the soul experiences its own true nature and unity with Transcendental Consciousness. People who have successfully awakened this energy have paranormal powers and access to higher realms of extrasensory perception.

TRIAD OF GUṆAS

Sattva, Rajas, and Tamas

Prakṛti is the creative aspect of Shakti responsible for all physical creation. As the efficient cause, she is the one who creates and as the material cause, she is the matters of creation. Once disturbed and excited, she has the power to move and act, condense into numerous elements, and confine consciousness by veiling it in various ways within the physical boundary of a body consisting mind and matter. This step-down embodiment of the transcendental soul, *Puruśa* to immanent and finite form of an individual is a quantum process. Shakti's innumerable energies in all types of manifestation have three fundamental attributes, the modes or Guṇas through which she operates. They are the mode of goodness or neutral force *Sattva* (sentient), the mode of passion or centrifugal force *Rajas* (mutative), and the mode of ignorance or centripetal force *Tamas* (static). Hence, she is often called *tri-guṇatmika*. She moves through these modes and just like the three primary colors that variously combine to give rise to an incomprehensible array of other colors and shades, she designs and shapes, creates and sustains endless forms of life and matter.

Even in the subtle substratum of unmanifest *Prakṛti*, these three Guṇas are present separately, but quite balanced, equipoise and therefore, inactive. When duly inspired, gently provoked, and so catalyzed by the desire of the soul, *Puruśa* to manifest, the polarity movement of *Rajas* is set into motion initiating the expansion phase. Sustained by *Sattva* and contained by *Tamas*, it deftly weaves the three Guṇa strands in innovative combinations, imparts them distinctive qualities, and creates the fabric of all objective reality. In each individual, they come together in specific proportion to create diverse system of energy fields constituting a unique corpus of the mind and body. *Rajas* operates between the subtle mind attuned to *Sattva* and the confines of the gross body, *Tamas* to create unique life patterns programmed by the individual destiny, *Prārabdha*. Inheritance of this specific *Sattva-Rajas-Tamas* complex is the predetermining factor that modulates the thoughts, speech, and behavior of a person. Not intelligent to think or act of their own, they perform under the control and guidance of the individual consciousness.

Sattva is the neutral force of equilibrium which is predominant in the crown of the brain, *Sahasrāra* Chakra. It gives discriminative knowledge and grants pleasure, illuminates mind and purifies thoughts, ethereal energy being its domain. An abstract principle of light, purity, harmony, and truth, it exists and operates beyond the limitations of time and space. It symbolizes the stillness of mind, undisturbed under all circumstances that always makes the proper choice and directs the rightful path of life. It manifests as the spiritual energy, higher knowledge, wisdom, noble character, charitable deeds, and selfless service in a person. In terms of time, equilibrium is the power of present that perfectly balances the past and the future. It is in control when consciousness happily dwells in the current moment and enjoys the natural flow of life. Such pure state of being is commonly seen in the infants and yogis.

Lord Vishṇu personifies this aspect of cosmic intelligence. As ethereal energy of all pervasive divine Self, he is the source of all physical manifestation. From its neutral ground, creative potency of *Rajas* arises as an impulse, acts with passion, rapidly expands, and duly evolves as the manifested world in all its motion and shapes. Initially dawning as curiosity and fascination, it gradually develops the nucleus of desire, grows the body of an idea, devises a plan of action, and then patiently waits for its timely execution. *Tamas*, passive force of inertia which follows it like a shadow, persistently creates various types of limits. *Rajas* expands as long as it overcomes these obstacles. But eventually *Tamas* prevails as all manifestation maximizes its potential over a period of time.

Manipura Chakra is the domain of ***Rajas*,** the force of movement, action, and passion as represented by fire. Power of movement is future driven in terms of time; past ideas translate into present action directed towards their fulfillment in the future. An abstract principle of motion, it is the driver behind all action. In its highest form, it is the divine will and creative potency of cosmic mind personified by **Lord Brahmā**. He is fully imminent in our self always creating through our mind and the body. He gives rise to endless waves of thoughts and desires, the force that initiates action and sustains all human activities. Mind is the ground that sprouts the seed of desire, nourishes and holds it until executed through action, at an appropriate time, directed by individual ego.

Sattva and *Tamas* greatly influence our inner intentions directing the nature of these desires. They also give us an aptitude, attitude, and abilities that highlight the appropriate profession for us to choose in order to ensure success in it. Various hobbies and hot buttons are the index of passions that define the dimensions, give direction, and determine the quality of life we live in the world we create. *Rajas* corresponds to the day, right side of our body, and all our conscious efforts to earn our living. A natural cause of attachments, it is the subtle force of fancies and wants as we set worldly goals and strive towards their fruition as achievements and accomplishments. It constantly externalizes awareness as we indulge in the outer phenomenal world of lesser experience.

Rajas is the self-starting, self-propelling, and self-evolving field of force that either acts independently or in association with *Sattva* or *Tamas*. It is the force of natural growth that transforms the spirit, quintessence of *Sattva* to visible objective reality, matter of *Tamas*. It is also the catalyst that connects *Sattva*, essence of subjective experience of mind with *Tamas*, the physicality of body, material objects, and the outer world. *Rajas* is the bridge and the medium that connects, as it blends the revealing light of *Sattva* with the veiling darkness of *Tamas* in innovative ways giving rise to various shades of manifestation.

Tamas is the passive force of inertia and inhibition, the cause of darkness, inactivity, and negativity well observed in solids and earth. It is the power of perseverance that holds on to the old knowledge and established way of life, the past in terms of time that resists change and prevents growth. Predominant in *Mulādhāra* Chakra, it restricts the flow of energy as it contracts to create limitations, provides stability of structure, and lays foundations. The plan that initiates in the mind, *Sattva* gets executed with passion, *Rajas* and finally comes to its inevitable end marked by *Tamas*. It relates to the night, left side of our body, and a period when all activities cease. Physical body is the domain of *Tamas* which veils consciousness in a material form and creates limits in space-time for us to live in. It is the power of negation, field of obstruction, and the force endowed with the blue-print of a successful return journey that ultimately trumps as it eventually completes the life cycle. An abstract principle of restraint, it patiently and persistently transforms material nature until the time it prevails, perishes whatever exists, and brings it back to the ground zero as personified by the ever graceful **Lord Mahesh**.

Sattva-Rajas-Tamas

Sattva, Rajas, and *Tamas* are the three modes of *Prakṛti* through which Consciousness operates to create as Lord Brahmā, sustain as Lord Vishṇu, and destroy as Lord Mahesh. These are the evolutionary energy states, in transition through which the infinite spirit descends and finites itself into diverse forms. They constitute three polarities of the unified filed of cosmic intelligence - the neutral *Sattva*, positive *Rajas*, and negative *Tamas* through which all kind of energy flows in nature. The evolutionary movement of *Rajas* arises from static origin of *Sattva* and duly expands even though *Tamas* constantly opposes it. Each grosser limit that *Tamas* gradually creates defines the step of evolution in material creation which essentially complements the act of *Rajas*. Though *Tamas* opposes *Rajas* through grosser matter, effectively it assists *Rajas* to create the final form it desires helping it to attain its ultimate goal. Their mutual interaction and interrelation is called *Guṇapariṇāma* which determines the play, processes and position of all material building blocks of the universe, *Tattvas*. It is only as *Rajas* reaches the peak of its potential that *Tamas* stabilizes and eventually contains it. In other words, *Tamas* defines the limits of its potential by resisting its motion and restricting its expansion to ensure that it does not continue indefinitely by ultimately ending it over time.

Consciousness moves away from the domain of *Sattva*, experiences through *Rajas*, and returns through *Tamas* in cycles. Quiescent *Sattva* harmonizes, as it maintains the rhythm and equilibrium between the two opposing forces, that of motion, *Rajas* and inertia, *Tamas* which spiral out and radiate in the opposite directions. Centrifugal *Rajas* and centripetal *Tamas* determine the state and structure of all the manifested systems in the universe. They also represent three levels of consciousness present in everything, though one of them always predominates. *Sattva* represents omniscience, *Rajas* sustains conscious mind, whereas unconscious mind is the domain of *Tamas*. Non-perceivable by means of the senses, they cannot be detected or known, spotted or identified. At all stages and in every process of creation, they operate interactively, each having a tendency to try, dominate, and suppress the other two. *Sattva* is associated with white color, *Rajas* with red color, and *Tamas* with black color.

Rajas is the only active force that renders static *Sattva* and *Tamas* active. Also, it is the mediator and the medium through which they connect. As we face the world, it acts for us according to its association with them governing the nature of our choices, likes and dislikes, receptions and responses. Coexisting in various proportions, they decide the degree of virtue, passion, and darkness of character which also determines the state of all human relationships. As people interact, exchange ideas, and communicate with each other, it may stir up conflict, strike compromise, or secure cordiality. Predominating *Rajas* gives rise to action, unending desires, sensual pleasure, and selfishness. It is the catalyst having the capacity to convert ideas and inspiration arising in *Sattva* into physical reality by reaching the final form created by *Tamas*. Buoyancy of *Sattva* gives passion for higher knowledge and happiness, clarity and contentment. It leads to light, purity, and clairvoyance, the power of divine grace and intuition that always gives clear perspective and right direction. When *Tamas* envelopes *Rajas*, it resists change, restrains action, and restricts awareness that produces ignorance, confusion, lethargy, and false pride. It is the cause of doubt, darkness, and delusion. All our actions are conditioned by these three interconnected, inseparable, yet quite interchangeable Guṇas complex; the particular Guṇa that dominates the other two shapes the nature of emotional, mental, and moral state at any given time.

Prakṛti, Vikṛti, and Sanskṛti

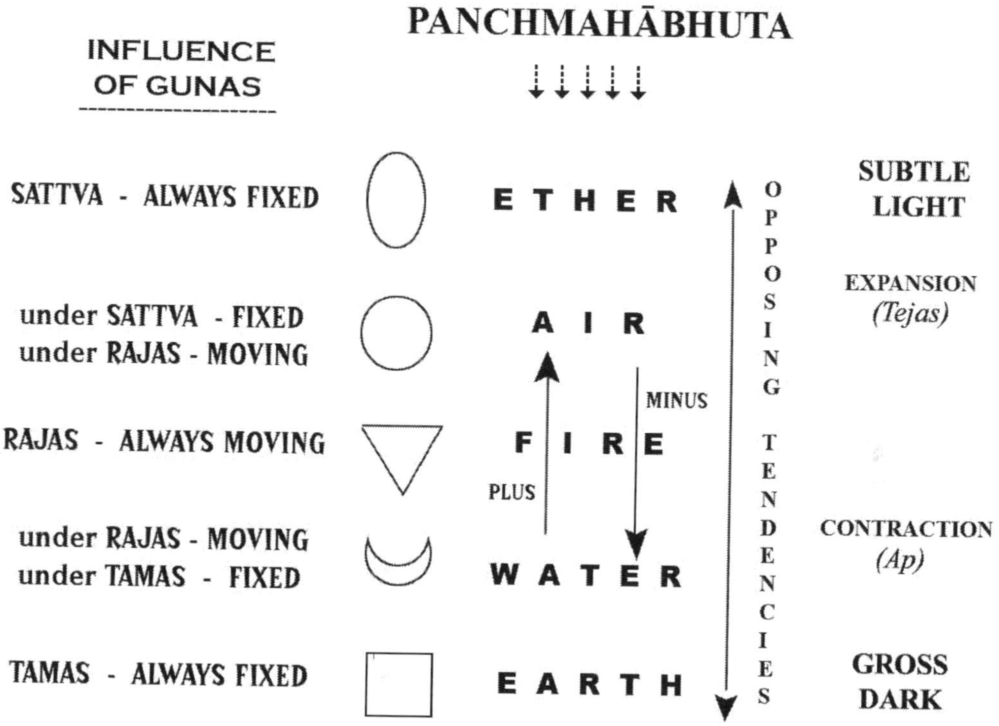

Thoughts and actions of most people are directed and dominated by *Rajas*, passion for worldly success and self-gratification consistent with the basic rules of nature, ***Prakṛti***. It is the natural mode of life to focus on acting, achieving, and enjoying. To make a career, earn money, buy clothes of choice, and eat favorite foods are some examples. Driven by need, lower passion, or greed when people steal or indulge in immoral activities, it illustrates the dominance of *Tamas* called ***Vikṛti***, the dark and fallen face of *Prakṛti*. On the contrary, virtuous and selfless acts like charitable deeds and helping others demonstrate the dominance of *Sattva* that is ***Sanskṛti***, the bright and shining face of *Prakṛti*. It is a spiritual expression that sets higher values in society.

Imagine being in a room having just a glass window with a curtain. The glass allows light to come in and have an outside view. It is like *Sattva* that reveals and takes us close to the consciousness. *Tamas* is like the walls which veil and obstruct, restrict our view and vision taking us away from the light of consciousness. The position of curtain determines how much light and view is available to us. The curtain of *Rajas* can be moved with the organs of action aided by thoughts of mind and senses. Opening the curtain is an active mode, where we need to make an effort that allows *Sattva* to dominate and suppress *Tamas*. Keeping the curtain as it is or close it is the passive mode, easy and effortless that does exactly the opposite. It is the role of *Rajas* to take us closer to consciousness, let us stay where we are, or take us away from it.

Lifelong, as we operate this curtain directed by free will, it allows us to enjoy its consequences subject to *Prārabdha*. Our passionate actions, consistent with the fundamental rules of *Prakṛti* have perpetually kept us at the same level of consciousness through eons. Creation by Lord Brahmā symbolizes our present life, a part of this endless wandering that will continue in the future. Most people do not realize the worthless nature of such life, devoid of a release from the cycle of birth and death. Also, just as gravity pulls down apple of a tree, lower passions and power of delusion make it easy for *Tamas* to dominate. It is effortless. As darkness dwells and ignorance prevails, it brings home anger, greed, jealousy, and other vices with direction to the hell and a key to its door. With sinking consciousness, falling down from the top as human and reincarnate later as an animal lower down the ladder of existence becomes a distinct possibility. Ever compassionate Lord Shiva, who represents *Tamas* and constantly carries out transformation relates to people even in this state of ignorance.

Each of us is bestowed with the power of volition to determine our destiny, *Prārabdha*. To contain the endless stream of desires and worthless worldly wandering propelled by *Rajas*, we need to have higher knowledge, strong will power, and firm determination. It is only after the pain and hard discipline, *tapas* which deprive us from the temporary pleasures of the world and the senses that we eventually ascend to such height. Life of *Dharma*, purity of thought, and action without attachment to its fruits brings peace and happiness. It raises the level of *Sattva* taking us closer to Lord Vishṇu. It also elevates the level of consciousness of our soul by the time we die rather than keeping it where it was or lower it compared to the level at which it was born with.

The mineral world is an exclusive domain of *Tamas* where consciousness is imprisoned to such an extent that materials have total darkness, heaviness, mass, and inertia. As plants grow, they exhibit an ability to move, *Rajas* and have a dormant consciousness, *Sattva*. However, elevation of its level is a gradual and very slow process spread over millions of years. It involves stages of evolution occurring through a vast number of plants and animals species. Man, the most evolved species has the unique ability of a higher conscious thought and action and therefore, human life is considered to be a boon and a blessing. It is meant to consciously choose such *Karma* that elevates *Sattva*, take it to the maximum potential, and achieve the level of purity and awareness that transcends the three Guṇas to be able to realize the Supreme Consciousness. This is supposed to be the ultimate goal of human life.

SCRIPTURES

WHY SANSKṚIT

Language of Creation

Sanskṛit is an ancient and classical language that, like Latin is no longer used in day to day communication. But many modern languages of Indian subcontinent are derived from Sanskṛit. Each evolutionary step of the entire Indian history, cultural heritage, philosophical thought, and religious life is embedded in various Sanskṛit texts, the most ancient being the Vedas. Sanskṛit mantras create unique vibrations called *Vāc* that truly capture the essence of the divine. Therefore, even though currently not used for daily communication anywhere, it has successfully retained its ceremonial status in all Hindu religious practices. It was only by the end of eighteenth century however, that it was rightfully accepted and widely recognized world over as the language of spirituality.

Sanskṛit and its Origin

The primordial sound Aum differentiates into a group of fifty audible root sounds for creation. Each sound is respected like a mother, *Mātṛkā* as it carries unique deity powers. Differentiation of Aum into these sounds occurs in steps that operate in tandem with the creative process. Their sequence shows the step-by-step unfoldment of spirit into matter leading to successive stages of evolution of the universe. Sanskṛit is directly derived from these sounds, each sound being one of its alphabets. Thus, it is an energy based language that casually and quite naturally developed for communication. Its uniqueness is in the fact that it uses such primary sounds the subtle vibrations of which are the basis of material creation. Therefore, it is perfect for the shortest ride back to the source. Consequently, it is the primary choice for spiritual exploration.

Sanskṛit alphabets and subtle energy channels

The fifty alphabets of Sanskṛit are classified into six different sound groups, each creating such vibrations that resonate with a specific spiritual plane. Each plane corresponds to one of the series of six major Chakras in our subtle body. Also, the number of alphabets in each group equals the number of subtle energy channels linked with the related Chakra, one alphabet for each channel. These channels were created by the associated alphabet sounds during gestation that constituted our subtle body. Hence all major subtle energy channels resonate with these alphabet sounds. It makes them an invaluable resource to tune in and harmonize our energies with nature in order to experience divinity.

Adequate and appropriate words in Sanskṛit

Sanskṛit mantras are Realized by sages that have specific sound combination which produces unique patterns of vibrations. Packed with psycho-spiritual energy, they influence various spiritual channels in our subtle body, invoke their powers, and activate them. Different mantras access different sets of channels and therefore, invoke different powers. These sounds are adequate in number and appropriate in nature. In various combinations, they cover the entire range of cosmic energy patterns having ability to access all our spiritual channels.

Sounds of ancient Hebrew and Native American languages are considered to be spiritual. But most other languages do not have words equivalent to those of Sanskṛit used in spiritual practices. For example, the word ‘mantra’ itself has no equivalent word in English. Thus, the arsenal of English words fails to provide appropriate sound combinations necessary to produce the range of vibrations in sync with those of universal energies. Using any other language misses out in connecting with wide range of the cosmic vibratory energy not allowing a meaningful and complete spiritual experience.

Spiritual and Physical planes

The sound vibrations of modern languages greatly differ from the cosmic vibrations of spiritual energies. Not being in tune with each other, we stay where we are, at the physical plane of existence by using any contemporary language. Pronouncing Sanskṛit mantras are expressions in harmony with the auditory energy that naturally exists in the universe. In other words, mantra sound vibrations reproduce and mimic these ever existing cosmic energies. Being in tune with each other, there is a smooth interaction between the two. In fact they acquire a greater strength. They, in turn, harmonize the energy flow within our subtle system raising our awareness. We feel like being a part of nature and in proximity to the higher spiritual plane. This is how mantra sounds allow us to harness divine energies for spiritual advancement.

As late Swami Rama describes it, Sanskṛit is the language of yogic union that is used to transmit and preserve human spiritual experiences. To bridge the wide gap and rise from physical to spiritual level, the sound vibrations of Sanskṛit mantras offer an incredible opportunity. Sanskṛit is an antiquated language, but when it comes to spiritual practices, it is the most appropriate and quite indispensable. Mantras containing Sanskṛit alphabets become the most potent tool making it an ideal spiritual language. For spiritual advancement, inner exploration, and meditation practice it is the language of choice.

THE VEDAS

Sacred Revelations

Vedas are the oldest known spiritual texts to mankind which are a sacred compilation and priceless treasury of Hinduism. The term Veda means spiritual knowledge that is the eternal essence of existence. Not pronounced by prophets, they are a collection of divine revelations called ***Śruti*** made by the Absolute, *Brahman* to the ancient sages enfolded in enlightenment thousands of years ago. The articulate sounds of these supernatural vibrations called *Vāc* were preserved with profound integrity as ***Smṛti*** and passed on to the qualified recipients by traditions of oral repetitions through generations. At the start of the literary tradition around 2nd century BC, they were first written down. The Vedas do not set forth any religious dogma, their content being universal in their appeal. They encompass the Eternal Truths known as *Sanātana Dharma* relevant at all times. Philosophy of the Vedas propound pantheism, the very roots from which other branches like *Sānkhya*, *Yoga*, and *Vedānta* emerged and thrived over time morphing it into Hinduism as we know it today.

While guiding everyday matters of life, they direct us to inquire the contents of our own heart to find the light of consciousness. They declare that effulgence of life within us is the same eternal source that pervades the entire universe. Vibrations of *Vāc* are the path with the power that connects our individual self with this divine source. Their nature is self-convincing and inspiring. They have a sense of intimate communion between nature and the ancient visionaries. The Veda mantras, hymns, and invocations are vocal adoration to worship various natural forces that were eventually visualized as deities. The most common deities referred to are Indra (Ruler of Devas), Agni (Fire), Vishṇu, Sun, Rūdra (Form of Shiva), and Brihaspati (Jupiter). From among these, Vishṇu and Shiva are the two most commonly worshiped deities today.

There are four Vedas – *Ṛgveda*, *Yajurveda*, *Sāmaveda*, and *Atharvaveda*. Each of them offers three levels of interpretation having four distinct subdivisions. The first part is known as Saṃhitā which consists of invocations, mantras, and hymns used to pray and eulogize the natural forces. Great importance is attached to the Meters used. It is followed by the second called Brāhmaṇa which describes, in details, the ritualistic aspect involved, in a prose form. Āraṇyakas go a step further from Brāhmaṇa in recognizing and exploring the spiritual meaning behind these rituals. Upaniṣads is the concluding part of Vedas that explains and teaches the underlying metaphysical philosophy. Of the four, the first three Vedas are an

FOUR VEDAS

Rgveda: Knowledge of Hymns.

Yajurveda: Knowledge of Liturgy.

Sāmaveda: Knowledge of Music.

Atharvaveda: Knowledge of Medicine.

TWELVE MAJOR UPANIṢADS

Iśa: Advocates both - life in the world and meditation.

Kena: Consciousness is beyond the comprehension of mind and intellect.

Kaṭha: Reveals the secret knowledge of the Self.

Praśna: Answers questions regarding life and body.

Mūṇḍaka: Higher knowledge realizes Ultimate Reality.

Māṇḍūkya: Explains three states of Consciousness and Beyond.

Taittirīya: Explains the creation of the Universe.

Aitareya: Shows that Pure Consciousness pervades through Universe.

Shwetashwatara: Mind, Matter, and *Māyā* are aspects of *Brahman.*

Chandogya: Advocates truthfulness as the highest virtue.

Bṛhadāraṇyaka: Teaches that *Brahman* is within all.

Kaivalya: Have faith in Scriptures and Guru.

independent collection representing the faculties of speech, mind, and breath. Sacred manuals of mantras and hymns, they are primarily used by the priests. However, some of these are recited as prayers and worship at religious functions and other auspicious occasions by everyone.

Ṛgveda is the first and the oldest Veda, premier of all as it is complete and by far the most interesting compilation. It was first written down around 1500 BC or before. Subtlest source of metaphysical thought, it consists of hymns having a sense of most elementary state of religious aspirations. Their Realization facilitated an outer worship of natural forces, later personified as deities. A fountain-head of Vedic science, it is a compilation of inner experiences, a source of light that defies the reasoned seeking logical convictions. Organized in 10 books known as Mandalas, each consists of Metrical hymns that total 1017. Each Mandala may be representing an ancient family tradition. All the other Vedas borrow heavily from it. Most aspects of the Vedic science like practice of *Yoga*, meditation, and mantra can be found in the *Ṛgveda*. The priests who recited the verses of *Ṛgveda* were respectfully called Hotris.

The mantras in ***Yajurveda*** combine prose with poetry in a form which is full of meaning and cadence. They consist of prayers and invocations used for the ceremonial consecration of utensils and altar before starting the actual fire ceremony. Also, they are supposed to be recited in lower voice while performing Homa, Yagna, and other sacrifices. There are two major recessions of this Veda – Shukla or White attributed to sage Yājnavalkya and Kṛṣṇa or Black attributed to sage Tittiri. These rituals and offering of sacrifices made during the fire ceremony direct us to make the ultimate and the most important sacrifice of the individual ego in the inner spiritual fire of awareness.

The third Veda is called ***Sāmaveda*** which is about half the size of *Yajurveda*. It is a special collection of reconfigured mantras, almost all derived from *Ṛgveda* having musical annotation used for singing and chanting during religious ceremonies. They are sung according to some fixed melodies known as Sāmgānās and their rendering is called *Yoga* of song.

Atharvaveda is attributed to two sages, Atharvan and Angiras who compiled the sacred knowledge of this last Veda. It consists of meditation methods and incantations which individuals can use. It also describes and glorifies the curative powers of herbs and waters, magical spells and healing charms. Quite unique to it, it also shows methods to call down disaster on enemy. Many consider it to be the dark and secret knowledge pertaining to the evil spirits and the after-life. Āyurveda, the ancient science of medicine is a part of this Veda.

Of all the mantras and hymns in these four Vedas, the **Gāyatri** mantra of *Ṛgveda* contains the essence and spirit of all the Vedas. Therefore, it is also called mother of the Vedas. It consists of twenty-four Sanskṛit seed letters, arranged in such a unique order that all of the wisdom, knowledge, and the entire Vedas are well concealed in them. Chanting of this mantra purifies the mind bestowing vitality and higher knowledge. All other mantras are contained in this mantra, which in turn merges in the primordial sound Aum.

Upaniṣad

The word Upaniṣad means 'sitting down near'. In a typical setting, this is the knowledge gained by sitting near the feet of Guru. If *Ṛgveda* contains nectar, the Upaniṣads contain nectar of nectar. It is a concentrated distillate of spiritual wisdom expounding the purpose of the Vedas. It clearly elaborates upon their spiritual aim, the content being direct in its language, purpose, and intention. Many of the Upaniṣads were written much later after the Vedic age. But their thought and vision originate from the Vedas upon which the old truths were recovered and recorded in a new format. They are relevant even today. Of the 108 preserved Upaniṣads, 12 are the major ones.

Revealing the soul of the Vedas, these Upaniṣads were the nascent pool of principles from which later came forth the more permanent and powerful philosophy of Vedānta. It speculates on all aspects of existence and evolution while covering metaphysics of thought and reason reflecting on the Divine. It advocates that essence of all things and beings is the divine Spirit called *Brahman* or Consciousness. It is the cause of all causes and what we see around us, including ourselves are various effects of this cause. In addition to describing doctrines of *Karma, Dharma*, and reincarnation, it discusses the philosophies of *Advaita*, oneness as well as *Dvaita*, separateness of individual soul and the Absolute. *Advaita Vedānta* is the ultimate crown as their teachings form the core and basis of Hindu thought and philosophy.

The ancient Vedas became less and less appealing over ages. Today all spiritual wisdom of Hinduism is considered to be contained in *Vedānta*. These scriptures are written in Sanskṛit, a language no longer used in day to day life. Also, they carry deep philosophical meaning which is difficult to comprehend for a common man. Therefore, though at the core of the Hindu thought and philosophy, they remain inaccessible and enigmatic for most of the people. However, many mantras and hymns from these are quite popular and commonly chanted during prayers, rituals, meditation, religious ceremonies, and many auspicious functions of life events like marriage.

BHAGVAD GĪTĀ

The Song of God

Bhagvad Gītā is the most authentic source of Hinduism. It is a truly memorable masterpiece written in a poetic form, in eighteen chapters having 700 Sanskṛit verses. It is embedded in the largest and ageless epic called Mahābhārat written around 500 BC. A holy compilation which contains pure distillate of the loftiest timeless Truths, it is the best recognized Hindu scripture extensively read and therefore, extremely famous worldwide. It is prophetic in nature, an exposition of the *Vedānta* philosophy, and truly a gospel. It is the conversation between Lord Kṛṣṇa and Arjuna that took place at the most crucial moment on the battlefield of Kūrūkshetra about 5000 years ago. The unusual setting of the dialogue signifies that there are constant moral conflicts within everyone while waging the war of life in which only the worthy and righteous emerge victorious.

Just before the start of war between rival sets of cousins, Pāndava and Kaurava, Arjuna the great archer, a Pāndava saw many of his close relatives, friends, and teachers on the other side making preparation. The prospect of fighting them made him sad and so he got dejected. He did not want to fight a war for any reason with the people he considered his own. At that moment, Lord Kṛṣṇa, who had gracefully accepted to be his charioteer reached out and pacified him. In his calm, confident, and reassuring voice, he explained to him the duties of a warrior. He further gave him detailed discourses on the philosophies of *Yoga* and *Vedānta*. It is the most profound knowledge, the greatest teachings of transpersonal psychology. Lord Kṛṣṇa is widely believed to be the eighth incarnation of Lord Vishṇu. Since pronounced by him, it is considered to be the most authentic and self-contained guide to life.

Lord Kṛṣṇa counseled his brother-in-law, Arjuna, who also was his close friend and now became his first disciple to follow his duty, *Dharma* which is the basis of all humanity. Creating *Karma* is the natural consequence of all acts of life. Everybody inevitably enacts *Karma* but it has to be consistent with the *Dharma* of each individual. *Karma* and *Dharma* are the two prime principles connected like two cotyledons so as to constitute the kernel of natural law which governs the universal world order. In the grand scheme of nature, each individual is obligated to act rightfully based on his unique situation and follow his *Dharma*.

He advised Arjuna to rise above the mode of passion, attend to his calling of the moment, and be ready to follow the path of martial action. There was no choice for him but to perform his duty. The ultimate goal of human life is to achieve union with the Supreme which is called *Yoga*. Following the path of action in the line of duty is called the *Yoga* of Action, ***Karma Yoga***. He advised Arjuna to give up the brooding over the fruit of action. To act is in one's hand, the outcome is not. Even if the duty is unpleasant and the outcome may be undesirable, one should not waver in carrying out one's duty. But Arjuna, in a deep state of melancholy and grief was not receptive to such persuasion.

Lord Kṛṣṇa continued with his discourse elaborating upon the nature of human life and its relation with the embodied soul. The soul is divine in nature, always eternal and therefore, immortal. Death is leaving the old body for a new one which is like changing clothes. Each life is a determined existence for it, one of the unending series of lives. Therefore, Māyā or illusion should not carry him away from following his *Dharma*. He then explained the unending cycle of birth and death. All human action is propelled by stream of desires aimed to harness material fruits which provide the power and pleasures of life. Such passion easily obscures awareness tempting us to follow the wrong path. Hence, often worldly goals are achieved through inappropriate ways and indecent means. It may yield the desired fruits and give temporary happiness, but such negative *Karma* eventually causes pain, grief, and misery. They sink the soul deeply in the objective world with bondages and attachments.

Therefore, action carried out without regard to the rightful act of duty, *Dharma* binds it to the cycle of birth and death. Unending desires are the chord that connects the soul to this cycle of reincarnation. The soul continues to come back to the world, *Saṃsāra* bound by the ever extending resume of its *Karma*. The only way of release from this cycle of transmigration is by severing the chord of worldly desires and material attachments. When one rises above the mode of self-gratification, pursues spirituality, and indulges in selfless service it leads one to the release from such aimless endless wandering. This philosophy forms the basis of all community and social services.

Besides the *Yoga* of Action, Lord Kṛṣṇa went on to explain Arjuna the other paths of achieving union, *Yoga* with the Supreme. They are the paths of Devotion, Knowledge, and Meditation. He further explained that everyone should live a life with detachment from the material sense of ego and pursue the path of righteousness. By consciously choosing any one or more of these *Yogas* that is appealing and seem appropriate to follow, one transcends the illusory mortality successfully entering the realm of the Supreme.

Yoga of devotion is also known as ***Bhakti Yoga***. This is the easiest, the simplest, and the best way to attain liberation in the current Dark Age. It is the highest form of worship where one focuses on the divine and completely surrenders to him. One's mind is constantly fixed on the Lord with never-ending love for him. All thoughts and actions of life are directed by the single minded motivation to please him. Anyone who follows his *Dharma* and lives a righteous life with such unswerving devotion is promised liberation from all sins and a release from the ocean of death and transmigration.

Yoga of contemplation is called ***Jnāna Yoga***. This is the process of acquiring higher knowledge to discriminate between what is real and what is not, what is eternal and what is not. The body is not eternal, the soul is. Death is only a transition for the soul from one body to another. The soul can never be destroyed; fire cannot burn it, and water cannot wet it. Such knowledge can differentiate between the physical body, the form of matter through which the spirit exists, lives, and experiences and the owner of the body,

Yoga of meditation is known as ***Raja Yoga***. The mind and the senses are always directed outward engaged in the material world constantly seeking pleasure, indulgence, and enjoyment. As lower passion and ignorance prevails, it is difficult to realize the true nature of the higher Self. Meditation is the practice to concentrate on our inner self which establishes a control over the mind and body. As the senses are directed inwards and the mind is rendered thoughtless, it establishes the state of awakening that allows realization of one's true nature. From the chaos and entanglement of the world, one enters the realm of calm, peace, and tranquility elevating his state of being.

Then Lord Kṛṣṇa imparted divine cosmic vision to Arjuna with which he was able to see his great universal form, Vishwaroopa. Arjuna saw his absolutely dazzling and magnificent form, in all splendor and brilliance, with various energies of the universe emanating from him. At that time, he also told Arjuna that whenever there is a decline in the moral values and *Dharma* in society, he incarnates to uplift the values and restore the balance of righteousness in the world.

Bhagvad Gītā, the song of God is one of the world's holiest scriptures also known as India's favorite Bible. A copy of Bhagvad Gītā can be found in most Hindu households. Different spiritual traditions, followers of different sects, and scholars of all ages have unanimously hailed it to be the most authentic source of *Vedānta* philosophy. Innumerable commentaries have been written on it and numerous adaptations and translations have been done in many languages. 'Bhagvad Gītā as it is' published by ISKCON is very popular.

DEVĪ MĀHĀTMYAM

Glory of Divine Mother

Devī Māhātmyam is a part of the scripture called Mārkaṇḍeya Purāṇa written around the year 300-400 AD. A sacred, esoteric, and poetic text dedicated to the glory of Divine Mother, it is also well known as Chaṇḍi Pāth and Durgā Saptashati. It is the most holy text for Shaktas who primarily worship her as the Ultimate Reality. All verses in the volume generally address her as Chaṇḍikā who has independent qualities of her own. She stands alone without being subsumed in others or having any complementary counterpart like a consort. She is portrayed as the Supreme Reality from whom all phenomenal existence proceeds. In each of the episodes throughout the text, numerous forms emanate from her singular aspect. They finally dissolve back in her after engaging in the phenomena of multiple battles against evil at various times and places. All events and episodes highlight the reasons of unending strife and struggle of life directing us to discover ways of psychological evolvement and awareness.

The whole work consists of 700 verses written in Sanskṛit language, in 13 chapters, classified into three categories called 'Caritra's. A rich synthesis of diverse philosophical strands, each Caritra revolves around the historical battles carried out by three major configurations of Divine Mother. They are *Mahākāli* Devī, *Mahālakshmi* Devī, and *Mahāsaraswati* Devī who destroyed the demonic forces that ruled the universe. These episodes are presented in the form of allegories. Each Caritra, in one or more episodes and chapters narrates the rise of demons who controlled the universe from time to time. It denotes the dominance of our lower nature and negativities that take control of our body and mind. Our morality suffers when it surrenders to such worldly instincts that dominate and direct our thoughts and actions. The inevitable end result of all material life is chaos and suffering. Ultimately we realize our mistakes, get frustrated with the circumstances, and pray for the help of Divine Mother. Kind and ever compassionate, she helps sincere devotees by destroying the negativities and raising awareness that ultimately grants us a release.

It begins as a story in which an honorable king, Suratha and a successful merchant, Samadhi happens to meet near the hermitage of a sage. As Suratha was betrayed by his ministers and deposed through a sinister plot, he had to escape to save his life. Likewise, Samadhi was cast out by his wife and sons who appropriated his entire wealth. Both were grief stricken and yet could not stop thinking about their families even after such betrayal. After sharing their sad stories, they approached the sage seeking an explanation of such undue concern and constant thoughts about their families. Describing the glory of Divine Mother who rules the universe, the sage said that it is due to her power of delusion and attachment for this world. He then narrated all her divine powers by describing her historic battles against negativities.

The **first Caritra**, the first chapter describes how Chaṇḍikā, as ***Mahākāli*** **Devī** helps Lord Vishṇu to win the battle against two demons, Madhu and Kaitabh. Lord Vishṇu who supports our life represents the existence of an individual. His fight is our constant battle against the energies of two major subtle channels in our body, Ida and Pingala personified as Madhu and Kaitabh. They give rise to illusions of life with such feelings as lust, anger, envy, greed, and pride. They cover our thoughts and control our actions leading us to the worldly path. By himself Lord Vishṇu, the individual with limited weapons of mind and senses is unable to control and defeat them. But with spiritual practices, as he invokes Divine Mother, *Mahākāli* Devī, she comes to the rescue. She is the latent power of *Kuṇḍalinī* that lies coiled three and a half time at the base of spine in everybody where these two channels meet. As she awakens, she absorbs their energies and rises up the spine along the path of liberation. Her action, *Kriyā* Shakti overcomes the mode of our ignorance, *Tamas*. As we overcome this first major hurdle, it marks the beginning of our spiritual journey. This episode establishes the cosmic status of Divine Mother. The verses of this chapter are considered to be equivalent to the first Veda, *Ṛgveda*.

The regal imagery of the middle or **second Caritra** consists of the chapters 2, 3, and 4. A very famous and well known episode, it describes the slaying of demon king Mahishasura by ***Mahālakshmi*** **Devī**. This demon represents individual ego, the 'I' which is the biggest hurdle in our spiritual progress. It always basks in the self-centered thoughts and activities which is the root cause of disharmony and discord, clashes and conflicts. It is an antithesis to love, compassion, and selfless acts necessary to establish peace and harmony, within and around. It also signifies energy of will, *Icchā* Shakti necessary to establish control over the mode of lower passion, *Rajas*. *Rajas* gives false perceptions and endless desires as the mind and senses constantly wander for power, pleasure, and self-gratification. To overcome this negative trait is a huge task for which the worshiper seeks the grace of *Mahālakshmi* Devī. Devī killing Mahishasura signifies overcoming this major obstacle which provides an exhilarating sense of freedom and release. This episode exemplifies the compassion with which Devī brings relief to all those who call upon her. As she raises them to the level of universal love and care, it makes these devotees virtuous. The verses in this Caritra are considered to be equivalent to the second Veda, *Yajurveda*.

The last or **third Caritra** consists of the chapters 5 through 13 and describes numerous episodes in which ***Mahāsaraswati* Devī** fights various battles with other demons like Raktabija, Shūmbha, Nishūmbha, Dhūmralochana, Chaṇda, and Muṇda killing them one by one. These are various impurities, personification of our unawareness, complacency, and spiritual ignorance of Reality. Engaged in the worldly affairs and entangled in daily chores, we fail to realize the futility of such a state of existence. Hence the worshiper seeks the grace of *Mahāsaraswati* Devī, bestower of higher knowledge and wisdom, *Jnāna* Shakti to impart higher knowledge, *Vidyā*. It breaks the last barrier of *Sattva* Guṇa, mode of goodness necessary to attain Self-Realization. Recitation of this Caritra is considered to be equivalent to the third Veda, *Sāmaveda*.

Saptamātrika is a group of seven goddesses ensuing from Divine Mother who help her fight these demons. They are the extremely aggressive, horrifying, and ferocious goddesses of the battlefield called Brāhmi, Māheshwari, Kaumāri, Vaishnavi, Vārāhi, Māhendri, and Chāṃunda. What is remarkable is that Chaṇḍikā, often referred to as Ambikā and Durgā is depicted as independent Supreme Self in Devī Māhātmyam. She releases these other powers she possesses to battle the antigods. She is the Great Goddess, *Mahādevī* who even sends Lord Shiva as her messenger to the antigods before engaging in the final battle with them. In an absolute contrast, in Shiva-Shakti concept, she shares her supremacy with Lord Shiva as they duly complement each other.

The entire work is primarily a recited text which has strong spiritual influence on the surrounding as its sound vibrations carry unique powers. Each verse is an extraordinarily potent mantra the recitation of which pleases Devī. When Devī Māhātmyam mantras are chanted, the energy released has a transforming effect that burns the negativities, purifies the body and mind, and gives the right direction to bring about spiritual elevation. The description of Devī fighting various battles against the demons is essentially our fight against the negative energies and impurities in our system. She provides us the armor and protection against the influence of all such negative forces, rising outside and within us. With her grace, we overcome these obstacles to ultimately qualify and merge with the Divine, thus winning the battle of our life.

The ideal time to chant Devī Māhātmyam is Tuesdays during the week, the eighth day of the waxing fortnight of the lunar calendar, and the nine special days of worship called **Navrātri** in the month of *Āso* of Hindu calendar. The tenth day after Navrātri is the day of her victory over the demons that is celebrated as Vijayadasami or Dassera with a fire ceremony called Chaṇḍi Homa. It is the most auspicious day of the Hindu calendar.

RĀMĀYAṆA

The Most Read Epic

The most popular epic of all the Hindu scriptures, it is the life story of Lord Rāma, the seventh incarnation of Lord Vishṇu. It was first narrated by sage Vālmiki in Sanskṛit some 3500 years ago. That and the later adaptation written by saint Tūlsidas are the most famous among many other versions. Divided into several books called Kānda, each of it chronologically describes his major life events interspersed with devotional and philosophical elements.

Born to king Dashratha in the kingdom of Ayodhyā, Lord Rāma was the crown prince. He was an epitome of virtue and integrity who demonstrated the highest moral values and ethical standards of any human being. It is a tale of his exemplary thoughts and actions at every stage during his entire lifetime. He did not waver in following his *Dharma*, the path of righteousness even under the most trying circumstances. He presented a role model of an ideal son, husband, brother, and human being for others to follow.

From the very young age, Lord Rāma showed his unique abilities, noble character, and upright nature. Various demons were harassing sages during sacrificial rites, rituals, and homas in their Āshrams. A great sage named Vishvāmitra took initiative, approached king Dashratha, and requested him to send prince Rāma to his Āshram for protection. Lord Rāma, with his younger brother Lakshmaṇ received archery skills and powers from the sage and then killed all those troubling demons to relieve the sages from their menace. He then married Sītā Devī, an incarnation of *Mahālakshmi* Devī, by winning her hand in a competition called *Swayamwara*. He succeeded in wielding a divine bow, which broke down, when other suitors failed miserably. This unusual feat showed his strength, superiority, and divine powers.

When his father decided to hand over the rein of his kingdom to Lord Rāma, his stepmother asked his father to redeem her two pending boons: first that instead of Lord Rāma, her son, Bharat to be anointed as king and second that Lord Rāma should proceed to live in exile for 14 years. When Lord Rāma learned about this, he had no hesitation in renouncing the throne, accepting the exile, and leaving the kingdom to keep his father's word. It is a glowing example of deep love, respect, and sacrifice of a son for his father.

His wife Sītā Devī and brother Lakshmaṇ accompanied him in exile. They went to a forest and lived there in a hut. One day Rāvaṇa, the demon king of island of Lanka abducted Sītā Devī by deception. While searching for her, they met Hanuman who introduced them to the monkey king Sugriva, also living in exile. Rāma befriended Sugriva and extended his help to regain his kingdom by killing Bāli, his brother. Sugriva then sent searchers, including Hanuman all around to find Sītā Devī. After a long search, Hanuman finally succeeded in locating her in the island of Lanka, the kingdom of Rāvaṇa.

Lord Rāma then planned an invasion of island of Lanka with the help of Sugriva and his army of monkeys. For the entire army to cross the ocean and go to the other side was a formidable task. Huge rocks were inscribed with the name 'Rāma' and thrown into the sea to build a bridge. Surprisingly, the stones with this name written over remained afloat and the bridge was thus completed. The whole army of Lord Rāma then crossed the sea.

Vibhishaṇa, the younger brother of Rāvaṇa advised him to let go Sītā Devī and avoid the war, but in vain. Instead Rāvaṇa threw him out of his kingdom calling him a traitor. Vibhishaṇa then met Lord Rāma, apologized on behalf of his brother, and offered his help in fighting the war against his own brother. A fierce battle ensued between Lord Rāma, the side of *Dharma* and Rāvaṇa, the side of *Adharma*. Rāvaṇa used all the evil spells and dark forces under his command, but did not succeed in winning the war. One by one all of his family and friends were killed. In the final phase, Lord Rāma defeated and killed Rāvaṇa ultimately releasing Sītā Devī. Every year, this day called Dassera is celebrated with great funfair by burning an effigy of Rāvaṇa.

When Lord Rāma returned to Ayodhyā after the exile, his stepbrother, Bharat welcomed him with tears and open arms gladly returning him the throne of Ayodhyā. Lord Rāma efficiently ruled the kingdom so that every citizen lived happily. It was considered an ideal kingdom, Rāmrājya, a perfect place to live. All the characters of Rāmāyaṇa show very high moral values of life. Sītā Devī as a dedicated wife and Lakshmaṇ as an ideal brother accompanied Lord Rāma through his years in exile and stood by his side. At the end of exile, Bharat gave him back the throne setting another example of brotherly love and affection. Sugriva helped Lord Rāma with his army to reciprocate the help he had received. Hanuman always stayed in his service exemplifying dedication and true devotion.

Rāmāyaṇa is a literary monument that highlights potent truths and true values of life through the life story of Rāma. It has tremendous impact and influence on the literature, temple, dance, and theatre. Held in much reverence, parents commonly narrate this story to their children to instill higher values of life.

MAHĀBHĀRAT

World's Longest Epic

Mahābhārat is another major epic of Hinduism written by sage Vyāsa who is also a character in it. It is a great tale of the dynasty of King Bharat and his decedents, written in thousands of Sanskṛit verses. Through various characters and events, it highlights basic human nature and conflicts in the relationship of individuals at all levels. Though separated by time, it is relevant to every society, at all times. It shows that follower of the path of righteousness ultimately wins the battle of life. It also shows how a man, once powerful and mighty to rule others, becomes helpless and surrenders to the demands of time. It consists of 18 different books called Parvas that elucidate the four goals of life – *Dharma*, *Artha*, *Kāma*, and *Moksha*. Bhagvad Gītā is a part of this epic.

King Shantanu of Hastinapur had a son named Devavrata. One day, while on a hunting trip, Shantanu saw Satyavati and fell in love with her. He returned very sad and restless. Devavrata took the initiative to identify the cause of his misery. Then, to facilitate their marriage, he took a great vow: never to get married and never to be the king so that the future son of Satyavati would get the throne. Since then he is known as Bhishma, the great vow taker.

Satyavati's son Vichitravirya became the king and married two women. Each had a son named Dhrutarāshtra and Pandu. Elder son Dhrutarāshtra was blind from the birth and so the throne was passed on to younger Pandu who was pale in complexion. However, Pandu died at young age and since his five sons called Pāndava were little, Dhrutarāshtra became the caretaker king. Dhrutarāshtra had a hundred sons called Kauravas. The core story of the epic is the struggle for the throne of Hastinapur between the five Pāndava brothers and the hundred Kaurava brothers. The eldest Pāndava, Yudhishthira was virtuous who followed the path of *Dharma*, whereas the eldest Kaurava, Duryodhana, guided by his cunning uncle Shakuni, followed the path of *Adharma*.

Since early childhood there was an enmity and rivalry between Pāndava and Kaurava that only grew with time. Duryodhana was always looking for an opportunity to get rid of Pāndava brothers. To accomplish this goal, he built a special palace using flammable materials and then arranged for their stay in it with an intention to set it aflame and burn them alive. However, Pāndava were warned by Vidur, their uncle about this scheme and so they left the palace by a secret tunnel when it was set on fire escaping unharmed.

Pāndava then started living in a disguise. Arjuna, the third Pāndava brother won Draupadi in an archery competition held by her father. As they returned home, they announced winning a prize by shouting out loud. Their mother Kunti was inside the home. Not knowing what it was, she asked to distribute it among them. Since Pāndava brothers always obeyed and carried out their mother's word, Draupadi ended up being wife of all five brothers.

When the family elders and relatives came to know that they were alive, they brokered a peaceful split of the kingdom of Hastinapur between Pāndava and Kaurava so that they can live without any future conflicts. In due course of time, Yudhishthira then built a new city named Indraprastha as the capital of his new kingdom. Kaurava brothers were invited along with others to attend its grand opening ceremony. While visiting, Duryodhana was deceived by the appearance of one section of the floor of palace and fell down in what actually was a pool of water. Draupadi, who watched him fall, laughed and taunted that son of a blind is also blind and thus humiliated him.

Duryodhana was insulted and he was consumed with anger. For revenge, he planned that his uncle Shakuni, an expert in the game of dice plays with Yudhishthira. He forced his father to send such invitation. Yudhishthira, always respectful of the elders, accepted the invitation. Shakuni kept on winning and, one by one, Yudhishthira lost all his wealth, his entire kingdom, his brothers, and finally Draupadi as well. Dushāsana, a Kaurava then brought Draupadi to the court by pulling her hair and started pulling her sari to strip her naked. Draupadi cried out while Pāndava brothers sat and watched helplessly. Then she cried for Lord Kṛṣṇa who miraculously saved her as her sari became endless around her waist and so Dushāsana finally had to give up.

Once again, the elders intervened and Pāndava brothers with their wife Draupadi were sent to live in exile for thirteen years, the last year to be spent in a disguise. On their return after the term, Duryodhana refused to give them even a small part of his kingdom. Lord Kṛṣṇa, on behalf of Pāndava, asked Duryodhana to give them just five small villages to settle the dispute, but in vain. War became inevitable and both sides summoned vast armies. Family members and relatives, friends and teachers started taking sides. Lord Kṛṣṇa, related to both sides, offered them a choice: Lord Kṛṣṇa as charioteer who would not take any active part in the war or his vast army that will fight the war. Duryodhana, who had the privilege to choose first, happily chose the army and so Lord Kṛṣṇa became the charioteer of Arjuna. The great battle of Kūrūkshetra ensued. Both parties adopted dishonorable tactics throughout the war. With the guidance of Lord Kṛṣṇa, Pāndava brothers finally won the war.

MISCELLANEOUS

TYPES of BODIES

Five Sheaths of Soul

When we mention body, we generally refer to the physical body. But our existence and ability to think and act is not only due to the body that we see. *Taittiriya* Upaniṣad recognizes five layers of bodies or sheath called Kosha that cover our self, the soul like the peels of an onion. They work together in complete harmony and govern our day to day life. Depending upon their nature, integration, and efficiency they ultimately project our unique personality presenting the state of our inner self to the outer world. Starting from the innermost sheath, they are called Ānandmaya Kosha, Vijnānmaya Kosha, Manomaya Kosha, Prāṇamaya Kosha, and Annamaya Kosha. The outermost sheath is the grossest whereas the innermost is the subtlest closest to the spirit. Manifestation of spirit to matter takes place in a step-down manner as each Kosha is a progressively grosser phase of our physical expression. They together make our being.

---

1. **Annamaya Kosha** – This is the outermost Kosha we are the most aware and conscious about. It is our physical body; the gross sheath made of matter which is nourished and supported by our food. *Tamas* Guṇa predominates in this Kosha as it defines the limits of our being. Depending upon the type and amount of food we eat and the activities we perform, it is possible to maintain its size and form. It is associated with our primitive instincts like urge for food, sex, and sleep. Made of five basic elements, *Panchamahābhuta*, it is associated with five organs of sense and five organs of action. Also, it has its origin in *Mulādhāra*, *Swadhishthān*, and *Manipura* Chakras.

> To start *Yoga* and meditation practice, we begin with different body postures called Āsanas. It is the first step that deals with this outermost sheath. Known as *Hatha-Yoga* practice, it balances the energy polarities to have its smooth flow within the body making it fit in its function.

---

2. **Prāṇamaya Kosha** – It is the subtle body of breath made of *Prāṇa*, the vital life force that provides an interface between the body and the mind. It is the unified field of living cosmic intelligence that sustains our life. Breathing is absolutely essential to life and therefore, it is considered a Kosha of our body. Made of air and ether, it consists of five different types of vital airs that

vitalize different functions of our body. They are called *Prāṇa* (respiration), *Apāna* (excretion), *Vyāna* (distribution), *Samāna* (assimilation), and *Udāna* (regeneration). *Rajas* Guṇa predominates in this Kosha which regulates and co-ordinates all body - mind functions and gives us personal aura. It has its origin in *Anāhata* and *Vishuddha* Chakras.

> After the Āsanas, the next step is to practice breath control and retention exercises called *Prāṇayama*. As it balances the flow of *Prāṇa*, it improves the efficiency of *Prāṇa* movement, revitalizes the subtle system, and enhances the integration of mind - body functions.

---

3. **Manomaya Kosha** – This is the body of the lower, conditioned mind, the mental faculty where *Sattva* Guṇa predominates. It receives information through the senses, organizes and analyzes the details, and then makes decisions. Necessary instructions are passed on to the organs of action. This is made possible as *Prāṇa* connects the mind with the physical body. Mind also processes our thoughts and emotions. Quite often, information of the external world doesn't make sense creating doubts and confusion. The next sheath is that of wisdom, higher knowledge, and consciousness. Mind seeks, and receives guidance from it for further action. Thus, it is the mind that truly represents us to the outer world. This Kosha has its origin in *Ajna* Chakra.

> Āsanas of *Hatha-Yoga* followed by breath control exercises of *Prāṇayama* balances the flow of *Prāṇa* in our subtle system and improve its efficiency. It is then followed by meditation that clears thoughts, stabilizes the mind, and establishes a control over it to experience peace and calm. This is a pre-requisite before dealing with the next sheath.

---

4. **Vijnānmaya Kosha** – This is the spiritual body, the sheath of individual consciousness having higher knowledge. *Sattva* and *Rajas* together predominates this Kosha. Purity, intuition, spiritual insight, and wisdom are its domain. Operating with the individual ego, *ahamkara*, it is the guiding force to the mind that discriminates, makes a choice, and decides the course of action. It has the ability to regulate actions that attach us to the world or detach from it. Each of its decision makes an impression on the sub-conscious mind, *Citta* carried by the soul as chronicle of *Karma* upon death. Spiritual practices strengthen it to have greater control over the mind, remove illusions, and enhance the ability to make right choices. It has its origin in *Nāda* and *Bindu* Chakras.

Regular practice of *Yoga* and meditation with a controlled mind gradually raises awareness that leads one to a higher level of consciousness. Improved efficiency of this Kosha influences and alters the way we think and act that changes the state and experiences of life. As awareness expands, it succeeds in reaching the next Kosha of eternal bliss.

---

5. **Ānandmaya Kosha** – This is the body of eternal bliss. The innermost sheath closest to the soul, it is the center of consciousness. *Sattva* Guṇa predominates here. There is great difference between the experience of happiness and enjoyment by the mind and by this sheath. The mind feels happiness because of an excitement, an external sensory stimulus. It is a temporary feeling that changes over time. Ānandmaya Kosha is the state of eternal bliss and peace, an ecstatic condition that enjoys the mere state of existence regardless of the external situation. It has its origin in *Sahasrāra* Chakra.

This is the final stage of meditation, where a state of supreme bliss and peace is achieved. At this stage, the *Kuṇḍalinī* energy rises from the base of the spine and unites with Shiva in the crown of head. This is the state of enlightenment, **Realization of the Ultimate Truth.**

Annamaya Kosha is the physical body whereas Prāṇamaya and Manomaya Kosha together constitute the subtle body. As *Prāṇa* leaves the physical body upon death, the mind also dies. Thus, these three sheaths are given up by the departing soul, *Puruśa*. The casual body of *Puruśa* is made of the fourth and the fifth sheath. It is a repository of the chronicle of past *Karma*, impressions, and desires. They determine the future time and place of rebirth of the soul. Upon reincarnation, the soul acquires the first three sheaths anew consistent with its destiny, *Prārabdha* to further life experience.

To the world, light of the soul is projected through these five layers. Each of them changes the original light of the soul according to its color, strength, transparency, and operational efficiency. The out-coming light therefore, has a different color, hue, intensity, and the effect, unique to each individual. A spiritual aspirant, under the guidance of a Guru, identifies suitable ways and means, follows the directed paths and practices, and finally succeeds to penetrate these layers to reach the center. As he successively passes through each sheath, a purer and clearer picture of his true self emerges. Barriers of the material body, logic and doubts of the rational mind as well as individual ego are destroyed to experience eternal peace.

LAW OF KARMA

Principle of cause and effect

The simple maxim of *Karma* is that each thought, speech, or act always bears consequence, either in the present or in the future. It is the natural law of cause and effect which makes one responsible for the state of one's life. Intrinsic to our existence, we inevitably create *Karma* as we act with passion to enjoy and experience its material effects, saw its seeds while harvesting the fruits of those sawn earlier. *Karma* regulates the way all inextricably interrelated parts of the entire universe interact with each other. The unitive field of living cosmic intelligence connects and relates all individuals in such strange ways and means so as to influence each other's lives. Creating *Karma* is a cause that often times may not translate in an immediate experience of its effect. But once created, it stays with us forever until resolved. Transcending the divisions of time, it encompasses the past, the present, and the future lives operating even beyond the boundaries of birth and death. Therefore, *Karma* adds to the soul profile, lies dormant, and waits patiently until the time when each effect to its originating cause is eventually experienced before it is neutralized.

All individual minds are well attuned to the ever vigilant cosmic mind which invariably catches our minutest thought, speech, and action. It etches these causes in its consciousness to ensure that it has its appropriate effect consistent with the natural law, *Ṛta*. The infinite power of this immutable law effectively restores the order and balance of all finite aspects of the material world. As an efficient, impartial, and attributeless administrator, it is well above such dualities as good and bad, positive and negative. Judiciously executing its authority, it not only provides equal opportunity for advancement to both but also offers them fitting fruitage. Whether the human mind chooses to be a Saint or a Satan, the cosmic mind provides equal avenues to excel. Thus, we have infinite potential to rise and reach the peak of heaven or fall down below and touch the bottom of hell.

Time and place construct the operating stage of this phenomenal world where we enact *Karma* as the cause to reap their desired effects. It is an incredible platform upon which we perform under our own direction which defines our role. It also determines our destiny, *Prārabdha* under the law of *Karma* which governs the entire show in inconceivable, strange, and most secret ways. Its rule is not restricted by spatial dimensions whereas the often elapsing time between the cause and its effect practically becomes non-existent after its ultimate justice. It not only rules the physical but also the metaphysical realms of the psychic and spiritual planes. Our happiness or sadness, including all other emotions we live through is the experience of such effects as due adjustment of our previous acts. Thereby it enforces order and restores equilibrium at those levels.

The casual body is a repository of the soul which carries *Karma* load called *Sanchita Karma* accumulated from all its previous lives. At birth, a part of this *Karma* defines the unique purpose which determines the basis to serve for that one lifetime. To discharge all obligations and reap the harvest of all accumulated *Karma* in a single life may not be viable. The physical body, mental faculty, and the course of life become the determinative factors limiting it to experience the selected set of *Karma*. The planetary energies at the time of birth are consistent with, and indicative of the nature of *Karma* brought to bear fruit. It is known as ***Prārabdha***, the initiation it gets and the general direction it is given to further its life experience. Therefore, by evaluating the birth chart, an astrologer can predict the major events and general direction of life.

Prārabdha encases a soul within the physical body and locates it at specific place and time. It provides a unique set of living conditions, endows instincts and aptitudes, and imparts distinct driving force of life. Ingrained images, latent desires, and past impressions called *Saṃskāra* determine the inborn tendencies through which it makes choices at every stage of life. These are molded by factors such as society and surroundings, heredity and ancestry, class and culture. Therefore, there is an apparent inequality between people as each soul manifests at a specific level of consciousness. Everyone acquires unique look and personality, nature and temperament developing areas of interest and aptitude which leads them to pursue distinct paths of life.

The past impressions, memories, and desires carried in sub-conscious, *Citta* is the unreasoning mind which instinctively makes a choice and instantly reacts. It is well hidden underneath the surface of conscious awareness, the reasoning mind which makes a logical choice and intelligently responds to any situation. Their cumulative aspect surfaces as such thoughts and passion as to lead all intent, purpose, and expectation laden actions of life. They bear appropriate fruits, in conjunction with past *Karma* consistent with destiny. New mental images after the spiritual lessons learned through life experiences alter the impressions carried by *Citta*. It renews the dimensions of conscious awareness modifying the effect on future thought, speech, and act accordingly.

This perpetual flux of actions, experiences, and impressions are the causes that, as a consequence, yoke the spirit to spatial and temporal confinement of the conditioned existence, *Saṃsāra*. Vibrations of good *Karma* create positive influence whereas those of the bad ones have a negative effect. It creates

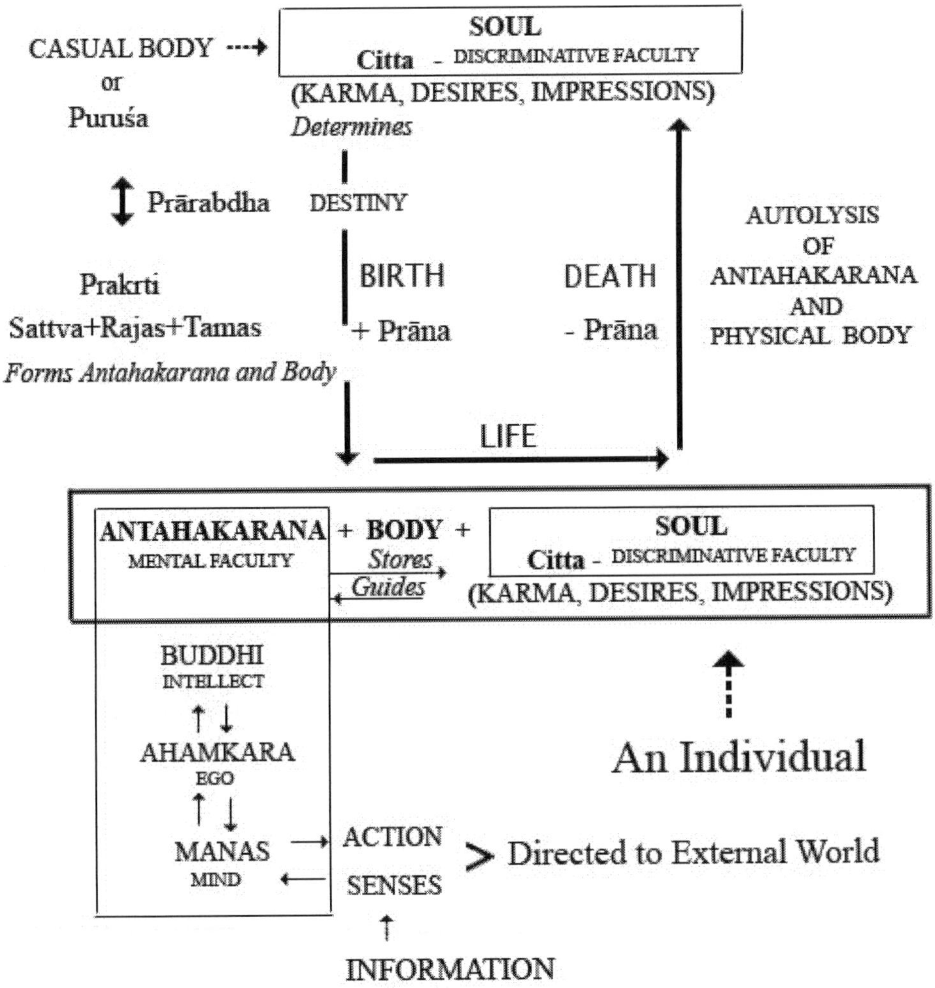

THE CYCLE OF SAMSARA

predisposition to follow the trend of impulses that get set in our unconscious mind. As we go along it, it strengthens it. But negating it makes it weak. The choice every moment is ours as it is subject to free will. All throughout the life this play continues. *Kriyamana Karma* is the *Karma* on physical level without mental or emotional involvement that bears fruit immediately. As an example, physical exercise raises the heartbeat and blood pressure.

One interesting facet of *Karma*, good or bad, is that it does not have a consequence like 'eye for an eye'. In other words, *Karma* produced now does not predetermine an exact same event at a specific time and place. It may not simply translate into a fixed reward or a specific punishment. However, it leads to a comparable experience anytime in the future until resolved. *Karma* also does not cancel free will, nor does free will neutralize *Karma*. We enjoy the merits of good *Karma* as luck, good health, comforts, and success in our endeavors whereas our failures, miseries, and obstacles are due to bad *Karma*. The best way to deal with *Karma* is not to produce any, eliminate them altogether. True purpose of life is to completely burn all *Karmic* seeds so as to eliminate all future possibilities of their germination which ensures liberation.

Upon death, soul leaves the physical body but carries along *Citta*, the sub-conscious mind with chronicle of *Karma*, desires, and impressions. This determines the basis of rebirth at an appropriate time, in an appropriate body, and this perpetual wandering continues. As Swami Vivekananda has said, our thoughts, words, and deeds are the threads of the net which we throw around ourselves. *Karma* can be endlessly patient, waiting for the right time till all the circumstances and conditions for its resolution get so perfectly lined up. This is how the law of *Karma* binds one to *Saṃsāra*, the cycle of birth, life, death, and rebirth. Most of us are unaware that our worldly knowledge, *Avidya* rules lower passion and ignorance binding us to this perpetual cycle.

The unique advantage of human life is the ability to control emotions and ever growing desires through power of volition, conscious choice-making that changes *Prārabdha*. There is no escape from it as we do have to resolve past *Karma*. The most we can do is transform them to a more desirable and bearable experience. Mantra chanting is an excellent tool that gradually burns and eradicates the huge granary of such seeds that we carry over several lifetimes. *Karma* can be transcended only by realizing the true Self. Mode of goodness overcomes ignorance and develops a spiritual personality that directs us to rise above the sense of individual ego, acquire higher knowledge, *Vidya* and reduce *Karma* load. The best *Karma* is zero-sum entity that assures no rebirth and an ultimate liberation. Human life is meant to pursue and achieve this ultimate goal.

Lord Kṛṣṇa has shown a way in the Bhagvad Gītā to get a release from this endless cycle. Desires are the thread that connects the effects to the initiating cause, the ultimate fruit to the original action. By severing this connection while tagging along the natural order of action, we achieve the freedom from such attachment. By following the path of *Dharma*, performing duty without yearning for fruits, doing selfless service, and by heartfelt love, devotion, and total surrender to him one can get freedom from the bondage of body and mind. Moksha is the true emancipation and liberation from *Saṃsāra*.

ASTROLOGY

Elusive Science of Prediction

Astrology is a part of the Vedas where stars and planets, believed to have consciousness are associated with deep spiritual meaning. Each of them acts through its specific powers that either punishes or rewards all living beings according to their deeds and destiny. Since ages, their subtle influence on humans was keenly observed by ancient sages. These experiences were duly recorded, classified, and categorized. It was carefully analyzed and intuitively interpreted which led to the understanding of their effect on us. Sages Bhṛagu, Parāśara, and Varāha-Mihira have made significant contributions to Vedic Astrology and their works are considered an authentic source.

The influence of visible Sun and Moon is quite obvious due to the direct experience of their daily affects. But more subtle influences of other planets and stars are not so readily realized. A planet, worshiped as a deity wields its power through distinct energies. It imparts specific traits and character at birth, constantly influences thoughts and action, and orchestrates as well as times the events of life. Together, their array decides, designs, and develops patterns, colors, and texture weaving the inimitable fabric that fashions each individual life. Their radiating vibrations interact to create an energy field unique to their relative positions at any given moment. All major subtle energy centers in our body are attuned to them, each receptive to the energy of a particular planet. As these psychic centers resonate with the energy field, its influences on the *Prāṇa* flow determines the overall state of our being. As planets tread along the path of their respective orbits, it changes the dynamics of the field and its effect. We deal with, and respond to this ever-changing vibratory field around us, always in a state of flux. It reflects in our changing thoughts, perception, and activities. Such a shift in their positions also changes surrounding circumstances in the objective world to deliver the destined life experiences.

A horoscope is the birth chart of a person which maps the position of planets in the sky as determined by the date, time, and place of birth. It describes the nature and extent of influence of each planet on the constitution and course of his life. Also, it gives an insight into the latent traits and past impressions, *Saṃskāra* carried from the past lives which reflects his character and personality. It also identifies the cycles of vibrations with which he resonates giving him a specific and a unique place in cosmos. Using the rules laid down by the ancient sages, the chart is analyzed to know the initial vibratory field with which he starts his life journey. Besides an overview of the general physical attributes, character, mental capabilities etc., truly gifted astrologer can also predict things like level of education, relations with parents and siblings, preferable field of work for success in it, income and financial status, love life and marriage etc. with precision. To foresee his future, the cycles of vibrations with which he resonates and their interaction with those to be created around him on a future date by the planetary field is analyzed. Many other calculations add to the accuracy and refine this prediction. Besides the knowledge of astrology, the power of intuition and gut feeling also play a vital role in such predictions.

In fact, when a soul takes birth, the planetary configuration is consistent with the merits of its past lives, the cause which determine the destiny of the newborn. The position of planets and the energy field at the time and place of birth shows the part of *Karma* brought to fruition. As it takes birth, things like the physical and mental traits, the parents and the community, the living conditions and upbringing are well defined. These are the things that it cannot change and has no control over. This is the field within which it gets to begin life and has a chance to make progress, learn spiritual lessons, and advance.

The *Saṃskāra* of its past lives has a bearing on the thoughts and actions. But it also has a free will to change the course and alter its destiny. Every day it makes conscious choices to act in particular ways. Each action has a natural consequence that operates on the basis of cause and effect. Based on the overall balance of good and bad actions, *Karma* it reaps the fruits, either in the current or in some future life. This is how luck and work both determine its worldly as well as spiritual status at any particular time, during the entire lifetime.

Twelve signs of Zodiac

The sky, divided into twelve equal parts, each occupied by a major star constellation makes the signs of the zodiac. They always remain fixed in their location and retain the same order. Each has a name that duly represents its characteristics. The star constellation occupying the sign visually helps us to identify its actual location in the sky by its shape. Imagine this as an outer 'sky dial' above our earth that always remains fixed. These signs form the backdrop against which we observe all the planetary movements.

Each sign carries specific characteristics and is ruled by a particular planet. Sun and Moon rule only one sign each whereas the other five physical planets rule two signs each; one of them, odd numbered active sign and the other, even numbered passive sign. For example, Mars rules Aries, an active sign of the zodiac that shows an aggressive and fierce nature as well as a passive sign, Scorpio. Saturn rules an active sign of Aquarius as well as a passive sign Capricorn that signifies hard work, organization, and order.

Twelve Houses

The sky viewed from our position on earth at any time, starting from the eastern horizon can be divided into twelve equal parts called houses. Six of these houses are in the visible sky above whereas the other six houses are in the invisible sky below the earth. Their order is fixed with respect to the observer on earth. The first house is invariably at the eastern horizon, the next five are under the earth, and the seventh on the western horizon. The remaining five houses are above in the visible sky. These houses form the inner 'earth dial' that keeps on changing with the rotation of the earth.

1 Aries 2 Taurus 3 Gemini 4 Cancer
5 Leo 6 Virgo 7 Libra
8 Scorpio 9 Sagittarius 10 Capricorn
11 Aquarius 12 Pisces

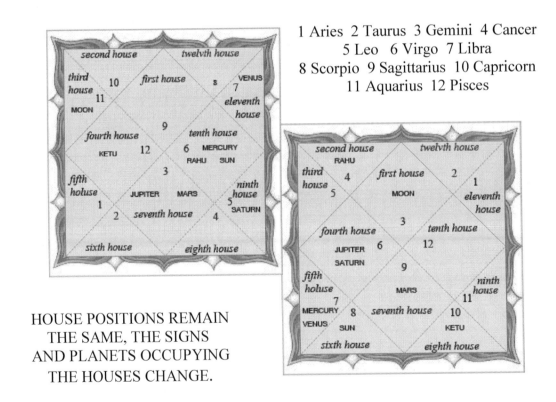

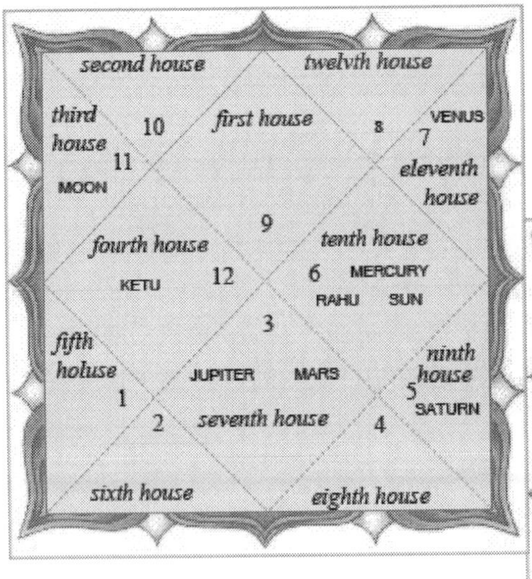

HOUSE POSITIONS REMAIN THE SAME, THE SIGNS AND PLANETS OCCUPYING THE HOUSES CHANGE.

TWO TYPICAL HOROSCOPES

At any given time, each house of the inner 'earth dial' coincides with a certain sign of the zodiac of the outer 'sky dial'. A sign is said to occupy the house it coincides with. The inner 'earth dial' turns with rotation of earth, but to us, on earth, it appears that the outer 'sky dial' is turning. So with time, the signs of the outer 'sky dial' enter, occupy, and move through the houses of the inner 'earth dial'. With one rotation of earth in twenty-four hours, all signs pass through all the houses completing a cycle. This daily cycle continues.

Each house is indicative of some specific aspects of our life. For example, the seventh house in the chart of a person indicates success and happiness in the marriage and partnership, the nature of spouse, vacations etc. whereas the type of profession, status, position, and success are seen from the tenth house.

Nine Planets

Seven of the nine major planets have a physical presence. They are Sun, Moon, Mercury, Venus, Mars, Jupiter and Saturn. Though Sun and Moon are not planets, they have the greatest influence on our lives and therefore, they are considered so for astrological purposes. In fact, these two planets are central to all astrological predictions; the Western system emphasizes Sun whereas the Vedic system emphasizes Moon. Two remaining planets, Rahu and Ketu do not physically exist. The two points of intersection of the orbit of Earth around Sun and the orbit of Moon around Earth are known as nodes; Rahu is the northern node and Ketu is the southern node. As they have very strong energy fields having influence like other planets, they are also considered planets.

At any given time, a planet occupies a certain position in the backdrop of a particular sign with respect to us. It is considered to be in that sign. Also, it is said to occupy that house which coincides with the sign it is in at that time. As we see the signs moving through the houses, the planets occupying those signs also move. Some of the signs may not have any planet in them whereas others may have just one. And there may be signs with more than one planet.

A planet occupying a certain sign, in a certain house, indicates a specific outcome as signified by that combination. Presence of other planets in the same sign as well as those occupying other signs and houses that aspect it modify this indication. Some special combinations and aspects called *Yoga* impart the involved planets strength, special characteristics, and specific advantages. The position of planets in the sky at the time of reading a birth chart and their current influence on them also matters. Factors like the strength of each planet, Moon chart, the birth star etc. are also weighed in. Thus, innumerable calculations, its careful evaluation, and an interpretation of their effects refined by Astrologer's intuition finally results in a prediction.

The Vedic and the Western systems of Astrology have a different orientation. The Vedic astrology uses phases of the moon to calculate a month and absolutely relies on sidereal system where the star constellations determine the zodiac signs. For the Western astrology, relation of Earth with Sun is the basis of all calculations. Therefore, the number of days in a month and a year is not the same in these two systems. Every year, they do not coincide but vary. Also, based on more refined data and calculations, Vedic astrology predictions are more accurate as compared to that by the Western system.

Because these planets influence our lives just like the other deities and demi-Gods, images of their presiding deities are also installed and worshiped in Hindu temples. There are specific attributes carried by each of them that determine the form of their worship. Each of the seven major planets is worshiped on specific day of the week associated with it. Also, there are specific mantras to propitiate each of these deities to seek their power and acquire protection. Chanting of mantra invokes their grace and binds their energy which acts as an anti-dot and neutralizes their negative influence caused by affliction. Fasting, donating specific grains and articles, and wearing associated gems are some other practices carried out to make peace with the planets.

Twelve signs, twelve houses, and nine planets provide an infinite number of combinations within the 360 degree sky. It has unlimited potential to produce individual charts that represent countless energy plays. Besides these, the influence of other distant stars and planets also do exist. No wonder that we all are different individuals who undergo very different life experiences. The science of prediction is an attempt to figure out the future by deciphering the divine will which, therefore, is always shrouded in mystery.

Sun ☉

Sun is the central planet of our Solar system. It is a *sattvic* planet and represents our soul. In the birth chart it is indicative of father, social status, the rational mind, level of ego, and eyes. Just as sun is central to solar system, it rules the bones, heart, and vitality of the physical body. Personal power and authority, ability to govern and control are seen by its placement. It indicates law and order at all levels. It is ruler of the sign Leo of the Zodiac. Its position is that of a King. The gemstone associated with Sun is red ruby.

Moon ☾

Moon is the next most important planet that influences us and is also a *sattvic* planet. It indicates our mind, memory, emotions, and eyesight. It is the one that rules and controls our senses. It is also indicative of mother and mother's family, relation with females in general, agricultural land, love, mental peace, home, happiness and the overall personality in the birth chart. Like the phases of the moon, our mood, mind and emotions also keep on changing. It rules the Zodiac sign Cancer and matters of the fourth house in a chart. Moon holds the position of a Queen. Natural pearl is its gemstone. Fourth house in a birth chart is the most comfortable position for Moon.

Mars ♂

Mars is a *tamasic* planet which represents fire, aggression, and energy. In the birth chart it indicates brothers, friends and enemies, land, injuries and accidents. The intensity of our actions to fulfill our goals is determined by Mars. Physical strength and courage, ability to argue, skill to use machines are all due to Mars. Warriors and surgeons dealing with the weapons, tools, and blood invariably have a strong Mars. It is the ruler of two Zodiac signs, Aries and Scorpio. Mars is considered to be the chief of Army. Red coral is the gemstone for Mars. In a chart, tenth house is the best position for Mars.

Mercury ☿

Mercury is a *rajasic* planet which represents knowledge, language skills, astrology, and math. From its position in the birth chart the level of education, success in the fields of agency and commerce, overall intelligence and ability to change is seen. Mercury indicates all types of communications including speech, writing, and use of computer. Whereas Moon is the innocent mind, Mercury is the intellect discriminating between good and bad. It rules the Zodiac signs Gemini and Virgo. Mercury is considered to be the crown Prince. Green emerald is the gemstone associated with Mercury.

Jupiter ♃

A *sattvic* planet, Jupiter is the most benefic and generous of all the planets. Health, wealth, devotion and faith, good married life, children and happiness are all indicated by the position of this planet. Spiritual insight, wisdom, morality and righteous actions leading to overall happiness are due to the grace of this planet. Magistrates, lawyers, administrators of government, religious priests, and ministers have a strong placement of Jupiter. It rules the two signs of Sagittarius and Pisces. Jupiter holds the position of the chief Advisor and Priest. Yellow Sapphire is its gemstone.

Venus ♀

Venus is a *rajasic* planet and signifies love, art and beauty, comfort, luxury, and wealth. In a male chart it signifies the marital status and wife. Pleasures of the senses and body are indicated by it. All forms of music and dance, creative expressions with elegance and style are indicative of the influence of Venus. It also is a very benefic planet. Good house and vehicles, name and fame, gems and precious metals are all due to Venus. Ruler of the two signs Taurus and Libra, it holds the position of Treasurer and white Diamond is its gemstone.

Saturn ♄

Saturn, a *tamasic* planet is farthest of all physical planets. It takes thirty years for it to complete one rotation around the Sun signifying dull and slow, dark and cold, retardation and isolation. It indicates negative traits like limitations and sadness, hard work necessary to get fruit, disease and old age. As master of the discipline, lessons taught by Saturn are most helpful for spiritual advancement. It imparts wisdom that is born out of experience. It rules the nerves, the signs Capricorn and Aquarius, and has the position of a worker. Blue sapphire is its gemstone and the seventh House in a chart is most comfortable for it.

Rahu ☊

Rahu is a shadowy planet, as it does not have a physical presence. It is *tamasic* in nature. The northern node of Moon's orbit, it is indicator of greed and manipulation, obsessive behavior and dementia. It gives rise to worldly desires, success, and fulfillment on the materialistic level. Drugs and poison, psychic powers, black magic, communicable diseases, mental illness and falling from grace etc. are the influences of this planet. It does not rule any sign of the Zodiac and the gemstone associated with it is honey colored Hessonite.

Ketu ☋

Ketu is another shadowy planet without having a physical presence and *tamasic* in nature. The southern node of Moon's orbit, Ketu indicates fantasy, penetrating insight, and psychic abilities. If Rahu gives rise to worldly desires, Ketu does the opposite as it is the planet of spirituality. It is indicator of change and reorganization, wisdom, non-attachment, and liberation. Ketu energizes the planet it associates with. Ketu also does not rule any sign of the Zodiac and its gemstone is Cat's eye. It is the only planet stronger than Sun, capable of causing an eclipse.

ĀYURVEDA

Holistic Approach to Healthy Life

Āyurveda is an ancient science of medicine that is part of the Vedas just like Vedic Astrology. References to Āyurveda can be found in the last Veda, *Atharvaveda*. The word 'Āyurveda' means knowledge of long and healthy life that has emerged from a divine source. It describes various therapeutic measures having holistic approach with a great emphasis on the physical, mental, and spiritual harmony in everybody. It was first revealed by Lord **Dhanvantari** who is considered to be the First Physician. Suśruta was his first pupil who also practiced and mastered the science of surgery. He wrote Suśruta Saṃhitā which, along with Carak Saṃhitā later written by Carak are considered to be the two main texts and authentic source of Āyurveda.

Āyurveda acknowledges the fact that the physical body is a highly organized system made of matter whose function is fully integrated with the mind through the subtle body. It believes that all action and changes at the physical level are the effects of causes initiated within the subtle arena. Hence, Āyurveda practitioner always evaluates the physical and psychological aspects of the patient together. The central concept of this universal form of medicine is '**Tridosha**' system, the three bio-energies that work around the balance of five basic elements, *Panchamahābhuta* in the physical body. Tri means three and dosha means bodily humour. These three bodily humours are known as Vāta, Pitta, and Kapha. Vāta refers to the balance between ether and air, Pitta is that between fire and water, and Kapha is the balance between water and earth. Everybody has these three doshas but in different proportions, one of which always predominates. It truly determines the individual temperament, body type, and the physical constitution. Each of these doshas should be balanced for a person to have a normal health and efficient functioning of the body and mind.

Vāta dosha is considered to be the most powerful of the three as it affects the basic body processes like cell division, breathing, impulses in the nerve cells, pulse, and the heartbeat. Primary seat of Vāta in the body is colon. People with dominant Vāta dosha are said to have Vāta constitution. They are physically underdeveloped, too tall or too short. Person with this dosha out of balance is susceptible to various kinds of skin problems and mental diseases.

COMMON ĀYURVEDIC HERBS

NEEM *(Azadirachta indica)*	Blood Purifier, Beauty Enhancer
AMLA *(Emblica officinalis)*	Eye tonic, Purest form Vitamin C
BRAHMI *(Bacopa monnieri)*	For Memory, Anxiety and Tension
EUCALYPTUS *(Eucalyptus citriodara)*	For Blocked Nose, Sore Throat
BHRINGARAJ *(Eclipta alba)*	Essential Hair Tonic
ISABGOL *(Plantago ovata)*	For Constipation, Piles, Dysentery
ASHWAGANDHA *(Withania Somnifera)*	For Stress Relief of Body and Mind
SHATAVARI *(Asparagus racemosus)*	For Decreased Milk Flow
SHANKHAPUSHPI *(Evolvulus alsinoides Linn)*	For Chronic Bronchitis, Weakness
TURMERIC *(Curcuma longa)*	As Antiseptic, Fair Complexion
VIBHITAK *(Teminalia belerica)*	A Superb Hair Vitalizer
HONEY *(Mel Despumetum)*	Eyes, Obesity, Asthma, Nausea

Pitta dosha controls the functioning of digestive system, metabolism, body temperature, and hormones. The small intestine, stomach, sweat glands, blood, fat, eyes, and skin are the seats of Pitta. People with predominant Pitta constitution have a medium physique, but usually strong and well built. Also, they show emotional tendencies of hate, anger, and jealousy. When out of balance, it causes heartburn, ulcers, anemia, acne, heart disease, and arthritis.

Kapha dosha is the one that keeps up physiological and biological strength, provides immunity, and controls growth. People dominated by this type of dosha have well-developed bodies though they tend to be overweight. Kapha is present in chest, throat, sinuses, mouth, joints, mucus, and cytoplasm. Those persons having this dosha out of balance are vulnerable to diabetes, gall bladder problem, nasal congestion, and asthma.

An imbalance in any of these three doshas affects the gastric function, the fire of digestion which produces toxins that enter the blood stream and circulate throughout the body. Symptoms of a disease are manifestations of the effect of these toxins. Āyurvedic practitioner tries to identify the dosha that is out of balance and then treats to restore it to correct the problem.

The first step taken is called '**Panchkarma**' or five actions of rejuvenation that cleanse the system of accumulated toxins. These are recommended to be done regularly and periodically. These consist of therapeutic vomiting, purgation therapy, enema, Nāsya or elimination of toxins through nose, and bloodletting or detoxification of blood. It is then followed by Samana, use of herbs and medicines most of which are from the plant or animal origin or it may be an alchemical form of a mineral. Each of these is purified by specific processes before it is used as medicine in such treatments. They may be administered individually but more often than not, their various combinations are used.

Āyurvedic therapies are very slow in their effect as they act to address the underlying imbalance that manifests as the problem rather than alleviating the appearing effects. Therefore, the result of these treatments is not evident immediately. However, their greatest advantage is that generally they do not have any side effects like the drugs of allopathic medicine. Many formulations and herbal preparations called '**Rasāyana**' that promote youthful state, physical and mental health, and vitality are quite popular and routinely used. One such Rasāyana, 'Chyawanprash' is extensively used by people all over the world. Change in lifestyle, food habits, and exercise along with the administration of these medicines help cure the dosha imbalance. Oil massage, sauna, and *Yoga* exercises are also part of the therapy.

BASIC TENETS of HINDUISM

Guiding Principles

Rgveda, Yajurveda
Samveda, Atharvaveda
Dharma, Artha
Kāma, Moksha
Incarnation, Karma
Brahman, Soul

Divine revelations called *Śruti* compiled as the four Vedas are the main scripture and ultimate authority. Vedānta derived from Upaniṣads along with Agamas, Bhagvad Gītā, and Purāṇas form the core philosophy and other major scriptures of the religion. Tantra is well intertwined with Hinduism.

God is One omnipresent, omnipotent, and omniscient Reality. This Ultimate Truth can be realized through devotion, higher knowledge, and meditation with the grace of a Guru. God can be worshiped without form and attributes (*Nirguṇa*) or with a form and attributes (*Saguṇa*).

God visualized with the essence of specific attributes, in a particular form makes a deity. Different visualizations form different deities which have given rise to several concepts, belief systems, and practices.

Once consecrated, images and statues of deities have the same potency and power as the aspect they represent and therefore, they are worthy of worship. They help develop a communion with the unseen Divine.

All paths ultimately lead to the same goal of God Realization. 'Truth is one; wise call It by various names.' A person chooses a path consistent with his level of consciousness to realize this Ultimate Reality.

By extension, all true religions of the world are accepted and well respected thus creating universal tolerance and harmony. All of mankind is one family.

Every one of us basically pursues four goals of life - Follow *Dharma*, work for Artha, fulfill Kama and attain Moksha.

Law of *Karma* that operates on the basis of cause and effect always prevails. One invariably faces the consequences of his bad *Karma* whereas enjoys the merits of his good *Karma* either in the current life or in the future lives.

Rebirth and reincarnation of a soul is certain and unavoidable until Moksha. A soul undergoes the cycle of birth, death, and rebirth to evolve until all his *Karma* are resolved upon which it is liberated.

Māyā or illusion is the veil that prevents the individual soul to know its true divine nature as it identifies itself with the body, mind, and the world.

Whenever there is a decline in moral values, *Dharma*, or righteousness in the world, God incarnates in a human form to restore the balance.

Humans have the highest level of consciousness among all the living forms. To be born as human is a boon and a blessing. The human life is meant for the ultimate goal of God Realization.

All life forms are manifestation of the same Supreme Being. Peaceful coexistence is possible only through non-violence and non-injury. All life forms – animals, birds, fish or any other kind should be loved. Killing them to eat their meat hinders spiritual progress and therefore, it should be avoided.

The parents who gave us birth and supported our growth as well as the teachers who gave us knowledge should be treated with utmost respect.

This creation is eternal, with no beginning and no end. It exists and operates in cycles and its nature is evolutionary. At the end of a cycle the existing universe is destroyed and replaced by another one. In the current cycle we are passing through the dark phase called Kaliyuga.

ॐ

HINDUISM TIMELINE

Major Periods

6000 – 1500 BCE
COMPOSITION OF THE ṚGVEDA HYMNS
EARLY VEDIC PERIOD

4700 BCE
INCARNATION OF LORD RĀMA

3100 BCE
INCARNATION OF LORD KṚṢNA

3100 – 1700 BCE
INDUS VALLEY CIVILIZATION

900 – 600 BCE
LATE VEDIC PERIOD

700 – 300 BCE
COMPOSITION OF UPANIṢADS

400 – 100 BCE
COMPILATION OF
BHAGWAD GĪTĀ and MAHĀBHARATA

300 – 1200 AD
EPICS AND PURĀṆAS ARE WRITEEN

700 – 1100 AD
BEGINNING OF TANTRA MOVEMENT

GLOSSARY

Abhishek: Pouring water, milk etc. over a deity image for bathing
Adharma: Opposite of Dharma
Ahaṃ: Source of 'I'ness, Lord Shiva
Ahaṃkāra: The individual ego
Ajna: Name of the Sixth Chakra
Anāhata: Name of the Fourth Chakra
Anjaneya: Another name of Hanuman as son of Anjana
Antahakarana: The mental faculty
Antarmukha: The inward facing mode
Apāna: One of the five types of Prāṇa that rules excretion
Ardhanārishvara: A human figure with half male and half female
Arjuna: One of the five Pāndava brothers
Artha: Money or Wealth, Meaning
Āgama: Special class of Hindu scripture
Āsana: A body posture in Yoga exercise
Ashta Lakshmi: Eight aspects of Lakshmi Devī
Atharvaveda: The last of the four Vedas
Āvarnas: Different levels of consciousness in Sri Chakra
Avidya: Worldly knowledge which is considered to be lower knowledge
Āyurveda: Knowledge of long and healthy life

Bahirmukha: The outward facing mode
Bhagvad Gītā: The most authentic source of Vedānta philosophy
Bhairava: Fearful aspect of Lord Shiva
Bhakti Yoga: The mode of loving devotion to God
Bharat: A brother of Rāma
Bhishma: Son of Shantanu named Devavrata, the great vow taker
Bhukti: The power of enjoyment
Bija Mantra: A seed sound
Bilva: The special leaves with three lobes offered to Lord Shiva
Bindu: The point of origin, abode of Lord Shiva
Brahmā: The creating aspect of God
Brahman: The Divine Consciousness, abstract principle of God
Brāhmaṇa: The section of Veda that elaborates the meaning of Vedic Mantras
Buddhi: Ability to make proper decision

Chakra: The psycho energy center in the subtle body
Chaṇḍi Pāth: Another name of Devi Māhātmyam

Caritra: Part or Section
Citta: Sub-consciousness with chronicle of Karma, desires, and impressions

Dakshināmurti: Form of Lord Shiva as archetype teacher that faces south
Devī: The Divine Mother, Ultimate Reality as female Supreme Being
Dharma: Specific duty of each individual. Path of righteousness and virtue
Dhātu: A basic element that constitutes the body
Dhrutarāshtra: King of Hastinapur, father of Kaurava
Durgā Devī: Aggressive form of Divine Mother
Dassera: The most auspicious day of the Hindu calendar
Draupadi: Wife of Pāndava brothers
Duryodhana: The eldest Kaurava

Gaṇesha: Son of Lord Shiva who removes obstacles
Gāyatri: The mantra of Veda that encapsulates all its wisdom
Guṇa: The mode or way through which energy operates
Guru: A religious and spiritual master

Hanuman: The great devotee of Lord Rāma
Hastinapur: Name of a city in ancient India
Hiranyagarbha: The cosmic womb from which creation flows
Homa: Sacred fire ceremony

Icchā Shakti: Power of will
Ida: The subtle energy channel ruled by moon
Idaṃ: The entire physical phenomena that evolves from the source
Indra: The god of heavens
Ishta-Devtā: The deity of choice for worship
Īshvara: The state of Lord Shiva who conceives the entire universe

Jagadamba: Mother of the universe, name of Divine Mother
Japa: Repetition of a mantra in cycles
Jnāna Shakti: Power of knowledge
Jnāna Yoga: The higher knowledge about the divine Self
Jnānendriya: Organs of knowledge

Kailāsa: The abode of Lord Shiva
Kalā: The creative expression of any kind
Kāla: The power of time
Kāla-Chakra: The circular wheel of time that creates birth, death, and rebirth
Kalasa: Special pot filled with water for religious ceremony

Kālikulā: The tradition that worships the terrible form of Divine Mother
Kalpa: A day in the life of Lord Brahmā
Kaliyuga: The current Dark Age
Kāma-Kalā: The subtle body of Divine Mother having desire to create
Karma: Act of thought, speech or action
Karma Yoga: Following the path of action consistent with Dharma
Karmendriya: Organs of action
Kārtikeya: The leader of the celestial army, son of Lord Shiva
Kauravas: The 100 sons of King Dhrutarāshtra
Kṛṣṇa: The eighth incarnation of Lord Vishṇu
Kriyā Shakti: The power of action
Kuṇḍalinī: Latent energy residing at the base of the spine in everybody

Lakshmaṇ: A younger brother of Lord Rāma
Lakshmi: A form of Shakti, goddess of wealth and consort of Lord Vishṇu
Leela: Past times of Lord Krishna
Linga: Form of the stone pillar symbolizing Lord Shiva
Loka: Spiritual level of existence

Mahābhārat: The world's longest epic poem
Mahākāla: Lord Shiva as lord of the time
Mahākāli: Ferocious goddess of time, consort of Lord Shiva
Mahālakshmi: Goddess of wealth and prosperity, consort of Lord Vishṇu
Mahāsaraswati: Goddess of learning and inspiration, consort of Lord Brahmā
Mahāvidya: The wisdom Goddesses
Mahā Yuga: A period of 4.32 million years of existence
Mahat: Field of cosmic intelligence, the center of creation
Mālā: Garland or rosary made of 108 beads
Manas: The lower mind attached with senses
Mandala: A geometric diagram representing energy pattern of a deity
Manipura: Name of the Third Chakra
Mantra: The sound body of divine cosmic energy
Manvantara: A temporal period within each Kalpa
Mātṛkā: An alphabet sound with special powers
Māyā: The power of limitation and illusion
Moksha: Liberation from the cycle of birth, death, and rebirth
Mṛtyuṇjaya: The conqueror of death, Lord Shiva
Mudras: Specific hand gestures having meaning
Mukti: Release from the constraints of life
Nāda: The subtle sound waves that is the source of all creation
Nāda Brahman: Subtle substratum of the universe, manifested aspect of God

Nādi: A subtle energy channel
Nāma-Rupa: Two linked aspects of sound and shape, name and form
Nandi: Bull, the vehicle of Lord Shiva
Nārāyaṇa: The one who floats on cosmic waters, Lord Vishṇu
Natarāja: The rhythmic moments of time, dancing posture of Lord Shiva
Navrātri: Nine auspicious days of 'Āso' month of Hindu calendar
Nav-Durgā: Nine different forms of Durgā Devī
Nirguṇa: Without having any attributes
Niyati: The cause of confinement in a place with a form
Nyāsa: A ritual of touching body parts while chanting mantras

Panchamahābhuta: Five material elements
Pāndavas: The five sons of King Pandu
Pārā Shakti: Shakti as the Ultimate Reality but in a state of slumber
Pārvati: Embodiment of Shakti, the consort of Lord Shiva
Paśupati: Lord Shiva as the master of all embodied souls
Pingala: The subtle energy channel ruled by sun
Prajāpati: The sons of Lord Brahmā who assist in his creation
Prakṛti: Efficient and material cause of manifestation
Prāṇa: The subtle universal energy, life force of the universe
Prāṇayama: The breath control exercises to control Prāṇa
Praṇava: The source of Prāṇa
Prārabdha: The path of destiny consistent with Karma, past and present
Purāṇa: Popular scripture with stories and legends of Hinduism
Pūrṇa: Complete, Total
Puruśa: Soul, part of Lord Shiva having limitations

Rādha: The consort of Lord Krishna
Rāga: The power of attachment
Rāja Yoga: Path to control the body and mind for Self-realization
Rajas: Mode of passion, action, and movement
Rāma: The seventh incarnation of Vishṇu
Rāmāyaṇa: The life story of Lord Rāma
Rāvaṇa: The demon king of Lanka who was killed by Lord Rāma
Ṛgveda: The first of the four Vedas
Rūdra: The ferocious form of Lord Shiva
Rudrāksha: Dark berries of a tree that is favorite of Lord Shiva

Sadāshiva: The ever benevolent form of Lord Shiva
Saguṇa: With attributes
Sahasranāma: One thousand names

Sahasrāra: The Chakra located in the crown of the brain
Sāligram: The fossilized shells worshiped as emblem of Lord Vishṇu
Samāna: One of the five types of Prāṇa that rules assimilation
Sāmaveda: The third of the four Vedas
Saṃsāra: The cycle of birth, death, and rebirth
Saṃskāra: Latent tendencies and impressions of the past
Sanātana Dharma: The path of life guided by Eternal Truths
Sanchita: Accumulated Karma yet to bear fruit
Sanskṛit: The ancient language of spirituality
Saptamātrika: Seven warrior forms of goddesses
Saptarishis: The seven mind sons of Lord Brahmā
Saraswati Devī: Goddess of learning and inspiration
Satcitānanda: Supreme state of eternal bliss and peace
Sattva: Mode of goodness and equilibrium
Satyanārāyaṇa: Form of Lord Vishṇu prayed on full moon days
Shabda: Name or sound
Shaivait: Followers of Lord Shiva
Shakta: Followers of Divine Mother or Devī
Shakti: The primordial energy that is the source of all objectivity
Shaktipāt: Transfer of energy to a disciple by a Guru
Smṛti: What is retained by the power of memory
Siddhi: Unique powers
Sita Devī: Wife of Lord Rāma
Smartas: Believers in all aspects of God
Śrīkulā: The tradition that worship Divine Mother in her most auspicious form
Śrī Vidyā: Worship of Divine Mother as Lalitā Devi in Śrī Chakra
Spanda: The subtle substratum of vibrations created by Nāda
Śruti: What is heard in the form of subtle vibrations
Sugriva: A monkey King
Sushumna: One of the three major energy channels in subtle body
Swadhishthān: Name of the Second Chakra
Swayambhū: Self born

Talas: Seven Chakras of lower consciousness
Tamas: Mode of ignorance and darkness
Tanmatra: Subtle essences that connect with organs of sense
Tantra: The universal belief system that harnesses power of ubiquitous energy
Tapas: Control over the mind and senses
Tattva: Building block in the universe
Ten Mahāvidyas: Ten wisdom goddesses
Trimurti: Three aspects of God; Brahmā, Vishṇu and Shiva

Tripurari: Lord of the three cities, Lord Shiva
Tulsi: A holy plant worshiped by Vaishṇava

Udāna: One of the five types of Prāṇa that rules regeneration
Upaniṣad: The last explanatory part of each Veda

Vaikhari: The articulate speech
Vaikūntha: The celestial abode of Lord Vishṇu
Vaishṇava: Followers of Lord Vishṇu
Veda: The oldest and sacred scriptures of Hinduism
Vedānta: The latest interpretation of the Upaniṣads
Vidyā: Female mantra, higher spiritual knowledge
Vighneshwara: Another name of Lord Gaṇesha
Vijayadasami: Also known as Dassera, the tenth day of Navrātri.
Vikṛti: Action guided by lower passion and animal instincts
Viniyoga: The basis of invocation of mantra energy
Vishṇu: The God as preserver of universe in Trimurti concept
Vishuddha: Name of the Fifth Chakra
Vishwaroopa: The universal form
Vyāna: One of the five types of Prāṇa that rules distribution

Yajurveda: The second of the four Vedas
Yantra: Geometric template that represents energies of a deity
Yudhishthira: The eldest Pāndava
Yuga: One of the four phases of Mahā Yuga.

ॐ

Shanti Mantra

Aum sarveshām swastir bhavatu
Sarveshām shāntir bhavatu

Sarveshām poornam bhavatu
Sarveshām mangalam bhavatu

Sarve bhavantu sukhinah
Sarve santu nirāmayāh

Sarve bhadrāni pashyantu
Mākaschit duhkha bhāg bhavet

ॐ

Meaning

Auspiciousness be unto all; peace be unto all;
fullness be unto all; prosperity be unto all.

May all be happy!
May all be free from disabilities!

May all look to the good of others!
May none suffer from sorrow!

26609293R00126

Made in the USA
Charleston, SC
13 February 2014